The place was Gettysburg. For both South and North, the stakes were extremely high. The Confederacy envisioned a victory of great significance. The Union feared a major disaster. "We've got to fight our best today," announced one Federal sergeant, "or have those Rebs for our masters." At the end of three days' fighting, combined casualties were at least 50,000 in the biggest and bloodiest battle of the Civil War. With now legendary sites of conflict like Seminary Ridge, Cemetery Ridge, and Little Round Top, the Battle of Gettysburg, like few other events in our nation's history, still resonates powerfully for Americans today.

Praise for Richard Wheeler's *Witness to Gettysburg*

RICHARD WHEELER is a former U.S. Marine and the author of sixteen previous books of military history, including *Voices of the Civil War* and *Voices of 1776: The Story of the American Revolution in the Words of Those Who Were There* (available from Meridian). He is a winner of the New York City Civil War Round Table's Fletcher Pratt Award and the Christopher Medal.

OTHER BOOKS BY RICHARD WHEELER

The Bloody Battle for Suribachi

In Pirate Waters

Voices of 1776

Voices of the Civil War

We Knew Stonewall Jackson

We Knew William Tecumseh Sherman

The Siege of Vicksburg

Sherman's March

Iwo

A Special Valor

Sword over Richmond

Witness to Gettysburg

Witness to Appomattox

On Fields of Fury

Lee's Terrible Swift Sword

A Rising Thunder

GETTYSBURG 1863

Campaign of Endless Echoes

RICHARD WHEELER

A PLUME BOOK

PLUME
Published by the Penguin Group
Penguin Putnam Inc., 375 Hudson Street,
New York, New York 10014, U.S.A.
Penguin Books Ltd, 27 Wrights Lane,
London W8 5TZ, England
Penguin Books Australia Ltd, Ringwood,
Victoria, Australia
Penguin Books Canada Ltd, 10 Alcorn Avenue,
Toronto, Ontario, Canada M4V 3B2
Penguin Books (N.Z.) Ltd, 182–190 Wairau Road,
Auckland 10, New Zealand

Penguin Books Ltd, Registered Offices:
Harmondsworth, Middlesex, England

First published by Plume,
a member of Penguin Putnam Inc.

First Printing, September, 1999

10 9 8 7 6 5 4 3 2 1

Ⓟ REGISTERED TRADEMARK—MARCA REGISTRADA

LIBRARY OF CONGRESS CATALOGING-IN-PUBLICATION DATA:
Wheeler, Richard.
Gettysburg 1863 : campaign of endless echoes / Richard Wheeler.
p.   cm.
Includes bibliographical references (p.   ) and index.
ISBN 0-452-28139-3
1. Gettysburg (Pa.), Battles of, 1863.   I. Title.
E475.53.W54   1999
973.7'3493—dc21   99-19692
                                                              CIP

Printed in the United States of America
Set in Stempel Garamond
Designed by Julian Hamer

For one of the battle's
unsung heroes,
Frank Haskell's horse,
Dick

Contents

Illustrations

MAPS

Preface

PUBLIC INTEREST IN the Civil War as a whole waxes and wanes through the decades, but the lure of the Gettysburg Campaign is perennial.

This episode deserves all the attention it is given. It played a major role in the "new birth of freedom" Abraham Lincoln envisioned, in the preservation of a union that has become predominant in world affairs; and it is therefore one of the most significant military events in history.

Perhaps I'll be permitted to claim a special timeliness for this book. I'd like to think of it as an offering that helps highlight one of the pivotal episodes of the Second Millennium as we journey into the Third.

Gettysburg 1863, which interweaves the military and civilian sides of events, employs the campaign's drama as its central theme. But the campaign's technical details are also covered. The combination represents a departure from the way the story is usually told.

But the book is not merely a variant approach to things generally known about Gettysburg. I have made my own way through the campaign, unearthing a substantial amount of little-known material; and I believe I have also come up with some fresh insights.

I have deliberately avoided the scattering of numbers throughout the text as source-note indicators. This is narrative history written for a general audience, and I feel that the inclusion of such numbers would prove annoying by interrupting the narrative's flow. Nor would many readers be likely to find a complicated set of source notes especially useful.

The book, of course, is based upon material carefully analyzed for its credibility. A look at the bibliography will reveal that my sources include a great many writings by people—both military and civilian—who were involved in the campaign.

The book's illustrations were taken from *Battles and Leaders of the Civil War, Frank Leslie's Illustrated History of the Civil War, Harper's Pictorial History of the Great Rebellion,* and other publications of the postwar years. Many of the illustrations are adaptations of sketches or photographs made while the conflict was in progress.

Nutting Hall
Pine Grove, Pa.
Summer 1999

GETTYSBURG 1863

1

Hooker and Lincoln

THE SPRING OF 1863 found the Civil War rumbling into its third year.

Union efforts in the Western theater were prospering, with the columns under the relentless, cigar-smoking Ulysses S. Grant maneuvering for a stranglehold on Fortress Vicksburg, key to control of the Mississippi River, of great strategic importance to the contest.

In the East, however, the picture was different. Early in May, Robert E. Lee's Army of Northern Virginia climaxed a generally triumphant career against the Union's Army of the Potomac with a win at Chancellorsville, halting an advance on Richmond, the Confederate capital, about fifty miles to the south. The feat was of special note because it was achieved with less than half the Federal numbers.

At the battle's end, the two armies settled back into their old camps on opposite sides of Virginia's southeasterly flowing Rappahannock River, the Federals on the north bank at Falmouth and the Confederates on the south bank at Fredericksburg.

The Union general who instigated Chancellorsville, forty-four-year-old Joseph Hooker, a tall, statuesque, blue-eyed New Englander known as "Fighting Joe," tried to rationalize his defeat. Adding to Hooker's humiliation was that he had preceded his advance across the river with the boast: "My plans are perfect and when I start to carry them out, may God have mercy on General Lee, for I will have none."

Hooker's plans were almost as good as he claimed, but when he started to carry them out he showed General Lee mercy in abundance by losing

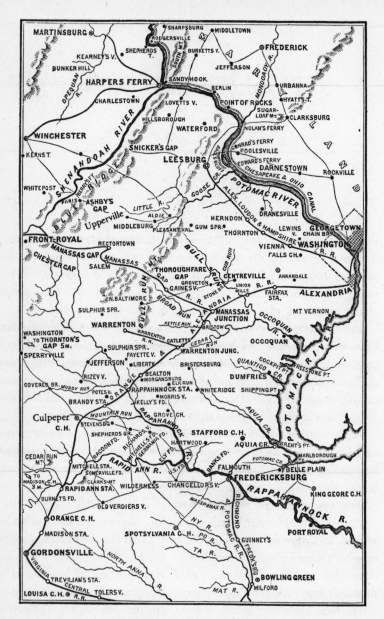

Field of operations in Virginia.

Joseph Hooker

his confidence. He withered under a counterattack, which included a daring flanking maneuver, and he retreated without even giving full battle.

It was all very strange. Joe Hooker was a West Pointer with a fine combat record going back to the war with Mexico, 1846–1848. In the present conflict he had shown uncommon skill and courage as a leader on the regimental, divisional, and corps levels. His organizational and training work as commander of the Army of the Potomac, begun in January 1863, had been outstanding. Performance was greatly improved, and morale rose. The pessimism occasioned by too many defeats was replaced by high optimism. Hooker convinced the men they comprised "the finest army on the planet."

Personally, the general's splendid appearance was coupled with an amiable down-to-earth style, and he was cheered enthusiastically wherever he rode.

It was true that Hooker had a reputation for heavy drinking, but he probably drank less than was believed. He seems to have had a low tolerance for alcohol.

There was no denying, however, that the general was an indiscreet talker. He entertained newspaper reporters with unflattering estimates of other officers, and with criticism of the authorities in Washington. Once he went so far as to say he thought the nation needed a dictator, and he indicated he might be available for the job. But there was a lot of rash talk assailing the air at that time, and no one took Hooker very seriously.

His soldiers drilled with bands playing and voices raised in song. A favorite ditty included these lines:

"For God and our country we're marching along.
   Joe Hooker is our leader; he takes his whiskey strong."

The whole bright new order of things was shattered at Chancellorsville. Here the troops learned, at the price of a sea of their blood, that Hooker's talents did not extend to the handling of a large army in the field.

Chancellorsville, one soldier averred, was a campaign the general "opened as with a thunderbolt from the hand of Mars, and ended as impotently as an infant who has not yet learned to grasp its rattle."

Army of the Potomac shaping up.

A Union burial at Falmouth.

In Washington, President Abraham Lincoln lamented, "My God, my God, what will the country say?"

Actually, the country did not protest as loudly as might have been expected. Hooker received a generally tolerant treatment among the war correspondents, who had been impressed by his preparational achievements, and who now glossed over his rationalizations.

These were ingenious enough. The failure was based on circumstances "not to be foreseen or prevented by human sagacity or resource." In withdrawing from the field after making only a partial effort, the troops had shown great confidence in themselves. "On fighting at a disadvantage we would have been recreant to our trust. . . . The Army of the Potomac will give or decline battle whenever its interest or honor may demand." There was special satisfaction in the fact that when the army returned across the river "not a rebel ventured to follow."

The heart of every officer and soldier, Hooker asserted, should be swelling with pride. "We have . . . surprised the enemy in his entrenchments; and . . . we have inflicted heavier blows than we have received."

The newsmen supported Hooker with statements like this: "Another such success to the rebels would be a terrible disaster. They cannot long stand such an expenditure of blood."

Casualties—in killed, wounded, captured, and missing—were about 17,000 for Hooker and 13,000 for Lee. But in relative terms Lee, with the smaller army, had the greater damage.

Joe Hooker had been President Lincoln's personal choice for top commander in the East after four other generals—Irvin McDowell, George McClellan, John Pope, and Ambrose Burnside—had been tested and had failed to measure up. Now Hooker had followed suit. Lincoln, nevertheless, did not hasten to replace him. There was no surefire replacement available.

It was the same old story for the President. To people who cried, "Abraham Lincoln, give us a man!" he could only say, "I can't *make* a general."

This lack of leadership in the North was a curious thing. The South had found competent leaders at once. The North, with the war more than two years old, was still groping.

The three generals who would settle the conflict at last—Ulysses Grant, William T. Sherman, and Philip H. Sheridan, all serving in the West—were still molding their reputations. People had not yet stopped worrying about Grant's drinking, and some still wondered about Sherman's strange brush with mental illness in 1861. Phil Sheridan's image as a hero was affected by his size. He had the heart of a gamecock, but he looked more like a bantam rooster.

The strongest figure in the army's command structure at this time was the commander-in-chief himself. But Lincoln's only military service dated back to 1832, when he was a twenty-three-year-old volun-

Abraham Lincoln

teer in the brief Black Hawk Indian War. For him, the conflict involved mostly a lot of drilling and marching. The closest he came to combat was to help bury some of the scalped victims of a skirmish.

In his present job, with so many of his generals letting him down, Lincoln had taken to studying strategy and tactics, and he was developing some first-rate ideas on how the war should be conducted.

But he was loath to condemn his unsuccessful generals for the way they had fought their battles. "I do not know that I could have given any different orders had I been with them myself. I have not fully made up my mind how I should behave when minie balls [common usage for minié balls] were whistling, and those great oblong shells shrieking in my ear. I might run away."

If ever a person was right for a job, it was Abraham Lincoln, the man who "bound the nation and unbound the slave."

Not that his greatness was evident from the start. A patchily educated farm youth, he managed to make his way into the law profession and into politics. He served in the Illinois legislature, won a term in the

House of Representatives, but failed when he tried for the Senate. His strength was that he became known for integrity, for logical thinking, and for incisive speaking.

Lincoln got his chance at the national presidency because his views on the slavery issue appealed to the newly formed Republican Party. He was not an abolitionist. His approach was not radical. He argued, in essence, that if Congress would act to keep slavery within its original boundaries as the nation expanded, the practice would eventually die through a lack of growth. The South would have plenty of time to adjust to the change.

Most Southerners wanted none of this, and Lincoln was given such labels as The Illinois Ape and The Original Gorilla.

Nearly six-feet-four-inches tall and signally rawboned, he had long hands and feet, a sallow rough-hewn face, and coarse black hair. He was awkward both in posture and in movement.

Lincoln campaigned as The Illinois Rail-Splitter, which made him seem a man of the people, though some wondered how such a talent qualified him to run the nation.

His election precipitated secession. The states began going out even before he was inaugurated. When he took office on March 4, 1861, at the age of fifty-two, he assumed a far heavier burden than any other incoming President in American history. But from that day on, as a period historian said later, "he controlled the helm of the Ship of State with marvellous wisdom and steadiness."

This was not to say that his course was always approved. He had plenty of critics, especially among newspaper people. Keeping his equanimity required that he ignore, in so far as he could, this battery of faultfinders.

"If I were to try to read, much less answer, all the attacks made on me, this shop might as well be closed for any other business. I do the very best I know how—the very best I can; and I mean to keep doing so until the end. If the end brings me out all right, what is said against me won't amount to anything. If the end brings me out wrong, ten angels swearing I was right would make no difference."

Lincoln's great Emancipation Proclamation, issued on January 1, 1863, went against his original views on how the slavery problem should be handled. He was thinking politically then. The proclamation was a war measure, one urgently needed. It infused new strength into a faltering Northern effort, at the same time undermining the rebellion's foundations.

Lincoln was totally committed to saving the Union. During crises, he skipped meals and got little sleep. He took on a weary, haggard look. Fortunately, he had a strong constitution. He had a tendency toward melancholy, but this was balanced by a sense of humor. He seems to have remembered almost every amusing story he ever heard, and he used these freely in his conversation. He also enjoyed quoting Shakespeare, which he could do at length. This represented one of his few aspirations to higher culture.

The President was not without personal problems. At the end of his first year in office, a young son, Willie, died of typhoid fever. The blow nearly crushed Lincoln, but the funeral was barely over before he was back at work.

The New York *Evening Post* reported: "Mr. Lincoln . . . is again . . .

Mary Todd Lincoln

spending, not infrequently, eighteen out of the twenty-four hours upon the affairs of the nation."

Thereafter Lincoln drew even closer to his other small son, Thomas, whom he called Tad, shortened from Tadpole. Tad spent much of his time playing in his father's office, even while the country's business was being transacted. Lincoln's eldest son, Robert Todd, was a student at Harvard at this time.

The President's wife, Mary Todd, was a high-strung woman on her way to serious mental problems. She was jealously proud of her position as first lady, and was not above throwing a tantrum in public if she felt she was being slighted. On such occasions, the extent of Lincoln's reproof was for him to say, "Now, Mother; now, Mother."

The President's chief concern in May 1863 was Joe Hooker, who had to be counseled as he weighed new courses of action. Hooker was hoping to make another attempt to capture Richmond. Lincoln believed—and correctly—that the primary aim of the Army of the Potomac should not be to take the Confederate capital but to destroy the Army of Northern Virginia.

2

Lee and Jackson

LEE'S SOLDIERS EMERGED from the Battle of Chancellorsville making great sport of Hooker's nickname, "Fighting Joe," and reveling in the way they had bested "the finest army on the planet." Their own reputation as an army, they knew, was now securely established, their ragtag appearance notwithstanding.

There was no uniformity in the cut or the color of their clothing. All shades of gray were manifest, with light brown, or "butternut yellow," also well represented. Most of the men wore sweat-stained felt hats, and many a jacket lapel was adorned with a toothbrush stuck like a rose in its buttonhole. Footwear was various, much of it in poor condition.

The troops may have been sartorially deficient, but they were well armed. Most carried first-rate muzzle-loading rifles. In the beginning, while the men were still inexperienced, many had even bedecked themselves with revolvers and bowie knives, a practice that had amused Lee.

"Gentlemen," he said, "I think you will find an Enfield rifle, a bayonet, and sixty rounds of ammunition as much as you can conveniently carry in the way of arms."

The lesson was soon learned, and now these extras were seldom seen.

It wasn't only the soldiers in the ranks who had been encouraged by Chancellorsville. Lee himself had begun to believe he'd be able to prevail indefinitely against the Army of the Potomac, whose superior numbers and bountiful resources had thus far counted for little.

But the war's western theater had to be considered. Affairs in the regions of the Mississippi, where the Confederates were doing poorly, were of equal importance. Lee's eastern army would have to perform a near-miracle in order to win the war by itself, and Lee, of course, was well aware of this.

It must be noted that Lee's triumph at Chancellorsville had a very serious downside. His ablest corps commander, Thomas J. "Stonewall" Jackson, was wounded, in a twilight accident, by his own men. His left arm had to be amputated.

At first it was believed that Jackson would survive, and Lee said to an officer who was about to pay him a visit: "Give him my affectionate regards, and tell him to make haste and get well and come back to me as soon as he can. He has lost his left arm, but I have lost my right."

With the battle barely over, Lee was already thinking in terms of further action, and he could not imagine operating without Jackson.

The two were a phenomenal team. Their success was based not only on strategic and tactical acumen, but also on friendship and mutual trust. Jackson's soldiers liked to say that he would assault hell if Lee

Typical Confederates.

Robert E. Lee

gave the order. Jackson himself said that Lee was the only general he knew that he'd be willing to follow wearing a blindfold.

Lee, on the other hand, declared that it was never necessary for him to provide Jackson with more than a broad idea of what was needed of him in order to get the desired result.

"Say to General Jackson," Lee told a courier as the Chancellorsville crisis was developing, "that he knows just as well what to do with the enemy as I do."

A notable sidelight on these generals whose military instincts were so much alike was that they were men of entirely different molds. About all they had in common was that both were Virginians, both were West Point graduates (Lee second in his class, Jackson seventeenth), and both served with distinction in the Mexican War.

Lee enjoyed the loftier family name. The Lees were prominent in Virginia for two hundred years before the Civil War. Son of Henry "Light Horse Harry" Lee of Revolutionary War fame, Robert E. married Mary Custis, the daughter and heiress of G. W. Parke Custis,

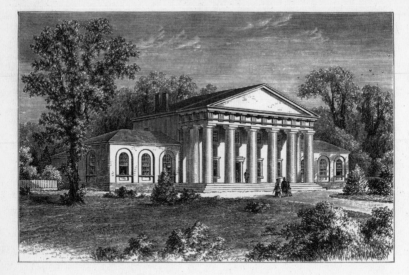

Arlington as the Lee family knew it.

adoptive son of George Washington. Through Mary, Robert E. became master of magnificent Arlington House on the Potomac River. The place contained many Washington relics. One of the couple's sons inherited the White House plantation on the Pamunkey. Washington had been married on these grounds.

By 1863 the Yankees had been occupying Arlington House for two years, and the Washington relics had been scattered. [The Lees would never return.] As for the White House plantation, the Yankees burned it during the Peninsula Campaign of 1862.

Jackson's pedigree can be simply stated. He was born of pioneer stock in western Virginia (later, West Virginia). He had no name to help him in his rise to prominence. This is not to say that Lee wasn't required to work hard for what he achieved, but Jackson had to work harder.

Lee, in his later fifties during the Civil War years, was a superb figure of a man and a soldier, and a fine horseman. He was one of those rare people endowed with an extraordinary measure of presence, needing only to walk into a room to command absorbed admiration.

Stonewall Jackson

A measure of vanity was suggested by the way he covered a balding pate by combing a long shingle of hair from the side. (We are left to wonder what happened when the picture-book general removed his hat in a high wind.)

Seventeen years younger than Lee, Jackson was about as tall, but was awkward on foot, uninspiring in the saddle, and much of the time shabbily uniformed. He had odd mannerisms, and he self-doctored for mysterious health complaints. His nature was one of deep seriousness, and he was often ill at ease in social situations.

Though Lee could affect an aloofness when thrown in with people he did not like (and these people found him difficult to understand), he had an almost magic way with people he liked. They were charmed by his kindness and consideration, his equanimity, his humor. Few realized that he was not immune to flashes of anger, nor to moments of visible anguish.

Lee's wartime amiability was all the more impressive because it was preserved in the face of his myriad burdens. To begin with, he carried the great responsibility of being the heart and soul of the Confederacy. He knew that millions were looking to him to find a way to resolve the war in the South's favor. His role was likened to that of Washington in 1776.

Maintaining and directing his army required the most diligent efforts, sometimes by night as well as by day, and Lee was often deprived of sufficient rest. Unfortunately, he hadn't the soundest of hearts. Five weeks before Chancellorsville he suffered a debilitating illness that wasn't fully diagnosed but was almost certainly a mild heart attack. Although he soon rallied, he never regained all of his former strength. This was distressing to one who had taken satisfaction in being known as tireless.

Lee was seldom without family problems. His wife Mary was badly crippled by arthritis, and he was her mainstay. He not only sent her letters of sympathy and encouragement, but also kept abreast of the treatments she was trying.

In 1862 one of Lee's daughters died at the age of twenty-three. She was a great favorite with him, and he wrote, in a letter to another daughter: "In the quiet hours of the night, when there is nothing to

Mrs. Robert E. Lee

lighten the full weight of my grief, I feel as if I should be overwhelmed. I have always counted, if God should spare me a few days after this Civil War has ended, that I should have her with me, but year after year my hopes go out, and I must be resigned."

Lee's concerns included two sons in the army who were often in harm's way. It wasn't that he had time to give them any special attention. Sometimes he was out of touch with them for weeks on end. He actually had an almost paternal interest in all of his soldiers and was ever mindful of their welfare. It was a special cross for him to bear that the lives he was risking in battle included many family friends. A number of these were already dead.

A few months before Chancellorsville the general, for moral reasons, involved himself in a civil matter he did not really have time for, and which he might have put off. When the Lee family inherited Arlington and the White House, one of the provisions of the will was that the Custis slaves be freed within five years of G. W. Parke's death. Legal complications had caused the proceedings to drag, and the period was about up.

Lee chose now to press things to a conclusion, saying of the slaves, "They are entitled to their freedom, and I wish to give it to them."

To be sure, the Lee family had its own slaves. Lee, however, was not easy in his conscience about this. He had no quarrel with the moralists who condemned slavery. But he and his Southern contemporaries had *inherited* the institution.

The original villains, born generations earlier, were the slave-procurers in Africa (and this included black tribal chieftains), the Yankee shipowners who conducted the trade, and the colonists who were eager to buy. The South had provided the better market: its population was modest, and labor was in short supply. Now a great part of the economy was based upon slavery. A sudden end to the institution would shatter the region's prosperity.

Even so, Lee had been opposed to secession as a means of preserving the Southern economy, had hoped to see the Union sustained. He had taken pride and pleasure in his thirty years of service under the Federal flag, had risen in stature after the Mexican War until selected

Southern agricultural scene.

for a three-year stint as superintendent of West Point, which brought him to national notice.

When the Civil War broke out, Lee was offered command of the Union forces then taking the field. But, like most other Southern officers in the Federal service, he felt he must resign his commission and side with his home state against Northern invasion measures.

Jackson's attitude toward the crisis was paradoxical. His front-line service in Mexico had given him a strong aversion to warfare. "I have seen enough of it to make me look upon it as the sum of all evils." But when war came at home, he was ready to fight the Northern "aggressors" with no holds barred. He believed they should be made to feel war's fullest fury, and he went so far as to say that the South should adopt a general policy of "no prisoners." This viewpoint was all the more astonishing in light of the fact that Jackson knew he'd be fighting many of his former military comrades.

Sometimes it seems that Old Stonewall was a little crazy.

Lee's belligerency was far more subdued. There were no bitter diatribes against the North. His chief way of showing that he no longer considered the Yankees to be his countrymen was to refer to them, in a cool manner, as "those people."

Still another way in which Lee and Jackson were markedly different was in their relationship with females.

Lee had a great affection for womanhood: relatives, family friends, casual acquaintances; and they adored him, doubtless as much for his appearance and style as for his celebrity status. Young females in his sphere got many a kiss on the cheek, a practice he playfully claimed was one of the privileges of his rank.

The story was told that, at a military review well attended by women, a young one exclaimed to a female friend, "General Lee kissed me twice!" The other shot back, "General Lee kissed me *four* times!"

This kind of conduct was not for Stonewall. Indeed, when irrepressible female admirers rushed up and kissed him, he usually reacted by blushing and losing his verbal coherence. He submitted with less embarrassment to requests for buttons off his uniform. This sometimes required the substitution of pins until new buttons were available.

Both Lee and Jackson were devout Christians, but only Jackson was publicly preachy. All who knew him were aware of the profundity of his beliefs. Although Lee was openly religious, he reserved most of his deepest feelings on the topic for letters to his wife and children.

Even in an age when Christianity was resurgent, Stonewall's faith seemed extreme to many. But he remained the same to the end. When his arm was amputated, he said, "I consider these wounds a blessing.

They were given me for some good and wise purpose, and I would not part with them if I could."

Jackson lingered for a week, providing time for his wife Mary Anna and their infant daughter Julia to reach his bedside, a reunion that moved its observers to tears. When Mary Anna, in tears herself, told him the doctors said he could not live, Jackson was at first unbelieving but finally declared, "I will be an infinite gainer to be translated."

News of the general's situation stunned Lee.

"Jackson will not die! He cannot die! God will not take him from us now that we need him so much."

On May 10 Stonewall succumbed with a smile after saying quietly, "Let us cross over the river and rest under the shade of the trees."

Later, Mary Anna wrote a long, dramatic account of Jackson's last week. It is filled with the names of medical people and army officers who were a part of the story. Along the way, brief mention is made of a servant named Jim who "nursed Jackson faithfully to the end." The nearly anonymous Jim must have been a prominent figure in the drama of Stonewall's passing.

Lee's loss of Jackson was a severe blow to the Confederate cause. Many Southerners, however, tried to view the general's death in the light of divine will. A Virginia diarist, Mrs. Judith McGuire, wrote: "How can I record the sorrow which has befallen our country? General T. J. Jackson is no more. The good, the great, the glorious Stonewall Jackson is numbered with the dead! Humanly speaking, we cannot do without him; but the same God who raised him up . . . can lead us on without him. Perhaps we have trusted too much in an arm of the flesh; for he was the nation's idol. His soldiers almost worshiped him, and it may be that God has therefore removed him."

Although Jackson was gone, Lee still had James Longstreet, a senior subordinate he called, with affection and admiration, his "old war horse." In his early forties, the general was six-feet-two and weighed well over two hundred pounds. His broad-browed face was heavily bearded. A first-rate corps commander, Longstreet was firm as a rock under fire. He, too, was a West Pointer who had come out of the Mexican War with commendations.

During these early years, Longstreet became warm friends with

James Longstreet

Ulysses Grant, and the friendship, like many others between Northern and Southern officers of the period, survived the Civil War.

If Longstreet lacked Jackson's offensive vigor, it was at least partly because he believed that a commander should eschew risk-taking, should be cautious and deliberate. His troop held him in high regard, and they gave him such nicknames as "Old Peter" and "Bulldog." Those men who drank and gambled found him generally tolerant of the vices. He was known to indulge in them himself.

There was a good bit of humor in Longstreet, but this was not readily apparent. His blue eyes held a stern look, and he used words sparely. He had a temper, but it was usually under control. Right now his busy life as a warrior was helping him cope with a shattering tragedy involving his family life. A year earlier he had lost three children to scarlet fever within the space of a few days.

Longstreet headed the military delegation Lee assigned to Richmond to take part in the ceremonies honoring Jackson's remains before their transfer to Lexington, in Virginia's Shenandoah Valley, for burial.

Lee was unable to attend because he was keeping a wary eye on Hooker's men across the Rappahannock.

Mary Anna was gratified by the presence of the high-ranking Longstreet, but there was a certain irony in the situation. Longstreet was not an admirer of Jackson's derring-do, which was at odds with his own conception of warfare, and, indeed, had been putting his own career in the shade. In his heart of hearts, Old Peter was probably not too sorry to see Stonewall make his exit.

The ceremonies in Richmond included a procession that wound through the principal streets, with Jackson's remains in a dark hearse drawn by four white horses. In the wake of the hearse, on foot and in carriages, were hundreds of military men and civilians, including the Confederacy's President Jefferson Davis and his cabinet, a column extending for nearly a mile. The sidewalks were jammed with people, some waving small Confederate flags, many sobbing audibly.

Draped with a newly adopted version of the Southern colors and surrounded by arrangements of spring flowers, Jackson's casket was displayed in the Capitol, and some 20,000 people filed by. Young children were held up by parents to look upon the ghostly face beneath the casket's glass panel.

Everything was conducted with quiet solemnity until the end of the day. Declaring the viewing over, the men of the honor guard cleared the hall and began closing the doors. Still wishing to enter was a crippled soldier, a man who had served under Jackson. Denied access, the veteran protested. He was told to leave or he'd be arrested.

This stirred his dander. Raising the stump of an arm, he cried, "By this arm which I gave for my country I demand the privilege of seeing my general once more!"

The veteran's wish was granted, and a proper quiet returned to the scene.

It was about this time that, up at Fredericksburg, a Northern youth and a Southern youth who were doing picket duty on opposite sides of the Rappahannock exchanged a set of shouts that made the historical record.

The Southerner queried, "Where's Old Joe Hooker?"

He was answered, "At Stonewall Jackson's funeral!"

The Northern youth followed this with a question of his own. "How come you Johnny Rebs never have any decent clothes?"

The Southerner responded, "We-uns don't put on our best to kill hogs in!"

The exchange was reported to Abraham Lincoln in Washington, and the Southerner's retort made him laugh. He said, "There's a good deal of mother-wit in some of those fellows."

Lincoln did not rejoice at Jackson's death. When a Northern newspaper carried an article sympathetic to Jackson, the President wrote the editor: "I honor you for your generosity to one who, though contending against us in a guilty cause, was nevertheless a gallant man."

Lincoln was never anything but charitable in his feelings for the Southern people. He understood their wish to preserve and advance their political and economic power, their reluctance to abandon the lucrative slave system. But he never for a moment believed they had a right to establish themselves as a nation apart from the North.

The Richmond ceremonies for Jackson took place on May 12, 1863. Two days later, with the remains gone from the city on a train bound for Lexington, General Lee came down the rails from Fredericksburg.

The countryside gleamed with the fresh, yellow-green color of spring, and the scenes helped assuage the general's grief over his lost subordinate and friend. Lee loved nature, once having written his wife: "What a glorious world God Almighty has given us. How thankless and ungrateful we are, and how we labor to mar His gifts."

Richmond was still in a somber mood, and not only because of Jackson. Other victims of Chancellorsville had been brought to the city in coffins. There were also many stretcher cases; and, according to one observer, "the busy round of hospital duties again engrossed surgeons, stewards, and nurses, paid and amateur."

Mixed with the people in the streets were some of the battle's walking wounded, men who were proud of their bandages and who were gratified by the attention they received.

A novel sight was that of groups of captured Yankees being marched to Libby Prison. Some of these men were in deep gloom, while others managed to laugh when citizens called out such remarks as "On to Richmond, boys!"

Good-natured replies were even given:

"I guess we got here sooner than we thought."

"We didn't figure to come this route."

At least one Yankee said he was glad to be a prisoner. "I'm tired of fighting the Johnnies, anyhow."

A Confederate hero.

Jefferson Davis

General Lee had urgent business with Jefferson Davis and his cabinet at the Capitol.

Lee found the President looking worn and unwell. But Davis often looked that way. He seems to have been singularly unsuited, in nervous temperament, for the pressures of his office. He had no reserve of strength. Matters were not helped by the fact that life, for him, was a drama without comic relief. He was habitually sober and staid. Currently, his concerns were compounded by news from the West that the columns under Ulysses Grant, in their campaign against Vicksburg, were overrunning his home area of Mississippi.

Another product of Federal military training, Davis had served in the Black Hawk Indian War, like Lincoln, and in the war with Mexico. He also had a varied career in Washington politics, had been a congressman, a senator, and a secretary of war. Serving in the Senate when Mississippi seceded, he resigned at once and went south.

The Confederate presidency was not something Davis sought. It was thrust upon him. He would have preferred a military command. Though he was doubtless best qualified for the job he got, he did not relinquish his dream of service in the field, and he was known to say, "If Lee were to take one wing of the army, and I the other . . ."

Both Davis and Lee, as students of the military, knew that Lee's celebrated victories were not accomplishing enough. Principally, they were saving Richmond from capture. They were not wresting Southern independence from the North. They were not even weakening, to any significant degree, the North's resolve. Moreover, if Vicksburg fell, which had begun to seem likely, the Union would gain a tremendous edge in its pursuit of the war. Its control of the Mississippi River would cut the Confederacy in two, disrupting the flow of supplies and reinforcements from west to east; and the Federal army and navy would also have a convenient highway, extending to the Gulf of Mexico, for conducting further operations.

Lee believed it was up to him to attempt a dramatic blow in the East if the Confederate effort was to maintain a chance of prevailing. For three days he talked with Davis and his aides about a plan he had for carrying the war into Northern territory.

It was true the commander had failed in a try to invade the North the previous September, that he had been stopped by George McClellan at the Battle of Antietam, near Sharpsburg, Maryland. But that penetration had been a spur-of-the-moment affair, an attempt to expand upon the Confederate victory at Second Manassas (or Second Bull Run) on August 29 and 30. The present plan was based upon a careful consideration of the war situation as a whole.

To begin with, Joe Hooker's presence on the Falmouth bank of the Rappahannock remained a menace to Richmond, and a move by Lee around Hooker's western flank to Pennsylvania would compel the Union general to recoil northward to protect his own capital. An added benefit of his departure would be that the war-scourged sections of Virginia would get some relief.

Of special importance to the invading Confederates would be that Pennsylvania's prosperous towns and farms could be compelled to provide them with supplies, not only for use during the campaign but also for replenishing their stockpiles in Virginia.

A further consideration was that such an invasion might have an effect on the Vicksburg situation, might startle the North into hesitation in that theater. At the least, the spotlight could be expected to shift from Southern reverses there.

The Union's peace advocates, known to be numerous, were another element in the talks. With Lee's army on Northern soil, these people would surely heighten their clamor against the war, and this could lead to a peace negotiated to the South's advantage.

The ideal situation would be for Lee to shatter the Army of the Potomac and press to the eastern seaboard above Washington. This would doubtless convince the North that subduing the South was an impossible task.

Also discussed was that a Confederate victory of any nature on Northern soil might prompt England and France to recognize the Richmond government and even send a fleet to its aid. The South's cotton was important to these nations, and they were already helping the Confederate war effort with clandestine shipments of arms and other supplies. (It was not yet fully understood in the South that any real hope of foreign intervention had died with the issuing of the Emancipation Proclamation. Interventionists would appear to be fighting for the preservation of slavery.)

Everything considered, Lee believed that an invasion of the North was the best thing he could try; and Davis and his cabinet, with only one aide dissenting, voted agreement. It was known that the Southern people were ready to support just such a move, were actually clamoring for it.

It was believed then, and afterward, that Lee made the plans for his invasion with a supreme confidence and saw success as virtually assured. But the general's confidence does not appear to have extended beyond a strong faith in his army. No commander of Lee's experience could have undertaken such a campaign with expansive optimism. The risks were obvious.

The Union army might be expected to fight with a special determination on its own ground—even as the Confederates had done in Virginia. Certain supplies, notably ammunition, might run short. The army's supply trains could carry only so much, and the farther north Lee went the longer the reach back to his depots. Time itself would be working against him. Things must be brought to a climax without too much delay, else the North would be able to muster reserves enough to cut him off from the South.

All in all, there was more reason for Lee to be apprehensive than confident. He was entering upon a dangerous gamble, and this must have loomed large in his mind.

The train Lee boarded in Richmond to go back up the line to his army at Fredericksburg stopped for an hour at the town of Ashland, and the general used the time to enjoy a mid-morning breakfast at a house near the station that was occupied by several ladies, one of whom was a relative.

This woman, after studying Lee's features across the table, decided she did not like his shaggy beard. "Cousin Robert, it makes you look too venerable for your years."

Lee laughed and explained that he found shaving to be too much of a chore under camp conditions.

"Well," the woman responded, "if I were in Cousin Mary's place, I would allow it to remain now, but I would take it off as soon as the war is over."

A shadow fell across Lee's face, and he said something seemingly out of character, something decidedly strange.

"When the war is over, my dear, she may take my beard off, and my head with it, if she chooses."

At that moment the train whistle shrieked a summons for its absent passengers to reboard, and the general left the house without explaining the remark. The ladies decided it must have been prompted by worry about the military situation.

This was probably the case. It is difficult, in fact, to interpret the statement as anything but a lapse into pessimism. Lee seemed to be implying that he expected the war to end with his head a forfeit to failure.

3

Stuart at His Zenith

COMPRISING THREE CORPS of infantry and one of cavalry, all amply provided with artillery, Lee's Army of Northern Virginia was in the process of building to about 75,000 men. Healed casualties were returning to duty, and recruits were arriving from various parts of the South, the former receiving a back-slapping welcome, the latter meeting with the usual patronization that veterans extend to men of no experience.

As the Fredericksburg camps bustled with preparations for the campaign, the troops had no real knowledge of Lee's intentions, but it was enough to know he had something big in mind. Boisterous good humor and enthusiasm mingled with the shouted orders, the thump of marching feet, the rumbling and creaking of wagons and gun carriages, the measured clop of hooves, and the rousing music of numerous bands.

Lee's opening plans called for one corps of infantry to remain at Fredericksburg facing the Army of the Potomac while the other two, under cover of the hills and woods on the southern side of the Rappahannock, began a secret move to the northwest, the march bearing on Virginia's Blue Ridge Mountains but having as its first destination the town of Culpeper, some thirty miles from Fredericksburg.

The cavalry edged off two weeks before the infantry.

Commanding this arm, a corps of about 10,000 sabers, was thirty-year-old Major General James Ewell Brown "Jeb" Stuart. Too young to have fought in Mexico, Stuart was a veteran of service on the Western frontier, and he bore a bullet scar on his chest from a wound

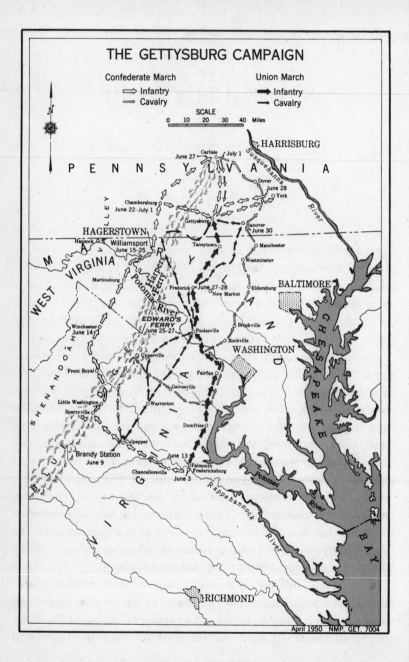

THE GETTYSBURG CAMPAIGN

Confederate March   Union March
    Infantry   Infantry
    Cavalry   Cavalry

SCALE
0   10   20   30   40   Miles

April 1950   NMP. GET. 7004

Jeb Stuart

received in a fight with a party of Cheyenne Indians. In the East in the autumn of 1859, he was a member of a detachment under Lee that captured the fanatical abolitionist John Brown during his raid on the Federal arsenal at Harpers Ferry on the upper Potomac.

A man of average height and sturdy build, Jeb Stuart was a laughing cavalier in the best romantic tradition. He courted danger with a song on his lips, carrying with him a personal band that included a banjoist and a set of fiddlers; and he survived by means of a splendid alertness. His career against the Yankees made him a legend throughout the South, and he was even admired by many in the North.

Colorful both in dress and manner, Stuart was ever an exhibitionist. He lived for praise and publicity, which he got in abundance, and which was usually well earned. But his obsession with his image, along with a delusion that he was infallible, sometimes made him difficult to work with; and, in his combat reports, he had a way of making even his setbacks appear to be successes.

Lee relied heavily on Jeb's expertise as an intelligence officer. Known for endurance in the saddle, he numbered among his exploits two raids entirely around the Union army while it was commanded by George McClellan in 1862.

Such a man, to be sure, was very attractive to women, and Stuart did not let the fact that he was married (and a father) spoil his enjoyment of female company, which, in spite of his constant round of duties, he managed to find in copious measure. Like Lee, he was a public kisser. But he was by no means a womanizer. He considered himself to be a knightly figure, and those who knew him well insisted he was "as pure as the girls he kissed."

(Lofty sexual morals were far from universal among Civil War soldiers. Prostitutes were readily available, and the incidence of venereal disease was high.)

Jeb Stuart's cavalry corps held six brigades, those of Fitzhugh Lee, Wade Hampton, W. H. F. Lee, Albert G. Jenkins, Beverly H. Robertson, and William E. "Grumble" Jones.

Robert E. Lee's family was well represented here. Fitzhugh Lee was his nephew, and W. H. F. Lee was his son. The latter was known as "Rooney" Lee to his intimates, and as "Alphabet" Lee to Yankees who found his use of three initials a curiosity. Another son of the commander, Robert E. Lee, Jr., was serving as an aide to his brother Rooney.

Stuart's staff officers included one of particular interest, young Major Heros von Borcke, a Prussian aristocrat (his family lived in a towered castle) who had resigned a cavalry commission in Berlin in order to cross the Atlantic and embrace the Confederate cause.

A Virginia woman who knew von Borcke described him as "a man of noble presence, standing over six feet without his shoes, and of size corresponding to his height. He was remarkably handsome, of a pure German type of beauty, and his manners combined a courtly ease and elegance with much dignity. . . . He was quite the rage with the girls, and his attractions were enhanced by his speaking English very brokenly. That made him altogether charming."

Not to be ignored is that von Borcke was a gifted writer. His word-

Rooney Lee

pictures (translated from the German) are exceptional. He says of the arrival of Stuart and his staff in Culpeper County: "Our tents were pitched in a beautiful spot, overshadowed by magnificent hickory and tulip-poplar trees, and surrounded by broad clover fields where our horses were richly pastured, and through which the pretty little river, Mountain Run, rolled its silver waters between picturesque banks, and afforded us the chance of a magnificent cool bath and plenty of sport with the rod and line."

Other troopers of Stuart's command who wrote memoirs agreed with von Borcke as to the beauty of Culpeper County. But neither von Borcke nor the others mentioned that it held one farm of 2,200 acres, located about three miles northeast of the town of Culpeper near Brandy Station, that the men deliberately abused—and with Stuart's blessing. (This sidelight of Jeb's career, incidentally, seems to have been overlooked by all of his biographers.)

The cavalry's abuse of this Virginia farm was not a new thing. Stuart and numbers of his men had been there before, and more than once.

Owner of the farm was John Minor Botts, a wealthy Virginian with a long career in politics, both state and national, and a well-known

John Minor Botts

figure in South and North alike. For thirty years before the war Botts had worked in opposition to the South's drift toward secession, and when the war started he continued his pro-Union talk, which got him into serious trouble with Confederate leaders. He was even confined, for a time, in a "filthy Negro jail." Residing in Richmond then, Botts had moved to Culpeper County early in 1863, hoping to find exemption from persecution.

But he'd barely settled in before Jeb Stuart arrived with a large force of cavalry and occupied the entire estate except for its house, yard, and garden. Hundreds of Stuart's horses were turned loose to graze in the choicest pastures. And when the troopers left, a good many of Botts' own horses, along with numbers of his cattle and hogs, went with them, appropriated for Confederate use.

From then on, detachments of Stuart's cavalry had returned regularly for further harassments. And now the entire corps was assembling in the area. Botts said later: "Daily and hourly I was subjected to all sorts of vexatious annoyances."

One of the things that brought such wrath upon Botts was the remembrance of a prediction he'd made at the war's beginning.

"The history of the world in 6,000 years has furnished but one instance of a David and Goliath. I do not think this is likely to prove a second. Five millions of people [probably eight or nine million, with blacks included] ... without money ... without a sufficiency of the necessaries of life, without a navy, and without commerce—to overthrow 22,000,000 of people with an abundant supply of both money and credit ... provisions, and other appliances of war, with a most powerful navy and a commerce unrestricted with all the world, would be a miracle that could be worked out by the hand of the Almighty alone. . . .

"I am compelled, therefore, to conclude that the rebellion will prove in the end a most signal and disastrous failure, unless the Administration at Washington shall be guilty of some act of most absurd and stupid folly."

This prediction threw a shade on the glorious dream of Southern independence. It laid bare realities that could not be denied, but that most people *wished* to deny. Even those who knew in their hearts that Southern chances were slim did not vocalize the thought.

Some, however, came close. At the war's start, Jeb Stuart said to a friend, "I regard it as a foregone conclusion that we shall ultimately whip the Yankees." Then he added, "We are bound to *believe* that, anyhow."

While Stuart's corps was massing in Culpeper County, it had little to do but to await the approach of Lee's infantry from Fredericksburg. The troopers, making free use of the Botts farm, spent much of their time drilling and engaging in other preparations for the campaign.

(At about this time it became known among Lee's forces, both cavalry and infantry, that affairs in their theater of the war had risen to a new level of importance to the cause. Word arrived from the West that Ulysses Grant had begun besieging Vicksburg, his army forming an arc that pinned the garrison against the Mississippi, which held cooperating Union naval vessels. Grant was effecting his planned stranglehold, threatening a disaster to the South that only Lee's army could offset.)

On May 22, Jeb Stuart, who had a boyish love for military pageantry, conducted a review, a relatively small affair, since a good part of his command was not yet present. He took satisfaction in knowing there would be time for him to hold a more elaborate review in the same area, with Lee attending, before the cavalry began its active role in the campaign.

By the first of June, even before Lee made his initial infantry movement, Joe Hooker was aware that something grave was developing. Union spies and the Confederate deserters who came across the Rappahannock informed him that Lee had ordered the Army of Northern Virginia to ready itself for a campaign that would involve long marches beyond the range of the South's railway system. Hooker heard next that the move would carry the Confederates across the Potomac into Union-held Maryland. It wasn't clear, however, whether Lee intended more than a large-scale raid to secure supplies. Because of the situation's uncertainty, Hooker could make no immediate response, but an alert was established.

The Union lookouts peering southward across the river included men with telescopes in the basketlike gondolas of hydrogen-filled balloons. Far from being camouflaged, these balloons were orange in

One of Thaddeus Lowe's balloons. Left: *replenishing its gas.*
Right: *Lowe making a reconnaissance.*

color, their gondolas decorated with the hues of the national flag. During their ascension, the balloons often drew artillery fire, but they were safe enough at their observation elevations of from 500 to 1,000 feet. They were controlled by Manila cables in the hands of ground crews.

It might be noted here that not all of the business in Joe Hooker's camps at this time involved the new campaign. Loose ends from Chancellorsville were still being tied up, among them the disposition of men charged with cowardice under fire.

This was an era when failures of courage on the battlefield were not tolerated. There was no sympathy for those unable to master their fear. They were treated as criminals.

The lieutenant of a New Jersey regiment, tried by court-martial, was convicted of cowardice. The entire brigade to which he belonged was turned out at the hour of evening parade and formed into a hollow square. Marched to the center of the enclosure, the lieutenant heard his sentence. He was to be dismissed from the service in disgrace.

The brigade's adjutant-general took the officer's sword from him and broke it. The same was done with the man's revolver. His shoulder straps and buttons were cut off. Worst of all, the adjutant-general ordered that the man's hometown newspaper be informed of his dereliction.

That same evening there was a similar ceremony involving an enlisted man. His sentence was that he be sent to the Dry Tortugas, west of the Florida Keys, for a period of hard labor. The buttons and the blue cord of his coat were cut off, and a placard marked COWARD was hung on his back. A guard with his bayonet fixed marched the man off to the brig, while a band played "The Rogue's March."

In the words of an observer, a member of the brigade: "As we looked upon the execution of these humiliating sentences, we could not help feeling how much better it would have been to have fallen nobly on that field of battle, honored and lamented, than to live to be thus degraded and despised. It had never been so forcibly impressed upon our minds how much better it was to die nobly than to live in disgrace."

This comment goes a long way toward explaining the remarkably dedicated performances of so many Civil War soldiers.

Richard S. Ewell

It was on June 3 that Lee began moving his infantry from Fredericksburg to Culpeper. Leading the way were the columns of the First Corps under James Longstreet. Next came the Second Corps under eccentric, birdlike Richard S. "Dick" Ewell.

Smoothly bald (and often called "Old Bald Head"), Ewell had a pointed nose and protuberant eyes, and was nervously animated. Having lost a leg during the fighting of 1862, the general left Fredericksburg riding in a buggy and equipped with a wooden leg and a set of crutches. He was prepared to strap himself on a saddle horse when the need arose.

Ewell had recently married a widow, a Mrs. Brown, who had nursed him through his convalescence. As it happened, she had been an interest of his younger years, a woman he had loved and lost. As a result of wedding her at last, and of adopting her religious fervor as well, he had changed from a man known for irascibility and explosive profanity into one who kept himself passably controlled.

But the marriage did nothing to lessen Dick Ewell's eccentricity. He went around presenting his new spouse to his friends as "my wife, Mrs. Brown."

Remaining at Fredericksburg, for the present, to face Hooker was Lee's Third Corps under Ambrose Powell "A. P." Hill, a Virginian born in Culpeper County. Slender and weak-framed, and sometimes referred to as "Little Powell," Hill was chronically ill, but he had earned a considerable reputation as an aggressive and skillful fighter. Unfailingly concerned with the welfare of those he led, he held his life to be no more sacred than that of a private. He was endowed with a quick intellect and an engaging style, and had many friends and admirers.

Joe Hooker was beginning to worry. He was far from eager for a new clash with Lee. And he knew that Lincoln, whom he had disappointed, would be monitoring his decisions to a greater degree than before. Of course, having the President as a strong partner had a bright side. Hooker's own responsibility in the developing situation would be lightened.

It was on the morning of June 4 that Hooker's balloonists at Falmouth discovered that many of the enemy's tents were gone. But this could not be construed as proof that Lee was beginning a general exodus.

Ambrose P. Hill

The next day Hooker telegraphed Lincoln: "This morning some more of their camps have disappeared. The picket line along the river is preserved as strong as ever. . . . As I am liable to be called on to make a movement with utmost promptitude, I desire that I may be informed as early as practicable of the views of the Government concerning this army."

All he knew, he said, was that he was expected to keep in mind the importance of covering Washington and Harpers Ferry. (The latter's location on the upper Potomac at the northern end of the Shenandoah Valley made it an outpost of Washington's defenses, though not a vital one.)

Hooker's wire continued: "In the event the enemy should move, as I almost anticipate he will, the head of his column will probably be headed toward the Potomac, via Gordonsville or Culpeper, while the rear will rest on Fredericksburg. . . . I am of opinion that it is my duty to pitch into his rear. . . . Will it be within the spirit of my instructions to do so?"

Lincoln responded immediately that he was sending the request to the War Department for consideration by Henry W. Halleck, General-in-Chief of the Union Armies. This did not please Hooker, for he and Halleck were on bad terms. Their enmity predated the war, its origins unclear.

In the same wire, Lincoln expressed personal doubts that Hooker should cross the Rappahannock and attack Lee.

"If he should leave a rear force at Fredericksburg, tempting you to fall upon it, it would fight in intrenchments and have you at a disadvantage . . . while his main force would in some way be getting an advantage of you northward."

The President clinched his opinion with a line that became a part of the Lincoln legend.

"In one word, I would not take any risk of being entangled upon the river, like an ox jumped half over a fence and liable to be torn by dogs front and rear without a fair chance to gore one way or kick the other."

The general-in-chief's telegram reached Hooker shortly after Lincoln's. Halleck stated firmly that Hooker must make his first aim the security of Washington and Harpers Ferry. "It would therefore seem perilous to permit Lee's main force to move upon the Potomac while your army is attacking an intrenched position on the other side of the Rappahannock." There was a qualification: "Of course, your movements must depend in a great measure upon those made by Lee."

Hooker went so far as to send a division across the river in an effort to learn more of Lee's intentions. A. P. Hill quickly semicircled the incursion. During the skirmishing, a number of Confederates were captured; but they gave no useful information, claiming that the tents had vanished only because of reorganizational measures.

The episode became a stalemate, with the Federals and Confederates facing one another peaceably, the pickets very close. A feeling of sociability set in. The two sides began exchanging newspapers, and the bluecoats produced coffee and sugar they traded for plugs of Southern tobacco.

Hooker's disappointment over this reconnaissance was at least partially offset by some information he received from his upriver scouts. They had found Jeb Stuart's cavalry massed in the Culpeper area. This discovery required no special skill on the part of the scouts, for Stuart

A friendly meeting of cavalry pickets.

was making a lot of noise. It was on June 5 that he conducted his second review.

A regret for Jeb was that his arrangements for the affair had matured before General Lee, who was expected to attend, made his arrival from Fredericksburg. But the entire program, with Stuart himself the central figure, proceeded as planned.

Civilians for miles around had assembled, by invitation, the previous day, and a tent camp had been set up to provide for the overflow of the area's guest accommodations. On the eve of the review a candlelight ball was held in the Culpeper town hall.

Early on the morning of the 5th, a perfect June day, the troopers, with the exception of Stuart and his staff, assembled on the chosen site, farmlands that neighbored those of John Minor Botts. The formations stretched for a mile and a half, some of them trampling fields of corn, wheat, and oats. How Botts fared on this day is not a matter of record.

Stuart and his aides, in their best uniforms and on fine mounts, a battle flag rippling above them, soon made a cantering approach heralded by bugles. Their route took them through a cluster of houses, and some of the female residents ran out and spread flowers in their path. As the general neared the field, the troopers raised a tremendous cheer, and he was given a twenty-gun salute.

Jeb did the customary ceremonial riding among the formations, then took his station on a little rise, the gathering place of hundreds of civilians, many of them women whose eyes shone with adoration. The beaming general gave the signal for the "march past," which was done by squadrons, with three bands playing. Stuart's Prussian aide, Heros von Borcke, found that "the magnificent spectacle of so many thousand troopers splendidly mounted made the heart swell with pride."

The review closed with regimental sham charges, the galloping troopers yelling and swinging their sabers, and the artillery firing blank cartridges.

That evening there was another ball, this one out-of-doors, the couples using a stretch of turf illuminated by bonfires, the whole scene bathed in a ruddiness that, according to von Borcke, gave it "a wild and romantic effect."

Jeb Stuart would have been surprised to know that he was much on the mind of Joe Hooker at this time. Hooker wired Washington: "As the accumulation of the heavy rebel force of cavalry about Culpeper may mean mischief, I am determined, if practicable, to break it up in its incipience. I shall send all of my cavalry against them, stiffened by about 3,000 infantry. It will require until the morning of the 9th for my forces to gain their positions, and on daylight of that day it is my intention to attack them in their camps."

General Lee reached Culpeper on the 7th, and he sent word to Stuart that he'd be pleased to review the cavalry on the 8th.

Jeb was quite willing to perform anew, but many of the troopers grumbled at repeating the work of preparation, knowing they'd again be anonymous figures in pageantry slanted toward the greater glory of their commander. But they had no choice but to comply, and the review was conducted on the same ground.

This time Stuart came upon the field with his uniform and his horse's gear bedecked with flowers, even though the affair was strictly business, with the observers mostly army people, and with Lee having ordered that events be kept simple so as not to tax the horses or waste ammunition.

It is said that Lee, noting the flowers, recalled having heard that one of Lincoln's failed generals (it is not clear which one) had been known to adorn himself this way. Perhaps Lee teased Stuart about this.

All in all, however, the review sustained Lee's confidence in his cavalry. On the personal side, he was able to write Mary that their two sons, Rooney and Robert, Jr., were "well and flourishing."

Lee had no way of knowing that this review marked the zenith of his cavalry's preeminence.

Joe Hooker had a strong hand in this. His achievements as an organizer had included the strengthening of the army's cavalry, which, heretofore, hadn't made much of a name for itself. One of the reasons Jeb Stuart had done so well against it was that its performance was weak. Things would be different now.

The Yankee troopers had a new commander, not a great one, but at least a good one. Thirty-nine-year-old Alfred Pleasonton was a man of ready perception and a generally sound strategic and tactical sense. He

Alfred Pleasonton

was small, slender, and nattily uniformed, topping off the effect with a stiff-brimmed straw hat he wore cocked to one side. But he spoiled his image of jauntiness with a shifty eye, having a habit of taking only darting looks into the faces of people he talked with.

Pleasonton colored his battle reports shamelessly in his own favor, but there was enough substance in his leadership to enable him to get away with this. He had the full confidence of his men. His subordinates included experienced regulars John Buford and David McMurtrie Gregg, promising young Hugh Judson Kilpatrick, and British soldier-of-fortune Sir Percy Wyndham.

Even while Jeb Stuart's review was in progress, Pleasonton's forces—numbering, like Stuart's, about 10,000—were stealing toward the north bank of the Rappahannock at the fords bearing on Culpeper. Jeb himself was planning to cross the river in this area the next day. Both Longstreet's and Ewell's corps had reached Culpeper, and Lee wanted Jeb on the north bank in preparation to covering the right flank of these columns as they began their invasion march.

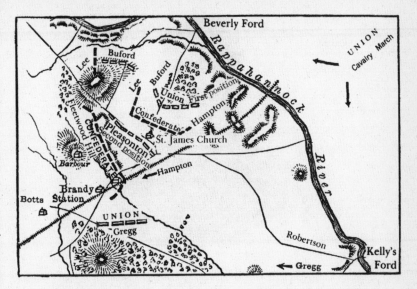

Battle of Brandy Station. Upper right shows Union approach to fords. Upper center shows foes in first positions (north of St. James Church). Lower right shows Gregg bypassing Robertson. All other troop delineations represent conditions as the battle neared its end. Hampton's charge has succeeded. Gregg's attack from the south has been repelled. Confederates hold all of Fleetwood Hill. Pleasonton and Buford have discontinued their attack from the northeast. Botts farm is shown at lower left.

After Lee had departed the review field, Stuart's troopers returned to their camps, most of which were now located northeast of Culpeper, in a great arc, on the plains between Brandy Station and the river. Part of one brigade, however, lingered on the Botts farm, as though to annoy the Union sympathizer to the last moment.

The forward units were all bivouacked a good distance back from the fords, but the fords were covered by pickets. Stuart had his headquarters at the southern end of Fleetwood Hill, about three miles from the river. The oblong elevation spanned three miles in a north-south direction, and it overlooked most of the surrounding plains areas.

Stuart had been so busy with his theatricals that he had neglected his security. He had no idea that Pleasonton's horsemen were making their

John Buford

bivouacs on the other side of the river only a few miles from his own camps. The bluecoats had been ordered to proceed quietly and to forgo campfires (which meant a cold supper and no coffee). It rained for a time late in the day, preventing Yankee dust from rising above the trees and drawing Stuart's attention.

Pleasonton's men were in two columns, the one led by the commander himself, with Buford second-in-command, and the other under David Gregg. Pleasonton and Buford faced Beverly Ford, which was nearest Stuart's headquarters on Fleetwood Hill, while Gregg was at Kelly's Ford, about six miles to the southeast, a spot that offered a route to the right flank and rear of Stuart's scattered camps. But the Yankees had no definite knowledge of the enemy's location. Last reports, in fact, had placed him back at Culpeper.

As the men of both sides settled down for the night, only the Confederates had the light of campfires for writing letters, for playing cards, for reading their Bibles. The Federals had little choice but to unroll their blankets when daylight failed.

Midnight found the camps on both sides of the river quiet and wrapped in darkness, though red embers and nubbins of flame marked the sites of the Confederate fires, around which men now slept. Movement nearly everywhere was limited to that of bored sentries making their rounds and to occasional stirrings among the clusters of unsaddled horses.

The atmosphere was sublimely peaceful—hardly indicative of the fact that the fiercest cavalry fight of the war was only a few hours away.

4

Flashing Sabers

It was still dark on the morning of June 9 when Alfred Pleasonton rode to the riverbank at Beverly Ford. The atmosphere was misty, and the general and his companions were ghostly in one another's sight. An aide, however, was able to detect that strong-faced John Buford had a pipe in his mouth, a centerpiece for his well-turned mustaches. Buford was seldom seen without his pipe, and he sometimes used its stem as a pointer while issuing orders.

Pleasonton and Buford had chosen Colonel Benjamin F. Davis to lead the advance across the river with his 8th New York Cavalry, backed by the other regiments of the brigade he commanded. Known as "Grimes" Davis, the colonel, an acting brigadier, got the job of launching the attack because he was one of the North's most promising cavalry officers. (He was actually a Southerner, a West Point graduate who had elected to abide by his vow of loyalty to the Union.)

Not only high in valor and determination, Davis was also one of those leaders who could make men accept rough work with a sense of pride rather than with grumbling reluctance, and he thus impelled them to peak performance. Though strict, he was well liked.

Pleasonton reconnoitered the ford with Davis, and they found conditions favorable for surprising the enemy. The water was only stirrup-deep. There was a dam just above the ford, and the roll of the water over the breast could be expected to help subdue the sounds of the

The 8th New York Cavalry at Beverly Ford.

crossing. Also advantageous was that a border of fog on the enemy's bank offered cover for the emergence.

It was decided that the attack should proceed at once, and at five o'clock, with daylight at hand, Grimes Davis led his 8th New York across, his other regiments poised to follow.

On the Confederate side, one of the off-duty pickets was nineteen-year-old Luther W. Hopkins. He had served a watch at the ford during the night but was now asleep, wrapped in a blanket, in a woods a few hundred yards back. The youth was rudely awakened by a cry from the camp watchman, who'd heard an alarm from the river.

Hopkins and the others of his company, about twenty men, jumped up and were shortly on horseback. Led by a captain, they formed a thin line at the edge of the woods astraddle the road that ran to the ford.

The first people to burst out of the fog were Confederate pickets on foot who were shouting and firing their pistols into the air to spread the alarm. They were soon followed and sent scampering right and left by mounted troopers in blue. As the Yankee host approached the woods at a canter with swords raised, Hopkins and his comrades opened fire, checking the surge for the moment.

But a return fire came at once. Two Confederates slumped from the saddle, dead; several swayed with wounds; and two horses went down heavily, their wounds fatal, their riders jumping clear.

Mounted Confederate couriers were now racing toward the rear, and the outmatched company decided to follow. Bullets snapped around the men as they urged their mounts to a gallop. To their great relief, they shortly met their parent regiment rushing forward.

This was the 6th Virginia, under Major C. E. Flournoy, and one of its members was another nineteen-year-old, John N. Opie, who was worried about his mount, a headstrong mare.

"My horse did what I too well knew she would do—that is, she shot out from the column like a thunderbolt and rushed down the road with the rapidity of lightning."

Unable to check the mare, Opie rounded a bend and found himself making a lone charge on the approaching Yankees. He hoped fervently they would realize what was happening and would be chivalrous about it, but several carbines were discharged at him. He and the horse went into a headlong tumble, the horse dead and the rider with a furrow in the sole of his boot.

By the time Opie was back on his feet, his friends were charging past him, and he secured a new mount as one of the men fell dead from the saddle under a second Federal volley.

In a skirmish in which the crash of carbines and pistols was joined by the clanging of sabers, the Yankees were at first pushed back. Grimes Davis succeeded in bringing about a rally; but then, even as he raised his sword and cried, "Come on, boys!" a Confederate lieutenant rode up to him and, dodging a whistling slash of the blade, shot him dead with a pistol.

The loss of their revered leader rocked the Federals, but their discipline soon asserted itself and they advanced with a new resolve, vowing vengeance. The Virginians, of lesser numbers than their assailants, discreetly turned tail (a literal move on the part of their mounts) and made for the rear.

Union troopers in swelling strength were now splashing across the river. The need for secrecy had passed, and the men were whooping and shouting. Wading in their support, muskets held high, was a detachment of infantry.

The leading Federals, pushing the 6th Virginia before them, were soon a mile from the river and were presenting a critical threat to Jeb Stuart's horse artillery, commanded by Major R. F. Beckham. These guns should not have been parked for the night at a spot so vulnerable.

Two of the pieces were shortly booming a desperate defense. At the same time, General William "Grumble" Jones, responsible for covering the ford and providing security for Beckham's camp, rushed forward with the 7th Virginia Regiment. The general's hat and coat were missing, and his bare feet shone white in his stirrups. Many of the others, too, were incompletely dressed, and some, though clutching their weapons, were riding without their saddles.

This Confederate charge was thrown back. Nevertheless, along with the artillery fire, it delayed the Federals long enough so that all of Beckham's guns and most of his camp equipage could be hurried to the rear. The major's headquarters desk, however, bounced out of a careening wagon and ended up in Alfred Pleasonton's hands. A drawer held some papers the Union general was to claim gave specifics on Lee's plans, but all the papers seem to have been were orders from Jeb Stuart to his commands to hold themselves in readiness to move at a very short notice.

Pleasonton gained another scrap of information, though nothing really new, through a letter found on the field. A Confederate trooper wrote that he believed Lee was making plans for "a grand raid toward the Potomac." (This writer had just seen Lee for the first time, and found him to be "a fine-looking man, but very gray-haired.")

The Confederate guns under Major Beckham were set up for action at St. James Church, about two miles from the river and a mile in front of Jeb Stuart's headquarters on Fleetwood Hill. The guns pointed generally northward. Grumble Jones's brigade—minus the casualties of his 6th and 7th Virginia Regiments, some of these left on the field—formed on the guns, creating an east-west line.

Pleasonton and Buford deployed their units under cover of an extensive woods separated from the Confederate line by a broad open area. The Yankees, of course, faced generally southward.

Jeb Stuart had awakened at the sound of the first shots coming up from the river, and he knew instantly what the firing meant. This is not to say he wasn't surprised. Such a thing was not supposed to be happening.

Even before the general began dispatching orders for Jones's support, most of the scattered Confederate units had begun reacting on their own to the sound of the firing.

Two brigades stationed to the north, upriver from Beverly Ford, moved toward Pleasonton's western flank, his right. These were the brigades of Robert E. Lee's son Rooney and his nephew Fitz Lee— with the latter unit under the temporary command of Thomas Munford, since Fitz was down with a bout of arthritis. An imperfect knowledge of what was expected of him would keep Munford from playing a prominent role in the fight.

Wade Hampton, the wealthy planter-politician from South Carolina, whose brigade was located south of the developing battlefield, moved northward on the Confederate right and confronted Pleasonton's eastern wing, his left.

When word reached Stuart that the Yankees were crossing also at Kelly's Ford, about five miles southeast of Fleetwood Hill, he ordered

Wade Hampton

Beverly Robertson's brigade, already in that vicinity, to counter this threat to his right and rear. The measure seemed adequate, and Stuart dismissed this worry from his mind. He gave his full attention to affairs at St. James Church, though he remained for a time at Fleetwood. His elevated position gave him a good view of the battlefield.

During these early morning hours, the open area between the church and the woods held by the Yankees was the scene of regimental charges and countercharges that were not productive of any special advantage to either side but were remarkable as military spectacles.

Young George Neese, observing the field as a Confederate artillerist, found the actions "fascinatingly grand beyond description.... Hundreds of glittering sabers ... gleamed and flashed in the morning sun, then clashed with metallic ring, searching for human blood, while hundreds of little puffs of white smoke gracefully rose through the balmy June air from discharging firearms all over the field in front of our batteries."

Unlikely pictures in the fray were those of color-bearers using their staffs both as lances and clubs, and those of black servants, Confederate and Yankee, who had secured muskets or carbines and were acting as sharpshooters.

The fruitless collisions ended with all of the Yankees falling back to the edge of the woods. According to Southerner George Neese, sixteen guns opened upon them "with a crash and sullen roar that made the morning air tremble." The Yankees "disappeared from sight and retired deeper into the woods."

Pleasonton's forces hadn't been driven off. It had become necessary for the general to look to his right, to his western flank, now threatened by Rooney Lee's approach from his upriver position.

The action here began with an artillery duel. Pleasonton used one of his artillery knolls as an observation post, and an aide said later that the general ignored enemy shells flying around the battery "like a flock of pigeons."

John Buford, smoking his pipe and maintaining the shade of a smile, led the fighting against Rooney Lee. The two were a good match, for Lee had inherited the spirit of his illustrious father. The contest churned over a broad area of farmlands marked by stone walls and patches of trees.

Lee at length gave way, swinging to the left of the Confederate line at St. James Church. Buford held to the right of the Union line, which kept him facing Lee.

Pleasonton was now in a position where he might have made a general advance, but he was worried about his strength. It had been a mistake for him to send David Gregg for a crossing down at Kelly's Ford. This had been done under the supposition that Stuart was still back toward Culpeper. Pleasonton had expected to make junction with Gregg at Brandy Station before engaging in major fighting.

Gregg, with his column raising a cloud of dust, was presently moving westward toward the station. Strangely enough, Confederate General Beverly Robertson had not interfered. He had been ordered to block the direct road from Kelly's Ford, and this he did. But Gregg had

Brandy Station, Virginia

made no attempt to use that road. He had swung to the south, around Robertson's right flank, on another road.

Gregg's wing numbered about 4,300 men; but he diminished his strength by sending a detachment of 1,900, the command of Colonel Alfred N. Duffié, on a southerly probe toward Culpeper. This force encountered two Confederate regiments stationed down that way, and the meeting ended Duffié's availability for Pleasonton's use, since the colonel was long delayed.

Among the mortal casualties of this skirmishing was a brother to Southerner Wade Hampton, Colonel Frank Hampton; and one of Jeb Stuart's favorite aides, Captain William D. Farley, who lost a leg to a cannonball. As Farley was being started away on a stretcher, well aware that he was dying, he bid a smiling good-bye to his comrades. He was clutching his bloody severed limb to his breast, and he explained, "It is an old friend, gentlemen, and I do not wish to part from it."

When, in mid-morning, Jeb Stuart galloped from Fleetwood Hill to his St. James front he found the battle arena to be relatively quiet. With Rooney Lee on Grumble Jones's left and Wade Hampton on his right, the Confederate line was now strong enough for a concerted effort; and, with this in mind, Stuart set about improving his dispositions.

At this time the general remained unworried about a threat to his right-rear. He assumed that Beverly Robertson was barring a Yankee approach from Kelly's Ford. When Grumble Jones sent a courier to Stuart saying he'd received word from the ford that things had gone wrong in that direction, Stuart responded, "Tell General Jones to attend to the Yankees in front, and I'll watch the flanks."

Not much had been left on Fleetwood Hill when Stuart went to the front. He had taken the precaution of ordering all of his headquarters equipage sent back to Culpeper. The hill, though a spot of great tactical importance, held only a few couriers, their horses, and Stuart's adjutant general, twenty-two-year-old Major Henry B. McClellan, a native Pennsylvanian who had moved to Virginia just before the war, and, with the zeal of youth, had embraced the Confederate cause. He had four brothers who fought on the Union side, and he was a first cousin of that very famous Yankee, General George McClellan.

David McMurtrie Gregg

It was a lucky moment for Jeb Stuart when Henry decided to become a Rebel, for on the day of the Battle of Brandy Station the young major did much to save Stuart's forces from disaster.

McClellan had been in charge on Fleetwood Hill for perhaps two hours when a scout from the Kelly's Ford area, one of Beverly Robertson's men who had been watching the Union troops under David Gregg, pushed his lathered horse up the slope to the skeleton headquarters. The major was told, in urgent terms, that the column of Yankees was moving, unopposed, upon Brandy Station. This was just south of Fleetwood Hill; and the news, if true, meant that the column was coming up directly in Stuart's rear.

McClellan was unbelieving. Beverly Robertson could not be allowing such a thing to happen. But a few minutes later the courier was able to tell the major to look for himself. Gregg could be seen approaching the station, the dusty column undulating in the late-morning sunlight, the leading horsemen hardly more than a cannon shot away. Gregg was coming on rapidly, obviously aware of the commanding nature of Fleetwood Hill.

McClellan shuddered at the thought of the column's taking the hill and getting its artillery into battery there. Stuart's forces at St. James Church would find themselves in the impossible situation of being menaced front and rear.

The young major's first move, of course, was to send word to Stuart to bring up troops, the message amounting to, "Kill your horses!"

But something had to be done to gain time, and McClellan had only one resource. Down the slope to the east was a single Confederate artillery piece, a 6-pounder howitzer. The gun had been brought to the rear from St. James Church because its ammunition was nearly exhausted. Only a few shells remained in its chest, and some of these were faulty.

Responding to McClellan's need, the crew got the gun up the hill as fast as its straining horses, with a whip snapping over their heads, were able to draw it. Utilizing the good shells, the gunners began lobbing a slow fire toward the head of Gregg's column.

The Yankees—all 2,400 of them—drew up. Gregg was obliged to assume that Fleetwood Hill was manned. He decided he would have to deploy for an assault. To cover this deployment, he unlimbered three of his guns, and things soon became very hot for McClellan and his few comrades.

The major's first courier reached Jeb Stuart at St. James Church while Fleetwood was still quiet, and the general rejected the report. To an aide he said, "Ride back there and see what all this foolishness is about."

Then up galloped a second courier, a man Stuart knew and trusted, who cried, "General, the Yankees are at Brandy!"

The cry was promptly followed by the booming of McClellan's lone howitzer. Then the Yankee guns were heard rumbling in answer, and all doubt was erased.

But Stuart was not yet aware of the full extent of the danger. He believed that only a small Union force had got past Beverly Robertson. A battalion and a regiment from Grumble Jones's brigade were ordered toward Fleetwood, but the men were not infused with a feeling of crisis, and they started the trip at a trot.

Stuart and his party soon followed. Visibility toward Fleetwood was excellent and it wasn't long before the general received what must have been one of the greatest shocks of his life. The fields extending from the southern end of the hill were filled with blue-coated troopers. Stuart's entire corps was imperiled, and so was his glorious career.

The general reacted by rushing orders to St. James for the entire line to start falling back toward Fleetwood. Rooney Lee, in the west, was expected to retrograde in such a way as to maintain enough contact with Pleasonton and Buford to retard the advance they would make.

In his eastern position, Confederate General Wade Hampton, who had decided on his own to do an about-face toward Fleetwood, was ordered to send a regiment ahead at a gallop. He dispatched Grumble Jones' battered 6th Virginia, then temporarily under his command.

The two units Jones had sent earlier were nearing Fleetwood, but without urgency.

In his position on the hill, Major McClellan had grown wildly anxious. His howitzer was out of ammunition and was being withdrawn. The blue-coated horsemen were beginning their attack. One regiment—the 1st New Jersey Cavalry of Sir Percy Wyndham's brigade—was already on Fleetwood's slopes. McClellan noted that the unit was advancing "in magnificent order, in column of squadrons, with flags and guidons flying."

At this moment the major saw the first of Grumble Jones's units arriving at the foot of the hill on his left. This was Asher Harman's 12th Virginia Regiment. Still not sure what was expected of him, Harman was holding his trot.

McClellan raced his horse down the slope and shouted to Harman, "For God's sake, charge! They're right on you!"

The surprised Harman put his troopers into a labored gallop up the hill, but they remained in column. There was no time to deploy for a regulation charge.

Onto the summit the column climbed, and came face to face with the Yankees. But only Harman's leading files could fight, and the entire column was shortly thrust back in disorder. A part of it careened into Grumble Jones's second unit, Elijah "Lige" White's 35th Battalion, now making a similar charge, and the battalion lost its effectiveness.

Both units were run off the hill, and the men of the 1st New Jersey whooped in triumph. Coming to their support during these moments were Wyndham's 1st Pennsylvania and 1st Maryland.

Jeb Stuart made his approach just in time to observe the Confederate retreat. His concern must have been high, but the situation quickly improved. The staggered units reformed; and Jones' third unit, the 6th Virginia, sent by Wade Hampton, was now on the scene. In spite of the punishment this regiment had taken in the action near the river, it was still in good morale.

Carbines, pistols, and sabers came into furious play as the fight for the hill was resumed; and this time it was Wyndham's ranks that were broken. Among the Confederates wounded in these encounters was Asher Harman.

Not all of the Yankees were cleared from the hill, but Lige White, with a part of his 35th Battalion and the 6th Virginia Regiment, was

The fight for Martin's guns.

able to break through to the southwestern base, where, on the road to Brandy Station, the three Union guns were in action. White rushed the guns, and the horsemen supporting them were driven away. But the guns were not immediately surrendered by their thirty-six Yankee crewmen.

The commander of the battery, Captain Joseph W. Martin, reported later: "It became a hand-to-hand fight with pistol and saber between the enemy and my cannoneers and drivers, and never did men act with more coolness and bravery."

In the end, Martin and the few others who hadn't been rendered casualties threw themselves on horses and rode away, leaving the guns to Lige White. But the Confederate officer wasn't able to keep them. He and his men suddenly found themselves surrounded by fresh Yankee troopers, and had to cut their way through to safer ground, losing heavily in the process.

Among those involved in another action in this area was Marcus W. Kitchen, adjutant of the 1st New Jersey. A Confederate with a revolver rode up to him and fired, but missed.

"Before he could again cock his revolver I succeeded in closing with him. My saber took him just in the neck, and must have cut the jugular. The blood gushed out in a black-looking stream. He gave a horrible yell and fell over the side of his horse, which galloped away."

During this part of the fighting, Jeb Stuart was riding everywhere, heedless of danger, shouting orders and striving for control. The fate of his corps was still decidedly uncertain.

Heros von Borcke was also in the thick of things, sometimes with Stuart, sometimes on his own. Once he rallied about a hundred troopers who had fled the field out of fear, gave them an inspirational talk, then led them in a charge.

He was nearing a unit of Yankees, his sword pointed, when things suddenly became very quiet behind him. Glancing over his shoulder, he discovered that the men had fled again. He himself whipped around just in time to avoid taking on the Yankees single-handedly, and it was only after a hard ride that he eluded their pursuit.

For a time, the advantage in the struggle for the southern part of Fleetwood Hill was gained first by one side, and then by the other. As yet, the

Deadly work at close quarters.

northern part of the hill was not involved. Rooney Lee was falling back to this area, but slowly, sparring with John Buford as he went.

The rest of Pleasonton's St. James line was making only a very cautious advance after the withdrawal of Grumble Jones and Wade Hampton. Pleasonton was concerned that Rooney Lee might turn his retreat, obviously calculated, into a sudden offensive. Buford might be bested, and this would enable Lee to swing around Pleasonton's right-rear and cut off his withdrawal route to Beverly Ford.

Early afternoon found David Gregg's bluecoats having gained a tentative upper hand on the southern slopes of Fleetwood. They also occupied the plains to the south and the west.

In the west, the farm of John Minor Botts was on the fringe of Gregg's deployments; and Botts, who was well known in the North for his loyalty to the Union, was sought out by at least one Yankee officer who wanted to shake his hand. There were likely other such meetings that went unrecorded.

Botts was doubtless hoping that his enemy, Jeb Stuart, would be soundly defeated.

It was Wade Hampton's brigade that brought the battle to a climax. These graycoats attacked from the northeast, across the open plains, in beautiful formation, four regiments of horsemen and a battery of artillery.

The right wing headed for the Yankees on the hill, the left wing for those on the plains that stretched from the hill's southern base. The brigade came on with hooves rumbling, men shouting, and uplifted sabers gleaming.

Gregg's Yankees were now outnumbered, but the regiments accepted the challenge.

Men on both sides rose up in their stirrups as the crash came. Sabers clanged, carbines and pistols rattled, artillery pieces boomed on the flanks. Men shouted in defiance, in fear, in pain. There were demands for surrender, appeals for mercy. Horses went down kicking. Others ran wild with empty saddles, some of which were bloodstained. Fallen men were trampled.

There was so much dust that all uniforms, Federal and Confederate, looked gray, and this added to the confusion. One Southerner who was captured said, "We can't tell you Yankees from our own men." Some

Brandy Station's climactic collision.

of the prisoners taken on both sides were incorrectly identified and released.

Gregg's resistance did little to weaken Hampton's attack. Soon, however, it lost its momentum in a way that was a great frustration to the South Carolinian. A Confederate artillery battery that had been put into action on Fleetwood Hill began firing into his regiments by mistake.

But the attack had progressed to a point where the issue was settled. Fighting at the southern end of Fleetwood diminished to minor brushes. The three disputed Union guns—Martin's battery—were again in Confederate hands, this time permanently.

Jeb Stuart began establishing a strong line on the hill, extending it northward to make contact with Rooney Lee's brigade, which had reached the upper end in its retirement before John Buford.

This northern fighting was winding down, too, after Rooney Lee was severely wounded in the thigh while fending off an effort by Buford to flank him.

It was now about 4:30 P.M., and Rooney's father, Robert E. Lee, had come up from Culpeper. He was aware that Stuart had been surprised, and he had begun to worry about the outcome. Some of Dick Ewell's infantry had been ordered up in Stuart's support.

Lee climbed to the cupola of the Barbour House, on a hill just west of Fleetwood, and observed the last of the skirmishing. At one time it swirled close to the house, and Lee and his aides were, for a few moments, in a precarious position.

But soon the Federals began drawing off in all quarters. The knowledge that Confederate infantry was arriving cemented their decision.

Colonel Duffié, who had split from Gregg in the morning and had been fighting in the south, came up and joined Gregg, and the aggregate made an easterly swing around Fleetwood Hill to join Pleasonton and Buford in their northerly position.

Pleasonton decided to take the entire force back across the Rappahannock at Beverly Ford and a downstream railroad bridge. The Federals had many of their dead and wounded with them, and they herded along numbers of Confederate prisoners on foot, some with bloodstained uniforms.

There were periods of artillery dueling at this time, as well as some lingering exchanges of small-arms fire. But Jeb Stuart chose not to launch an organized pursuit. He'd had quite enough of these unexpectedly pugnacious Yankees.

As for the Yankees themselves, they left the field without the slightest sense of defeat. Some wondered why they were withdrawing. All knew they had handled themselves extremely well.

Even Henry McClellan, Stuart's dedicated adjutant-general, gave them credit: "This battle . . . *made* the Federal cavalry. Up to that time confessedly inferior to the Southern horsemen, they gained on this day . . . confidence in themselves and their commanders."

When Robert E. Lee left the Barbour House for a closer examination of the battlefield and a meeting with Stuart, he came upon his son Rooney being borne toward Brandy Station for evacuation by train. The commander was relieved to find that Rooney's wound, though nasty, was not likely to prove fatal. In spite of his pain, Rooney seemed to be more concerned about his brigade's other casualties than he was about himself.

Later, Robert E. Lee wrote Mary: "He is young and healthy, and I trust will soon be up again."

The sun set while the Federals were crossing the river. As bugles sounded orders, a glorious afterglow put a yellow-red cast on the water, the fields, the woods, and on the weary troopers themselves. It was a strangely beautiful ending for a hellish day.

The sunset held less beauty for the Confederates, since they were left with the battlefield. It was already drawing buzzards.

As a matter of principle, Jeb Stuart wanted to reestablish his headquarters on Fleetwood Hill; but the spot, one of the hardest-contested, was strewn with dead men and dead horses covered with flies. Stuart had to settle for a camp well off the battlefield, back toward Culpeper.

The general would have hated to see this paragraph about his troopers that appeared in a Northern newspaper: "A [Confederate] captain who was taken prisoner said they were under orders to move on Wednesday morning at daylight. They moved a day sooner, and backward at that."

Casualties of Brandy Station (also called Fleetwood Hill and Beverly Ford), in killed, wounded, captured, and missing, were 866 for the Federals and 523 for the Confederates.

Jeb Stuart took no disciplinary action against Beverly Robertson for allowing David Gregg to march around his flank at Kelly's Ford. Robertson had violated no orders. He had covered the road he'd been ordered to cover. All he could be faulted for was failing to show initiative in an unexpected situation.

A curious thing about Brandy Station was the way its strategic significance was magnified by Union General Alfred Pleasonton. This involved some twisting of facts.

Joe Hooker's orders had been for Pleasonton to break up Jeb Stuart's concentration of troops, for they seemed to be poised for a raid into Northern territory; but the battle ended with Stuart's forces still intact, however severely handled. Pleasonton seems to have reacted to this by deciding that his mission hadn't really been a punitive one, but had been a reconnaissance in force.

Viewed in this light, the mission was more of a success. The general had learned that Lee had infantry at Culpeper. He had also captured

Major Beckham's desk, with its few papers. In Pleasonton's report to Hooker, this last became the capture "of Stuart's camp, with its orders, letters, etc."

In an article written after the war, Pleasonton further inflated his achievements, saying some remarkable things: "Stuart's headquarters were not more than a quarter of a mile from the ford, and we pushed our advance with such vigor that we captured it, with a copy of his orders and other important papers."

The attack was "a reconnaissance in force ... which ... accomplished more than was expected, by not only establishing that Lee was at Culpeper in force, but it apprised General Hooker of Lee's intention to invade the North."

The end result, Pleasonton claimed, was "to give the Army of the Potomac the initiative."

In truth, Hooker was not greatly benefited by Pleasonton's "reconnaissance." It turned up no certain evidence that Lee was undertaking a major mission. Not even Pleasonton believed it did—at the time.

On June 10, Hooker wired Abraham Lincoln: "General Pleasonton ... reports that he had an affair with the rebel cavalry yesterday near Brandy Station, which resulted in crippling him so much that he will have to abandon his contemplated raid into Maryland, which was to have started this morning.

"I am not so certain that the raid will be abandoned from this cause. It may delay the departure a few days."

Stuart's departure (for his role in Lee's invasion) *was* delayed a few days. And this, on the surface, seemed to be the only result of Pleasonton's work at Brandy Station. But there was more to the matter.

Poor Alfred Pleasonton, prevaricating seeker of glory! He seems to have gone to his grave with no awareness of the one truly important thing he'd done at Brandy Station.

He had humiliated Jeb Stuart.

Not that Stuart admitted this. He told his troops they had won a great victory, and he wrote a report of the affair in which he claimed he was in complete control from beginning to end, and was always sure of the outcome.

Even if all of this had been true, the fact remained that the enemy had surprised him. Of course, he even tried to deny this. But the South's newspapers tripped him up.

Said the Richmond *Examiner*: "The battle narrowly escaped being a great disaster to our arms. Our men were completely surprised, and were only saved by their own indomitable gallantry and courage."

Other newspapers were equally critical, and an official in the Confederate Bureau of War wrote in his diary: "Stuart is so conceited that he got careless."

One of Culpeper's female residents who termed herself "a true Southern lady" wrote Jefferson Davis to complain about Stuart. His conduct since his arrival in the area, with his emphasis on reviews to please his lady friends, had been "perfectly ridiculous." She had seen him decorate himself with flowers and ride up and down lines thronged with these ladies, "apparently a monkey show . . . and he the monkey." If Stuart was allowed to keep his command the Confederates were "lost people."

The numerous criticisms aimed at Stuart, even though groundless in his own estimation, were bitter buffets for a man accustomed to public adulation—and needing it as he needed food and drink.

As the Gettysburg Campaign developed, Stuart was surely looking for a spectacular way to restore his reputation, and this doubtless influenced his judgment when he adopted a course that proved upsetting to Lee's plans.

Such a case could have been made by Pleasonton in his writings after the war, when perspectives on the Gettysburg Campaign began to clarify. It is unfortunate that the general's thinking was dominated by fantasy.

A noteworthy postscript to Brandy Station grew out of the wounding of Rooney Lee. He was transported to Hickory Hill, his father-in-law's estate north of Richmond, to mend. Two weeks later he was captured and carried off by a Yankee raiding party. He was wanted in Washington as a hostage to insure the safety of some Federal officers in Confederate hands. Rooney was well treated, but was kept for many months. During his captivity, his wife Charlotte, a gentle and bright-natured woman, grew sick and died.

Upon his release in a prisoner exchange, Rooney, fully recovered from his wound under the care of Northern surgeons, returned to his brigade.

The whole situation was another burden for Robert E. Lee, one far beyond a concern for his son. He had to keep his wife reassured that Rooney was safe. While Charlotte was still well, he had to reassure her, too. When she became ill, she needed his sympathy and encouragement. Being very fond of Charlotte, Lee was much affected by her death.

[A word must be added about that Southern champion of the Union, John Minor Botts. After the war he wrote a book chronicling the rise and fall of the Confederacy, and used as a subtitle: *The Political Life of the Author Vindicated*. Botts died at his Culpeper estate, then a picture of rural serenity, in 1869.]

5

Villain on a White Horse

ALL THAT WAS clear to Joe Hooker at this time was that Lee was on the move. The Confederate objective was still a mystery. But even though at least one corps, that of A. P. Hill, was known to be lingering at Fredericksburg, it had begun to seem that Lee's entire army was going to be involved. And this prompted Hooker to approach Lincoln with a plan that must have stunned him.

The general wanted to wait until most of Lee's troops were gone from Fredericksburg, then make a dash for Richmond. Once the city was his, he would march northward and attend to Lee, whose advance, in the meantime, would be retarded, perhaps even stopped, by an assemblage of troops from Northern stations.

Hooker was obviously trying to put off a showdown with Lee—hoping, it appears, that he might even avoid one.

Lincoln, backed by General-in-Chief Henry Halleck, hastened to set Hooker straight, saying in his wire: "If you had Richmond invested today, you would not be able to take it in twenty days; meanwhile, your communications [with the North], and with them your army, would be ruined. I think Lee's army . . . is your sure objective point. If he comes toward the Upper Potomac, follow on his flank and on his inside track, shortening your lines as he lengthens his. Fight him, too, when opportunity offers."

Left with no other choice, Hooker, on June 11, acted to improve his deployment against Lee's maneuvering by ordering one of his corps to

Daniel Sickles

march up the north bank of the Rappahannock to Beverly Ford. For this first move of about thirty miles Hooker chose the Third Corps under Daniel E. "Dan" Sickles.

Sickles, a feisty New Yorker in his late thirties, was one of the army's "political generals," his prewar military training limited to militia duty. His civilian activities had included a law practice, work overseas with the diplomatic service, and ventures into state and national politics. Highly ambitious, Sickles managed to further himself more through self-assured pushing than through special abilities.

He was notorious as the man who killed Philip Barton Key, son of Francis Scott Key, composer of "The Star-Spangled Banner." Philip had been conducting an amour with Sickles' wife, and Sickles shot him dead on a Washington Street. Acquitted of murder through a plea of temporary insanity (one of the first such cases on record), Sickles gained further notoriety, in this Victorian age, by forgiving his adulterous wife and continuing the union.

Ever a man who cultivated "good connections" to advance his ambitions, Sickles was presently on close terms with Joe Hooker, who, hardly a saint himself, wasn't troubled a whit by Sickles' notoriety.

Sickles' men broke up their camps at Falmouth with a certain reluctance. The camps had been "home" for many months and consisted of cozy huts as well as tents, with some of the shelters festooned with evergreen boughs, and others bordered with transplanted saplings to provide their occupants a measure of shade.

The men had organized theatrical groups and glee clubs, and the drill field doubled as a baseball diamond. For the religious, there were camp meetings and Bible studies. Luxury foods and alcoholic beverages were available from the civilian sutlers (if one was willing to, or could afford to, pay their prices), and boys selling newspapers came shouting through camp on a regular basis.

All in all, life at Falmouth was not unpleasant.

Orders to prepare for the march were spread by galloping couriers. For no reason that was apparent, haste was urged. "Pack up, men! We

Selling newspapers in camp.

have no time to lose!" All that was known, one soldier said later, was that "Lee was making a move that had to be checkmated."

Much of the camp equipage—most of the larger tents, along with the stoves, cots, mess chests, and dishes—was left in charge of Hooker's quartermaster department for transfer to Washington. Some items were burned, others simply discarded.

Within three hours the corps was taking to the road, the soldiers laden with packs, blanket rolls, canteens, muskets, and ammunition. Put into creaking motion by sturdy horses or mules were baggage and ammunition trains, hospital ambulances, signal corps wagons. The rumbling artillery wheels made the widest marks in the earthen roadbed. Even a drove of cattle—rations on the hoof—were a part of the procession. In the very front was a detachment of Alfred Pleasonton's cavalry.

As the camp was abandoned, a horde of poor Virginia civilians, blacks and whites, swarmed in to comb the remains. Many useful things had been left. In special quantity were discarded overcoats, for the mid-June weather was hot.

Breaking up the camp at Falmouth.

The country along the north bank of the river had been a military province since hostilities began in 1861. For the past seven months it had been Union territory. One of the marchers wrote in his diary that the farms "had been ruined by the war, devastated by the hand of man."

For the most part, Yankee hands were to blame. The houses, partly stripped and abandoned by their owners, had all been entered. Windows had been broken, doors torn off, and much of the forsaken furniture, along with other accessories, had been taken away.

Not all of this damage was simply wanton destruction and thievery. Some of the missing items—even the doors—had been "appropriated" to further the comfort of Union winter camps.

The aforementioned diarist felt a little better in his conscience to note that "Nature, smiling in her new dress" was beginning to soften the region's desolate appearance.

The hot weather, along with the fact that the troops, due to their prolonged camp life, were not in top marching condition, made this trip a very hard one. Much of the route was through farmlands parched by the sun. The dust was choking, and good drinking water was in scant supply.

Spirits were not raised by the mounted officers who, monitoring the march from positions taken in the shade of wayside trees, called out, "Keep moving, men! Keep moving!"

Beverly Ford was reached on the second day. Signs of the great cavalry battle were still much in evidence. One man noted: "Wounded horses were limping about on the ground in the vicinity; the carcasses of dead animals that had 'fought like men' were scattered in every direction; and I saw one floating in the stream that was fully equipped, and still bore the rations, blankets, and overcoat of its absent rider."

It was the mission of the Third Corps to picket the Beverly Ford region and confront Lee if it turned out that his plan was to cross the Rappahannock at this point and march toward Washington, which lay to the northeast.

Lee, as a matter of fact, was already beginning to move northwestward. Dick Ewell's corps had passed through the Blue Ridge Mountains into the Shenandoah Valley. Longstreet, however, remained at

Culpeper, while A. P. Hill was still at Fredericksburg. In dispersing his forces so widely, Lee was acting boldly but not recklessly. Longstreet was in a position to support Hill if Joe Hooker attacked toward Richmond. Ewell was beginning Lee's invasion, but was not beyond recall in case of emergency.

While at Culpeper, Longstreet took a precaution that was to prove of great significance to the campaign. He hired a professional spy, a young Mississippian known only as Harrison, to go to Washington and learn what he could of the Union's reaction to Lee's movements.

Longstreet knew the man to be trustworthy, and gave him a considerable supply of gold for his expenses. But when Harrison asked, "Where will I find you when I return?" the general said only, "With the army; I'll be sure to be with it."

By this time Northern civilians were beginning to worry. This was especially true of the Unionist element in Maryland (this was a state divided in its loyalties) and the people of Pennsylvania. Ever since the Battle of Antietam, Maryland, the previous autumn, these citizens were aware that Lee, if he wished, could venture into their territory.

But not everyone in the North believed that an invasion was looming. Previously there had been many false alarms, caused by minor Confederate cavalry incursions. It had so often been a matter of "cry wolf" that some residents, even in vulnerable areas, adopted a wait-and-see policy.

Abraham Lincoln himself wondered whether anything of critical importance was really happening. His wife was visiting friends in Philadelphia at this time, and he assured her by telegraph that Washington was safe, if she wished to come home. His other wires to her included such homely things as "Have at last got new tires on the carriage wheels," and "You had better put Tad's pistol away. I had an ugly dream about him."

Lincoln seems to have been one of the few people in the North who did not fear a Confederate invasion. He saw the prospect not as a threat but as an opportunity. With the right generalship, an invading army might well be cut off and destroyed. But Joe Hooker was clearly not the right man for such a task, and Lincoln was seeking a replacement for him.

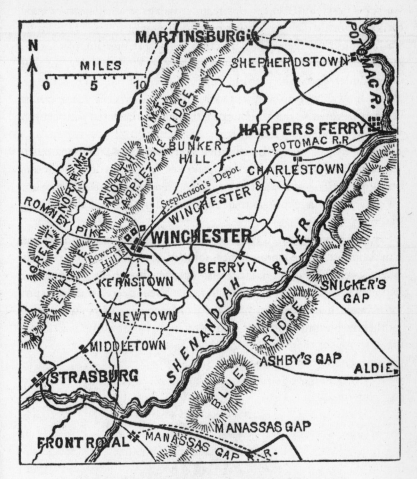

*Battle of Winchester. Heavy line south of the town
indicates Milroy's position at close of first day's fighting.
His northwestern forts are shown as three boxes.*

Confederate General Dick Ewell's entry into the Shenandoah Valley
did not mean that he had a clear route to the Potomac. In front of him
at Winchester, about twenty-five miles south of the river, was a Union
outpost. The garrison, numbering about 9,000 men, covered not only

Harpers Ferry but also the upstream crossings at Shepherdstown and Williamsport, which were best suited to Lee's use.

In addition to their role as an obstacle to Lee's invasion plans, these Yankees were a particularly irritating thorn in Virginia's side, for their commander, forty-six-year-old Major General Robert H. Milroy, a Mexican War veteran and a lawyer during his civilian years, was so fiercely devoted to the Union cause that he administered the occupied area with unremitting sternness.

"Our corps," one of Ewell's men said later, "was rather anxious to capture Milroy, as he had tyrannized over the citizens of Winchester, insulting ladies—so it was reported—and rendering himself obnoxious in different ways, more so than any Federal general had done during the war."

It was Milroy's harsh manner with Confederate womanhood that rankled most. By and large, Union soldiers on Southern soil treated the ladies, even the flag-waving zealots, leniently. But there were Federals who believed that the South would never be conquered until the spirit of its women was broken, since the Confederate soldiers got so much of their inspiration from that source.

Robert H. Milroy

Milroy may have been one of the latter group—or perhaps he just hated Rebels in general. At any rate, the commander's notoriety peaked with an incident that became known in the South as "The Logan Outrage."

It began when Mrs. Milroy and their children came to live with him. According to Winchester's aristocratic ladies, Mrs. Milroy was "a woman not above but below the stamp of servant." These ladies laughed among each other over her "general appearance and manners."

Especially amusing was the reception—or lack of one—that Mrs. Milroy got from the Yankee garrison.

"I'm the wife of Gener'l Milroy," she was heard to say to a group of soldiers in the street. "Why don't you hurrar?"

The soldiers reacted with a blank stare, remaining silent as she moved on.

If this story delighted the aristocrats, something soon happened that did not. The Milroys were occupying a modest house on the town's main street, amid a lot of commotion and dust, and Mrs. Milroy decided she wanted something better. She cast a covetous eye on a beautiful home in a charming spot, the abode of Mrs. Lloyd Logan, an invalid with five children whose husband was absent.

The general ordered the Logans to leave, taking only their clothing, and guards were set to watch them pack. It is said that Mrs. Logan was even denied the silver spoon she used to take her medicine. As she emerged from the house, she was confronted by the sight of Mrs. Milroy and her children drawing up in a fine appropriated carriage to take possession.

It was a tenancy marked by the free use of all the abode's elegant appurtenances, and the Confederate citizens were furious. One young woman, Mary Tucker Magill, vented her wrath in a letter she tried to mail to a friend. Intercepted by Milroy's censors, the letter got Mary into deep trouble. A courier, a "tall, lank specimen of humanity with a ratty expression of eye," pushed his way into her house and told her she must write an apology to General Milroy for the "defamations" or suffer banishment from Winchester.

Mary flatly refused the courier's demand. Even her mother, though aware the situation was serious, told the man, "Apologize to Milroy. Never!"

Mary recorded later: "By this time all the neighbors had gathered in. . . . They were weeping and wailing over the terrible revelation of our utter powerlessness—that this coarse, vulgar man, that these invaders of the sacred soil of Virginia had the power of breaking down the doors of our homes and forcibly taking away one of the inmates. . . . And our natural protectors were meeting death far away!"

A group of Yankee cavalrymen brought a carriage to the house, and Mary was taken eight miles from the town and left standing in the road. Friends came to her aid and saw that she got to Richmond, where other friends took her in.

It isn't hard to understand why Dick Ewell's men, while moving to clear the way for Lee, were also gunning for Milroy!

Many of Ewell's troops had a special fondness for this region, for they had been members of Stonewall Jackson's corps and had taken part in his great Valley Campaign of 1862. Some, indeed, had homes here. All were greeted as friends and saviors by the white-haired men, the aproned women, and the barefoot children who stood in groups and watched them pass. Even many of the black people, not yet attuned to the concept of freedom, were happy to see them.

In the soldier-civilian conversations, Stonewall Jackson's death, of course, was much discussed and lamented.

Robert Milroy had received no word that Ewell was coming. The Union general's job at Winchester was not to hold off a major invasion but to stand in the way of minor Confederate forces occupying positions to his south. He had been doing a good job during the past six months, keeping scouting expeditions ever at work to watch the enemy's movements. Nothing had developed that wasn't easily handled. Milroy had counted on the Army of the Potomac to take care of the Army of Northern Virginia. At the very least, he had expected to be notified at once if Lee made a move in his direction.

Milroy's immediate superior was Major General Robert C. Schenck, headquartered in Baltimore. Also in touch with Winchester was Henry Halleck in Washington. Because of their uncertainty over the situation between Hooker and Lee, both Halleck and Schenck had been urging Milroy to abandon Winchester and fall back to Harpers Ferry.

Milroy had responded with such arguments as: "I have the place well fortified and am well prepared to hold it. . . . I exceedingly regret the prospect of having to give it up; and it will be cruel to abandon the loyal people of this county to the rebel fiends again."

(The "again" indicates that this had been done before. In truth, Winchester exchanged hands many times during the war, keeping civilian affairs in a constant turmoil.)

Milroy did take the precaution of sending his surplus stores, about a hundred wagon loads, north toward Maryland and Pennsylvania.

On June 12, Robert Schenck telegraphed Milroy: "You will make all the required preparations for withdrawing, but hold your position in the meantime." Then Schenck reconsidered and decided to send Milroy orders to retreat at once. But by this time a Confederate scouting party had cut Milroy's wires. With Dick Ewell approaching in force, Milroy was in the dark about him, and was entirely on his own.

No help in the situation was that the general had bad luck with reconnaissance measures he launched at this time. One of his parties, proceeding about twelve miles to the south, actually encountered Ewell's van. But the party's commander brought back information so indefinite that Milroy decided that the troops were some of the nonthreatening kind that were usually encountered during such scouts—or, at worst, were a detachment of Jeb Stuart's horsemen that had ventured into the Valley. There seemed to be no reason to retreat.

Dick Ewell spent Saturday, June 13, attacking Milroy's outposts and advanced units, not only those in the south but also those in the east and the north, the actions forming a great semicircle. The strongest pressure against Winchester itself began with the work against the troops thrown out to the south. Still uncertain as to what they were facing, these troops fought back as they retreated, the crackling skirmishes involving infantry, cavalry, and artillery.

By late afternoon Milroy was setting up a two-mile defensive front south of the town. The line ran along a creek and a mill race, and utilized a scattering of stone fences. Artillery support was provided from

Federals making a stand.

an eminence called Bower's Hill on the western flank. Ewell's southerly troops, his main body, drew up in opposition to this stand.

During one of the last skirmishes before darkness fell, the Federals took a prisoner, and Milroy finally learned that he was facing a substantial part of Lee's army. The Union general, nonetheless, decided to keep fighting, believing that Joe Hooker would come to his relief.

Hooker, as a matter of fact, had no information on what was happening in the Shenandoah Valley. Nor was he planning to do anything in that direction. On that Saturday, June 13, he began moving his army northward from Falmouth and Beverly Ford to a position from which he could protect Washington. He had judiciously chosen Virginia's Manassas-Fairfax area, west of Washington and south of Edward's Ferry on the upper Potomac. The Ferry would be available for a crossing if Lee made it necessary for the army to continue into Maryland and Pennsylvania in order to cover Washington by keeping on his "inside track."

(At least one soldier who was a part of the migration from Falmouth speculated that the Federal units were leaving behind thousands of ghosts, victims of the battles of Fredericksburg and Chancellorsville, "an army of occupation forming a great permanent camp—the bivouac of the dead.")

At Winchester, the early part of the night of the 13th was shattered by a violent thunderstorm, and the lightning flashes revealed soldiers on both sides huddled on the ground under their "gum cloths," or rubberized blankets, trying to keep their muskets and ammunition dry.

It was about 2 A.M. when Milroy quietly withdrew his southern forces through the dripping town to join the troops in his main defenses on high ground to the northwest.

Most of Winchester's citizens had remained in their homes, and here and there a window was faintly agleam with the light of a candle or an oil lamp with its wick lowered; and a few wakeful people watched the Union procession from shadowed doorways. Dogs barked from behind picket fences.

Overwhelmingly Confederate in their sympathies, the citizens were hoping and praying that events were developing toward Milroy's downfall.

While the movement was in progress the Federals were joined by about a hundred hard-used men, some of them walking wounded, who had come from an outpost at the town of Bunker Hill, about ten miles to the north. They were the survivors of a 200-man detachment under a doughty old major named W. T. Morris. The detachment had been quartered in a brick church they had turned into a fortress by knocking out bricks at intervals to make firing ports for their muskets.

The previous afternoon Major Morris had learned that Confederates were approaching; and, unaware that the force was a large one, he had taken his 200 men out to offer combat. The collision occurred on open ground, and within a brief time about half the Federals were killed, wounded, or captured. The survivors made it back to their fortress and barricaded themselves inside. Poking their muskets through their small ports, they began exacting revenge for their defeat. The minie balls that were returned in showers merely pattered against the brick wall and fell, misshapen, to the ground.

When darkness came the Confederates sent in a flag of truce

demanding the garrison's surrender. Major Morris responded: "We are not doing that kind of business."

At midnight the Federals slipped out of the church "as silently as a funeral train," eluded the foe, and made their way to Winchester.

Sunday morning, June 14, dawned partly cloudy, but the air was fresh and clean after the nocturnal rainstorm. As the sun broke through for a temporary burnishment of Winchester's easterly windows, parties of Confederate cavalrymen slipped in from the south. They encountered only a few Yankee skirmishers they dispersed. The mounted invaders were greeted by groups of ladies described as being "perfectly wild with joy and excitement."

These horsemen were soon replaced by infantry patrols, and there was further skirmishing with Federals sent out from the forts. The morning saw skirmishing also in outlying areas, but the important development was a reconnaissance made by Confederate General Dick Ewell in the company of one of his division commanders, Jubal Anderson Early.

A Virginian in his late forties, arthritic, tobacco-chewing "Old Jube" was one of the Confederacy's most conspicuous personalities. He was

Jubal A. Early

earnestly religious, but just as earnestly profane. Though highly respected for his intelligence, resourcefulness, and courage, he was not an inspirational leader, nor a popular one. A grumpy man with a biting wit, he was snappish with his orders, intolerant of failure, and critical of his fellow officers.

Not even the great Stonewall Jackson, though Early's superior in command, had been safe from his tartness. One day after a hard march Jackson had an aide send Early a reproving note:

"General Jackson's compliments to General Early; and he would like to be informed why he saw so many stragglers in rear of your division today."

Old Jube made this reply:

"General Early's compliments to General Jackson; and he takes pleasure in informing him that he saw so many stragglers in rear of my division today probably because he *rode* in rear of my division."

Robert E. Lee called Early "my bad old man."

On that Sunday morning, June 14, Early was on horseback and the one-legged Ewell was in his carriage as the reconnaissance was made. They ascended Bower's Hill, southwest of Winchester, and trained their telescopes on Milroy's set of earthen forts northwest of the town. The attack plan was quickly formed. Ewell, with one of his divisions, would make a lot of noise—a diversion—on a hill east of Winchester. Early would leave a demonstrating detachment on Bower's Hill, taking the stronger part of his division, with twenty artillery pieces, on a wide arc to the west, and ascend to the farmlands atop Little North Mountain, which overlooked the fort system. Old Jube was to attack the system from the west as soon as he could organize to do so.

The westerly circuit, entirely out of the sight of Milroy and his people, was hours in the making. Early had a local man as his guide. Only a few people were encountered on the wooded country roads. Two "very ordinary-looking men" were taken into custody as a precautionary measure. A young girl on horseback, with a wide-eyed small brother behind her and clinging to her tightly, revealed herself to be very frightened at sight of the column's approach. Then, upon learning that the troops were Confederates, the girl doffed her bonnet and began swinging it over her head, at first a delight to the men with her tremulous cheering, then an object of compassion as, overwrought, she burst into tears.

It was about 4 P.M. when Early's troops reached the Little North high ground, a region of fields, orchards, and woodlands. While his infantry rested and his artillery pieces were manhandled into commanding spots, Old Jube found an overlook from which to study the earthen forts and assess the situation. He was gratified to note that the Confederate demonstrators were functioning successfully. Not a single Yankee was looking toward the heights that posed their real danger. All were concerned with the diversionary troops, especially those on Bower's Hill to the south. Dick Ewell's demonstrators could be seen on their eminence just east of the town.

Old Jube perceived that his infantry would have to cross a ravine and climb to a crest holding an outlying fort that would have to be taken before anything could be done against the main fort, some hundreds of yards closer to the town.

By the time the attack was ready, hardly more than an hour of light remained. The job, Early realized, was not likely to be completed that day. But he intended to see it well begun.

For the Federals in the forts the day had been one of terrible suspense. Artillery replies had been made to the demonstrators, but it was surmised that something else was afoot. Robert Milroy had not ignored the possibility of trouble from the west, but a reconnaissance he had sent out in that direction somehow missed making contact with Early. One of the things working in the Confederate general's favor was that, because of the heavy rain of the previous night, his progress was not marked by a column of dust.

The critical moment that evening found Milroy on an observation platform fifty feet up the flagpole of his main fort. He was scanning the countryside in every direction but the right one.

"On a sudden," according to a man who served in the main fort, "came the boom of cannon and rush of shell, as if hell itself had burst its bolts and bars and was bringing fire and tempest into the world. Every eye was turned west. Twenty rebel cannon were throwing shot and shell."

Confederate national flag (left) *and Confederate battle flag.*

The bulk of the fire was centered on the outlying fort as General Harry T. Hays and his brigade of "Louisiana Tigers" began an assault across the ravine.

For Dick Ewell and his staff, headquartered on their eastern hill, the moment was almost unbearably exciting. They had a clear view of the outlying fort on the crest of its rise. The Louisiana Tigers could not be seen as they dipped into the ravine and climbed the western slope, but they could be heard shouting. They were being punished by Federal fire, but suddenly their battle flags came rising into view beyond the outlying fort. The bluecoats who had been firing muskets from trenches out in front of the fort were seen running back to it. Then the fort emptied, its occupants streaming toward the main fort, not far from the town.

Dick Ewell, who had been jumping about on his crutches, paused to take a look through his glass.

"Hurrah for the Louisiana boys!" he exclaimed, his eyes misting over. "There's Early! I hope the old fellow won't be hurt!"

At that moment a spent minie ball struck Dick Ewell on the chest, almost knocking him down, but doing no serious damage. His surgeon, Dr. Hunter McGuire, lately of Stonewall Jackson's staff, took away the general's crutches, saying, "You'd better let these sticks alone for the present." Ewell made no protest. He simply started hopping about as best he could without support.

With the sun now setting and the red Confederate banner flying over the outlying fort, Jubal Early turned his artillery on Milroy's main fort. The Union commander, remarkably enough, had continued to watch the show and issue his orders from his flagpole platform. He was viewed with fascination by the Federal soldier quoted earlier.

"There still sat the intrepid but unfortunate general upon his elevated seat, the shells shrieking and whistling around him, and yet as calm and unmoved as if he were quietly taking his siesta at home." Milroy's guns were responding, and the noise was "like the mingled roar of ten thousand thunders, and only closed when night set in."

This day saw action also at Martinsburg, about twenty miles northeast of Winchester. A detachment of Dick Ewell's forces dispersed the Federal garrison there, taking many prisoners, five guns, and some valuable stores.

As for the situation at Winchester that evening, Jubal Early made this assessment: "It was very evident that the enemy's position was now untenable, and that he must either submit to a surrender of his whole force or attempt to escape during the night."

Robert Milroy summoned his brigade commanders to a council of war, explaining later: "Precedents which have occurred during this rebellion and in other countries would have justified a capitulation; but I thought, and my comrades in council thought, that we owed our lives to the Government rather than make such a degrading concession to rebels in arms against its authority . . . that we owed it to the honor of the Federal arms to make an effort to force our way through the lines of the beleaguering foe."

Preparations for the move involved the abandonment of everything that made noise: all of the wagons and all of the artillery. The cavalry units, of course, would keep their mounts. About a thousand workhorses were to be taken along, and these offered rescue to the sick and wounded with strength enough to ride bareback. The severely disabled would be forsaken, though surgeons would be left to care for them.

One thing especially painful had to be accepted. The officers' wives residing in Winchester would be safer left behind, however unfriendly their treatment at the hands of the townspeople.

Mrs. Milroy's situation at this time is a mystery. It might be supposed that, as the wife of the commanding general, she was spirited to Harpers Ferry before Winchester was surrounded.

Harpers Ferry

The Federal procession was formed in a mile-long ravine leading from the main works northward to the chosen road to the Ferry. Commands were given in subdued voices, and efforts were made to keep the workhorses from taking fright in this unfamiliar situation. It was about 2 A.M. when the march was commenced, slowly and cautiously. Two hours elapsed before the head of the column penetrated the darkness to Stephenson's Depot, about four miles out.

Arriving at this place at the same time was a Confederate intercepting column from the east, elements of Edward Johnson's division of Ewell's corps. General Johnson, riding with his van, was alerted to Milroy's presence by the sounds of neighing horses and tramping men. The neighing horses belonged to the troopers leading the column, who at once detected Johnson's nearness and fired a volley with their carbines, the muzzles flaring in the darkness, the crash signaling an end to all efforts, on both sides, to repress sound.

This was rural terrain, and, in spite of dim visibility and resultant confusion, the leading regiments of both columns were soon deployed. The night was now splintered by myriad flashes. Musketry began rolling, and Confederate artillery pieces started booming. As the shells shrieked and crashed, the Federal artillerists lamented having left their own guns behind.

The great herd of Union workhorses, mistaken for cavalry, were targeted by shellfire and went wild, unseating some of their riders and carrying the rest rapidly from the scene on a road *away* from Harpers Ferry.

The Federals fought gamely, but by dawn it was obvious that the foe was too strong. General Milroy, personally involved in the action from the start, now had his horse shot from under him. He had trouble locating another, but then procured a splendid white one, which made him a conspicuous figure, recognizable even to the Confederates.

The general rushed orders to the unengaged regiments to try to elude the fray and head for Harpers Ferry. Some of these units were captured in the attempt. Several of the front-line units were also taken. Among the regiments that managed to start along the desired route, some soon lost themselves on side roads.

Milroy himself, in company with components of his cavalry, managed to escape toward the Ferry. The Confederates who had recognized him watched unhappily as he and his party galloped out of sight. They had lost their villain.

Perhaps no one realized it, but there was irony in the fact he had ridden away on a white horse, the traditional mount of pure-hearted heroes.

Milroy's escape notwithstanding, this was a great moment for Dick Ewell. In the three-day action, pressed at low cost to himself, he'd accounted for about 4,000 Federals (most of them captured), which just about halved the numbers he'd fought. Twenty-three guns, along with 300 wagons and an abundance of stores, were also taken.

For the moment, at least, it seemed that Robert E. Lee had been granted the replacement for Stonewall Jackson he needed so badly.

Ewell lingered at Winchester long enough to attend a public flag-raising ceremony, during which he and Old Jube were embarrassed by the warmth of the approval they got from Winchester's liberated ladies.

For remaining at Winchester until it was too late to make a safe withdrawal, Robert Milroy came under high censure in Northern quarters, and later that summer his conduct was analyzed by a military court of inquiry. The verdict, endorsed by President Lincoln, was that the general deserved no particular blame, that he seemed to have acted as judiciously as the circumstances permitted.

With considerable justification, Milroy himself maintained: "I checked the advance of Lee's army three days. That was certainly doing something for the country. If they had been allowed to go on, they would have had three days longer for pillage and robbery in Pennsylvania, and probably ten times as much property as I lost would have been destroyed in that time."

6

The Troopers Clash Again

IT WAS ON June 15, the day of Milroy's rout, that Washington began issuing calls for the Northern states to assemble emergency militia units. Very active in these efforts was Lincoln's irascible but highly efficient secretary of war, Edwin M. Stanton. He seems to have been one of the first Northerners to surmise the truth about what was happening.

In his wires to the state governors asking for troops, Stanton said: "The movements of the rebel forces in Virginia are now sufficiently developed to show that General Lee with his whole army is moving forward to invade the States of Maryland and Pennsylvania, and other States."

Stanton was frustrated by some of the return telegrams. The men who were supposed to be rushing to arms had questions. What was the maximum time they would have to serve? Would this service give them exemption from the draft?

Restraining his anger, Stanton responded that the service period was not predictable but would probably be short. No, it would not exempt the men from the draft, but they would be given credit for the time. The governors were urged to get the men together, one way or another. But the response in many regions was sluggish.

It was not in all cases a lack of patriotism that held the men back. Numbers were reluctant to leave their home areas, feeling they might well be needed there. Informal groups of home defenders were formed,

Edwin M. Stanton

the membership including veterans of the War of 1812 who turned out with tarnished old muskets, pistols, and swords, some even in faded remnants of once-smart uniforms. As they joined in the drilling, brittle in their movements, the oldsters were the object of public amusement. Some even laughed at themselves.

Edwin Stanton had good reason to fret about Washington's inability to stimulate large militia turnouts. Already an element of Dick Ewell's forces—Albert G. Jenkins' brigade of cavalry, detached from Jeb Stuart's command—had crossed the Potomac at Williamsport, Maryland, for a raid thirty miles northward to Chambersburg, Pennsylvania. The audacious Jenkins collected about $250,000 worth of goods for the Confederacy.

Horses and cattle the general simply took as contraband of war—which meant that they were deemed morally confiscable. This measure had the effect of shutting down some of the area's farms. The other materials seized—such things as foodstuffs, clothing, and medical supplies—were paid for with Confederate scrip, which had no value to

Confederates entering Chambersburg.

Northerners and was even of failing value in the South, though Jenkins insisted it was good as gold.

The general took into custody scores of black people, both slave and free. The excuse for this was the Union's policy toward the South's escaped slaves. Those who came north, and even those who entered Federal lines in Southern places, were accepted as contraband of war, and many were given jobs related to Northern military efforts.

Many of Jenkins' black captives escaped, some with the help of Chambersburg's whites, some on their own. One black man wrested his guard's rifle from him, shot him in the head (seriously but not fatally), and won his footrace for freedom.

(Worthy of note here is the paradox that many of the black servants traveling with the Confederate army were intensely loyal to the South. These men delighted in seeing Yankee property confiscated, and they enjoyed their part in the work. They could not understand why the foraging was done with a certain moderation. According to one Confederate officer, these blacks were for "universal pillage." This officer had a servant who was "highly disgusted when he had to return anything.")

During Albert Jenkins' visit to Chambersburg, several of his cavalry horses were spirited away by venturesome Union militiamen. The general called upon the town council to reimburse him for his lost property. With little ado, the council paid the required amount—in Confederate scrip. Jenkins smiled ruefully and accepted the paper without protest.

The general had no admiration for the fawning Confederate sympathizers he met. To one, he said: "Well, if you believe we are right, take

Confederate scrip (reduced in size) of 1862 and 1863.

your gun and join our ranks." Another was told: "If we had such men as you in the South, we'd hang them."

Jenkins and his troopers soon fell back toward the Potomac to camp, for Lee was not yet ready to launch his invasion. But parties of the horsemen went out daily on minor raids in the Maryland–Pennsylvania border country, bringing back plunder to add to the materials moving southward.

Jenkins' work, coming on the heels of Milroy's rout, caused great consternation. The roads in western Maryland became crowded with people who had piled furniture and other possessions, including caged chickens, on the family wagons; and, if they owned livestock, had formed it into droves. With as much speed as could be mustered, these odd caravans were rolling toward Pennsylvania. At the same time, many Pennsylvania families living southwest of the Susquehanna River were hurrying, with goods of a like nature, along roads leading to the other side. For most of the fugitives, destinations were not an important consideration. The chief aim was to elude the Confederates.

The processions in both states were interspersed with crowds of blacks, most on foot carrying cumbersome bundles, a few in dilapidated carriages drawn by plodding horses, the barefoot children wide-eyed with anxiety. These fugitives, understandably, were in terrible fear of Confederate capture and delivery into Southern slavery.

It is not to be supposed that the refugees from the threatened regions represented the majority of the residents. Large numbers, particularly among the urbanites, remained in their homes. While the timid were leaving such vulnerable cities as Baltimore, Maryland, and Harrisburg, Pennsylvania, the stalwarts were taking up picks, shovels, and axes for the purpose of studding outlying areas with trenches and breastworks.

At Baltimore, crews of conscripted black laborers were heard singing the popular abolition song that utilized the tune of "The Battle Hymn of the Republic": "John Brown's body lies a-moldering in the grave . . . His soul is marching on."

By June 16 Joe Hooker was completing his move to the Manassas-Fairfax area. The men had suffered much during the periods of forced marching, and there were numerous cases of sunstroke, including fatali-

Citizens of Pennsylvania digging entrenchments.

ties. Some of the troops passed the fields of the two Bull Run fights (July 1861 and August 1862), and were shocked to learn that many of the Union slain had been left where they had fallen and were now skeletons in sun-bleached tatters. Some of the bones were in disarray as the result of assaults by scavengers.

Hooker kept in close touch with Washington. His relations with his old enemy, Henry Halleck, were a frustration. Halleck continued to be overly concerned with the status of Harpers Ferry, and this limited Hooker's freedom of action. In truth, Harpers Ferry wasn't even in danger. Lee planned to bypass it to the west. This would leave the Ferry unhindered in its contact with Hooker and Washington.

Hooker tried to gain release from Halleck's influence by petitioning Lincoln. The President responded that Halleck was general-in-chief of the nation's armies and was therefore Hooker's commander. There was no getting around this.

So Hooker continued to chafe. Compounding his distress was that he believed Lee had him outnumbered. This was not the case. He was probably superior to Lee by about 25,000 men.

Lee's army was now stretched over a westerly arc covering more than a hundred miles. Part of Ewell's corps was across the Potomac in Maryland, and the remainder was poised to follow. Hooker's departure from Falmouth had freed A. P. Hill from Fredericksburg, and his columns were passing through the Culpeper area, their aim to enter the Shenandoah Valley. Longstreet had left Culpeper, but not to make an immediate entry into the Valley. He was on his way north along the eastern slopes of the Blue Ridge. Lee wanted him to deploy at the mouths of Ashby's and Snicker's Gaps, which led into the northern part of the Valley.

Jeb Stuart's troopers were with Longstreet, their job to stay on his right and screen his march and his deployment. Longstreet and Stuart must keep Hooker from gaining intelligence of Ewell's position astride the Potomac, and of A. P. Hill's march through the Valley. Once all units of both corps were assured of a safe passage into Maryland, Longstreet and Stuart were to follow.

The morning of June 17 saw the stage being set for a new round of cavalry actions. Stuart's horsemen were taking up positions some miles east of Ashby's Gap, their mission to patrol the passes through the Bull Run Mountains, which lay west of Joe Hooker's Fairfax-Manassas

Union cavalry scouts.

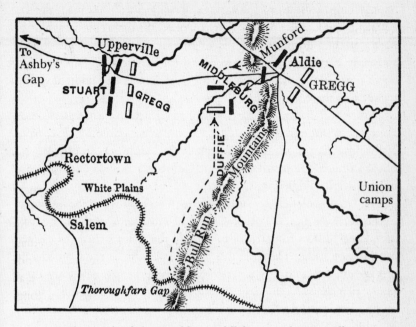

The cavalry fights at Aldie, Middleburg, and Upperville.

camps. The Union troopers under Alfred Pleasonton had left these camps, intending to make a scout through the Bull Run Mountains toward the Blue Ridge.

Pleasonton was heading west toward the very passes Stuart was coming eastward to patrol.

By early afternoon, Stuart had three brigades facing the Bull Run Mountains: Fitz Lee's, still under Tom Munford; the wounded Rooney Lee's under John R. Chambliss, Jr.; and that of Beverly Robertson. Munford, actually, was pushing through the gap at Aldie, the northernmost pass, intending to set up a camp near the village. Stuart himself was heading for Middleburg, five miles west of Aldie. Not expecting trouble, the general and a few others, including Heros von Borcke, were looking forward to socializing with the town's citizens, some of whom were friends.

General Pleasonton was equally unaware that contact was imminent. His main column, with David Gregg's division in the lead, was approaching Aldie from the east. A detachment of 300 men, the 1st Rhode Island Cavalry, led by Alfred Duffié (the same colonel who had been detached during the Battle of Brandy Station), was pursuing a southerly detour with orders to ride through Thoroughfare Gap and come north along the west side of the mountains to Middleburg and make camp there that night.

Duffié, who had got an early start, had sighted some of Stuart's men as he nosed through the gap. This should have given him pause, especially since his command was so small, but Duffié was an officer who obeyed orders. He brushed past the Confederates and rode doggedly north toward Middleburg.

The Union colonel was still en route to his goal when the bluecoats to the northward on the other side of the mountains, with Gregg having placed Judson Kilpatrick's brigade in the van, reached the eastern outskirts of Aldie. The time was about 2 P.M. Since the Confederate brigade under Munford was west of the town, the east held only a few mounted pickets. As these turned and retreated, Kilpatrick called to his leading regiment, the 2nd New York Cavalry, "Form platoons! Trot! March!"

Judson Kilpatrick

The Yankees went clattering through the streets, pushing before them not only the pickets but also a number of troopers surprised while using the town blacksmith's facilities to shoe their horses. Munford's main forces were encountered in the farmlands about a half mile to the west.

In a roaring give-and-take fight that lasted until late in the day, Gregg fielded five regiments, Munford four, with each side keeping a battery of artillery in hot play. Seemingly fearless as he led saber and pistol charges, Kilpatrick had his horse killed under him, but was soon remounted. His bluecoats succeeded in encircling one of Munford's squadrons, capturing it entire. The surrender was a formal one, apparently the first on Jeb Stuart's record. Even so, the fight ended with Munford having suffered a total of only 119 in killed, wounded, captured, and missing, as compared with 305 for Gregg.

As dusk settled in, the Confederates drew west toward Middleburg, summoned there by Stuart, who wanted to consolidate his forces after undergoing an embarrassing experience at the hands of Alfred Duffié and his 300 Rhode Islanders.

Jeb and his small party had reached Middleburg from the west at about 3 P.M., an hour before Duffié's arrival from the south. Sending a few mounted pickets to cover the southern approaches, Stuart gave his attention to the ecstatically excited women who had gathered about him even before he'd had time to dismount. The scene in the street, according to an observer, "looked like a dance around a maypole."

The handsome and dashing Heros von Borcke attracted his own admirers. He was comfortably seated in the living room of one of the houses, discussing his most recent adventures with "a circle of pretty young ladies," when he heard, above their cries of wonderment, a staccato of hoofbeats and a shout, "The Yankees are coming!" Von Borcke knew at once it was the southerly pickets returning.

"I had just time to rush out of the house and mount my horse when the enemy's cavalry poured into town. . . . I soon joined General Stuart . . . and the remainder of his staff, who were riding off as fast as their steeds would carry them."

Jeb was blazingly angry. He'd been forced to flee from Yankees under the very eyes of ladies who had been paying him homage as an invincible hero. Determined to redeem himself at once, the general rode to his nearest regiments, those of Beverly Robertson's brigade, and ordered them to clear the town.

As for Alfred Duffié, the citizens told him whom he'd routed, and he realized he'd made himself an object of vengeance. His best course would have been to take advantage of the confusion he'd created and attempt to force his way to Gregg at Aldie, five miles to the east.

But Duffié had been ordered to camp at Middleburg that night, and not even the prospect of doom was going to keep him from trying to do so. He barricaded the streets and slipped a courier toward Gregg, asking for reinforcements. But Duffié's numbers were too small to merit major risk-taking on the part of their parent division. The 300 men were left to their fate.

When Jeb Stuart returned as the sun was setting, it was Beverly Robertson who led the attack, with Heros von Borcke assisting. The big Prussian had the great satisfaction of charging with pointed sword, a shouting squadron behind him, under the rapt observation of the same ladies he had recently abandoned in haste.

There was a storm of resistance from Duffié, but his defenses were soon shattered. His good luck was that darkness had come, and he was able to get away southward with a good part of his regiment intact. But the men were exhausted and soon had to bivouac, even though they were still in dangerous territory.

The danger from the north, however, had subsided. Stuart, Robertson, and von Borcke were satisfied with having rescued Middleburg. They spent part of the evening there with their lady friends, who, as von Borcke wrote later, "were busy nursing the wounded, large numbers of whom were collected in several residences." The groups included some of the wounded of Duffié's command.

The Union colonel drew encouragement from the fact he wasn't pursued. He decided that once his men were rested he might be able to head for a reunion with Gregg in the Middleburg-Aldie area on a schedule fairly compatible with his orders, even though this would involve making his way through Stuart's lines.

The matter was brought to a head by the Confederates under John Chambliss, who had been scouting in the south and came riding north that night for the purpose of joining Stuart. They chanced upon Duffié's bivouac at about 3 A.M. and soon had it surrounded. Only now did the indomitable colonel decide that his mission might have to be given up. "But," he said later, "I decided not to surrender at any event."

As wild fighting sullied the luster of the dawn, the regiment was cut to pieces. Even so, numbers of the bluecoats managed to pierce the cordon and fade into the Bull Run Mountains, which they crossed for a return to Joe Hooker's camps. Duffié himself got through. In all, one-third of the valiant Rhode Islanders made a safe return from the ill-starred mission.

The regimental colors survived in a way that did further credit to the unit's spirit. When the color-bearer, a sergeant named Robbins, was wounded and saw that he must fall into the hands of the foe, he stripped the flag from its staff and thrust it inside his shirt. The move went unnoticed by the Confederates, who would have liked nothing better than to make a trophy of this worthy unit's emblem.

In the press of events, the sergeant's captivity was not maintained; and, not badly hurt, he was soon able to make his way over the mountains to the Union camps. He approached the headquarters of his own regiment hallooing and flourishing the flag over his head. The other survivors, who thought he'd been killed, cheered and swung their hats as they crowded around him.

Robbins got a lieutenancy out of his deed, and the proud 1st Rhode Island Cavalry was rebuilt around the colors he'd saved.

The news Joe Hooker got from Alfred Pleasonton on developments behind the Bull Run Mountains that first day, June 17, told him little, for there was no word on what Longstreet was doing. Early in the morning on the 18th Hooker telegraphed Henry Halleck in Washington that he had instructed Pleasonton to try to learn what was behind Stuart's cavalry, and that, as a precaution, he was sending a part of the Army of the Potomac northward to Leesburg, Virginia, to cover Edward's Ferry and the other Potomac crossings in the area, which might soon be needed.

In his return telegram, the general-in-chief reacted to a complaint Hooker had made that Washington was not providing him enough intelligence on Lee's movements. Said Halleck: "I can get no information of the enemy other than that sent to you. Rumors from Pennsylvania are too confused and contradictory to be relied on. Officers and citizens are on a big stampede. They are asking me why does not General Hooker tell where Lee's army is? He is nearest to it. There are numerous suppositions and theories, but all is yet mere conjecture. I only hope for positive information from your front."

Pleasonton's corps lost little of its strength through Duffié's misfortune; but, pending a decision on infantry supports he had requested from Hooker, the general moved from Aldie only very cautiously on June 18, sending out scouting parties and assuming a position east of Middleburg.

Jeb Stuart, stationed west of the town, was glad for the respite, since not all of his units were up from the Rappahannock. Moreover, Longstreet was not yet firmly established in the Blue Ridge Gaps he'd been ordered to cover.

That afternoon there was a change in the weather that both sides welcomed. First came dark skies and a high wind, then lashing rain, and finally a hailstorm that inspired whoops of delight. "For this atmospheric change we had earnestly prayed," a bluecoat wrote in his diary. "The heat had become so oppressive and the roads so dusty as to make our movements very unpleasant and disastrous to men and beasts, especially to the latter."

Though Pleasonton was still not ready for an all-out effort when the sun rose on June 19, he advanced Gregg's division through Middleburg to test Stuart's position, which was on a road leading first to Upperville and then to Ashby's Gap in the Blue Ridge.

The bluecoats began the action with shellfire, some of the missiles bursting in the trees above the Confederates, sending down patters of limbs and twigs. Stuart's guns were soon replying, and both fronts began to crackle with small-arms fire, with some of the men on horseback and others on foot. There was grumbling among the Confederates about the inconsideration of Yankees who made people defend themselves before they'd had breakfast.

Stuart commanded from a hill in the rear. At first his units had little trouble holding their ground, and the general was encouraged to believe they'd be able to drive the Yankees. When Heros von Borcke, upon returning from a scout at the front, expressed doubt about this, Stuart laughed and told him he was wrong. "I'll be in Middleburg in less than an hour."

It was David Gregg who did the driving. As the Confederate right began to give way, von Borcke rallied a counterattack that saved things for the moment. An abashed Stuart galloped forward with a group of aides to supervise a withdrawal to a position half a mile back. As the general joined von Borcke, the troops began to cheer his appearance at the front, and this drew the attention of some of Gregg's sharpshooters. A chance to kill Stuart himself!

But the marksmen aimed their shots at von Borcke by mistake. He slid from his saddle and went to the ground on his back, blood gushing from a critical wound in his neck.

Insensible for a moment, the Prussian revived to find a group of men trying to lift his heavy frame back into the saddle. Two of the number were quickly shot dead, and he urged the others to leave him and save themselves. But the effort was continued, and von Borcke found enough strength in his legs to help. Slouchily remounted, a horseman supporting him on either side, he was hurried rearward. With the retreat now in full swing and the Yankees closing in, his pain had to be disregarded.

There were shells bursting around the ambulance he was put into, and the frightened driver took off whipping the horses and bouncing the Prussian unmercifully despite his groans and his appeals that the gait be lessened.

"At last," he wrote later, "I could stand it no longer, and, crawling up to him, I put my cocked pistol to his head and made him understand that I should blow out his brains if he continued his cowardly flight."

Soon after the ambulance was slowed, Stuart's staff surgeon, Dr. Talcott Eliason, overtook it and stopped it to examine von Borcke's wound. The ball had entered the back of his neck, missing the spinal column but puncturing his windpipe, then had turned down into his right lung. His left arm was paralyzed. The doctor told him he had but a few hours to live. Eliason's home happened to be in Upperville, a few miles to the west, and von Borcke was taken there and put to bed.

By this time it was about noon. The fighting to the east had ended. Stuart had consolidated his new position, and Pleasonton chose not to press him any more that day.

Von Borcke's friends used their free afternoon to visit him at Upperville. He had been sedated with morphine. Though aware of what was going on around him, he could not move or talk. Seeing him lying there so still, his eyes closed, his face and neck badly swollen, and his skin pale, some thought him dead. He heard the doctor tell them he was still alive but would not survive the night.

"At last Stuart himself came, and, bending over me, he kissed my forehead, and I felt two tears drop upon my cheek as I heard him say, 'Poor fellow, your fate is a sad one, and it was for me you received this mortal wound.' "

Von Borcke was deeply grateful for his commander's sympathy, but he had no intention of fulfilling Eliason's prophecy. Thanks to his sedated sleep, the trooper met the next morning feeling both refreshed and strengthened, though he was far from out of danger.

Meanwhile, things were happening along the Potomac at the northern end of the Shenandoah Valley. Dick Ewell had started another move. His van—the van, in fact, of the entire invading army—was edging farther into Maryland.

Intending to take the toll road to Hagerstown, the column was obliged to draw up because the gate was down, its elderly tender standing before it.

"Who," he asked, "is going to pay for all the horses and wagons I see coming?"

He was told he'd be given an order against Jefferson Davis to take to Richmond.

This made the old man swear. Then, raising the gate, he said, "I'll charge the toll to profit and loss."

But he had a warning for the Confederates, telling them the smartest thing they could do was to turn around and go back to Virginia.

Down in that state, in the Stuart-Pleasonton arena, June 20 was a rainy day, and the action was limited to skirmishing and artillery duels. To the west, Heros von Borcke lay in his bed at Upperville and listened, relieved when the sounds remained distant. If his friends should be driven, it would be through Upperville, and this could result in his capture by the Yankees, which, in his condition, might well occasion his death.

That day both sides made preparations for a settlement of the issue. All of Stuart's units were now up from the Rappahannock, but there was no infantry with him. Longstreet's corps, however, had taken its place along the east slopes of the Blue Ridge from Ashby's to Snicker's Gaps. Ashby's was less than ten miles behind Stuart's position. Pleasonton's entire cavalry corps was on the scene and three brigades of infantry were on their way from Hooker's camps. Pleasonton had visions of doing the job of crippling Stuart that he'd failed to do at Brandy Station.

This time the Federal commander did not have the advantage of surprise, but he had a psychological advantage—one he wasn't aware of. Von Borcke's wounding had shaken Stuart, especially since he knew that he himself was supposed to be the target of the bullet, and had escaped it through a quirk of fate. For the moment, Jeb was not his usual aggressive self. To be sure, he did not admit this, but his actions that day were out of character. Later, he said in his report: "I was extremely anxious now to attack the enemy . . . but the next morning, 21st, being the Sabbath, I recognized my obligation to do no duty other than what was absolutely necessary, and determined, so far as was in my power, to devote it to rest. Not so the enemy, whose guns about 8 A.M. showed that he would not observe it."

Stuart did not counterattack, but began a fighting retreat. It was well conducted against a superior foe, but the general's personal participation was scant. This was noted by his adjutant-general, Major Henry McClellan.

"I asked the reason of this unusual proceeding, and he replied that he had given all the necessary instructions to his brigade commanders, and he wished them to feel the responsibility resting upon them and to gain whatever honor the field might bring."

Stuart even took the time that morning to ride into Upperville to give von Borcke a message that might have been sent by courier. It was possible, Jeb said, that he would not be able to bring the Yankees to a stand east of the town. If he failed to do so, von Borcke would be

Union troops at Upperville.

evacuated by ambulance. After Stuart left, von Borcke got out of bed long enough to struggle into his uniform. He had no intention of fleeing the Yankees in a nightshirt.

Later, Stuart gave as his reason for losing Upperville a reluctance to fight there and endanger the women and children. He wished to hurry through, he said, but the Yankees, with their "reckless and inhuman instincts," forced him to defend himself during the passage.

Von Borcke's ambulance arrived, but he delayed his departure until word came from Stuart that the situation was irredeemable and that he should go at once.

"I was carried by my friends to the ambulance in the midst of shells bursting in the streets and crashing through the housetops, fugitives rushing wildly by, wounded men crawling out of the way, riderless horses galloping distractedly about, whilst close at hand were heard the triumphant shouts of the pursuing foe."

Barely avoiding engulfment in the fighting, von Borcke's ambulance took him two miles along a road toward the Blue Ridge, then whisked him up a side lane to a plantation house, where he was secreted. A party of Yankees soon arrived, but the owner diverted them with food and drink. They said they'd been searching for a prominent Confederate, at first thought to be Jeb Stuart himself, who had been wounded, but that they'd reached the conclusion the officer had died.

[A few days later von Borcke was taken to Richmond to recuperate, and at once found himself the object of much female attention. Northern newspapers carried the notice that the "big Prussian rebel" who was so important to Stuart had been buried at Upperville.

Von Borcke's recovery was slow, and his days as a Confederate trooper were over. It was a strange twist that the Prussian, over whom Stuart shed tears when death seemed upon him, lived to shed tears of his own at Stuart's bedside when the general was dying of his Yellow Tavern wound in 1864.

Von Borcke returned to his family's castle in Prussia before the war ended, the proud possessor of a letter of thanks from the Davis government and a Confederate flag that he flew over one of the castle's towers. In 1866, during the brief Austro-Prussian War, he served on the staff of Prince Frederick Charles.

In his latter years, von Borcke returned to the States for a visit. His wife had just died, and he sought comfort in a change of scene. He was greeted warmly by his old friends, but all were shocked at his altered appearance. The once light-footed giant, the handsome dazzler of Southern womanhood, was now an almost helpless hulk, his weight having risen to well over 400 pounds.]

By the time the sun was setting behind the Blue Ridge on that tumultuous Sunday, June 21, 1863, Pleasonton's forces had pressed Stuart's to the hillocks of Ashby's Gap. The Union commander chose now to end his mission, and the decision was a wise one. Elements of Longstreet's infantry were moving down from the gap to bolster Stuart's lines.

During the early hours of June 22, Pleasonton withdrew eastward to Aldie in the Bull Run Mountains, and Stuart soon reoccupied much of the ground he'd lost. The series of engagements had cost the Federals about 800 in killed, wounded, captured, and missing. The Confederate loss was about 500—not enough to be crippling.

In the track of the fighting was a string of graves, men of both sides.

But not all of the dead were disposed of in this manner. The corpses of men of well-to-do families were sent to embalmers who prepared them for transfer home.

Pleasonton declared himself the victor in the encounters, but Stuart had been successful at screening Longstreet and the troops in the Valley. It was true that Pleasonton got a picture through information he received from Confederate deserters and black people: Lee himself was now in the Valley; Ewell was well across the Potomac; A. P. Hill was moving toward the river; and Longstreet was entering the Valley by way of the northern gaps. The picture happened to be accurate, but secondhand data like this was never fully trusted.

What Joe Hooker needed most from Pleasonton's mission was a penetration of the Valley that gained some positive intelligence.

There was a frustrating scrap at the end of Pleasonton's June 22 report: "General Buford operated independently yesterday. . . . He sent a party to the top of the Blue Ridge that saw a rebel infantry camp about

Longstreet entering the Valley.

two miles long on the Shenandoah [River], just below Ashby's Gap. The atmosphere was so hazy they could not make out anything more beyond."

The chief benefit of Pleasonton's work was that Jeb Stuart was prevented from pushing reconnaissance parties through the Bull Run Mountains toward the Union camps, which Lee had hoped his cavalry would be able to keep under close observation.

7

Early Visits Gettysburg

EVEN WHILE HE was reoccupying the territory west of the Bull Run Mountains, Jeb Stuart was in courier contact with Lee and Longstreet, then in the northern part of the Valley, regarding the cavalry's next move in the campaign.

Stuart's obvious course was to follow Longstreet into the Valley and proceed north to the Potomac. But the roads leading to the fords were limited in the amount of traffic they could bear. Till after the crossing, the cavalry might be compelled to stay in rear of the infantry. Moreover, if Stuart suddenly vanished into the Valley, the Federals might deduce that Lee's whole force was heading northward, whereas Lee wished to keep them guessing as long as possible, to keep them from following him until the Army of Northern Virginia was consolidated on Union soil, wholly prepared to meet any sort of advance they chose to make.

These considerations gave Jeb the opportunity to come up with an alternate plan, one that would make it possible for him to undertake the most ambitious raid of his career, a feat he believed would redeem his reputation with glory to spare. The idea was based on the knowledge that Joe Hooker was still in Virginia's Fairfax-Manassas area, south of the Potomac, and apparently had no immediate plans for a major move. Stuart proposed to swing southward around Hooker's rear to his right, pass northward between him and Washington for an assault on his communications, then cross the Potomac and swing back to Lee's right while the invasion was in progress.

Lee was uncertain about the feasibility of Stuart's proposal but sent him a set of orders he was able to construe as giving him discretion to proceed as he thought best. The lack of firmness was a serious mistake. Lee assumed that Stuart, whatever he chose to do, would retain sharp sight of the fact that his main responsibility was to operate on the invasion's right, screening it from Hooker and keeping headquarters informed of his movements. Stuart was expected to make short work of any deviation from this mission, the proper conduct of which was essential to Lee's success.

Unhappily for Lee, Stuart seized upon his prospective raid as an all-important effort. His mind became one-tracked. He envisioned a great triumph, and there was small regard in his plans for the time element as it related to Lee's movements. Inexplicably, Jeb seemed to feel that this would somehow take care of itself. It was almost as though he expected the campaign to adjust to his raid.

Lee would not be left without cavalry. Nearly half the corps, about 4,500 men, would remain with the army. But the efficiency of this segment would be limited by the absence of Stuart's leadership. His raid would utilize his three favorite brigades, those of Wade Hampton, Rooney Lee (under Chambliss), and Fitz Lee, now recovered from his debilitating siege of arthritis.

On June 23, the day Robert E. Lee dispatched his fateful orders to Stuart, Joe Hooker made a trip to Washington, less than twenty miles east of his Fairfax headquarters. At the War Department the general met with Lincoln, Stanton, and Halleck. Lincoln was in one of his sadder moods, and Hooker himself was a troubled man, still scratching for definite information on Lee's intentions, still harboring the false belief that his own army was outnumbered, and still hoping to be allowed to move upon Richmond.

Nothing special was achieved by the conference, but Hooker was told again that he must pay close attention to Harpers Ferry, even though that place did not seem to be figuring in the enemy's plans. Dick Ewell had crossed the Potomac upriver from the Ferry (west of

Fitzhugh Lee

it), and Hill and Longstreet, still south of the river, appeared to be bearing in the same direction.

Hooker lingered in the city long enough to get drunk; and he was drunk, it is said, while attending to the army's business at Fairfax next day. He wired the War Department that he was reacting to the situation as best he could with the information he had; and that he would doubtless be able to achieve "glorious results," whatever Lee did—whether he continued to advance or decided to withdraw after filling his supply wagons—if Washington took prompt measures to provide the army with reinforcements.

The wire closed with an appeal for orders covering the situation as a whole. "Outside of the Army of the Potomac, I don't know whether I am standing on my head or feet."

It was only a few hours after he sent his wire that Hooker finally learned the full truth about Lee's threat. Some of Hooker's scouts were headquartered across the Potomac at Frederick, Maryland, northeast of Harpers Ferry; and, by the general's orders, they had been using a peak of the South Mountains, near the Ferry, to observe the approaches to the upriver fords.

The party's chief, John C. Babcock, now reported: "I learn beyond a doubt that the last of Lee's entire army has passed through Martinsburg toward the Potomac.... The main body are crossing at Shepherdstown. Can see them from the mountain."

It was A. P. Hill's corps that Babcock saw. Longstreet was making for Williamsport, farther above.

Babcock was too distant from Hill's column to perceive the holiday mood of the crossing. Bands were playing on both banks, and the waders were shouting and laughing, many with their shoes and trousers removed and slung with their gear. Groups of civilians—both Union loyalists and Southern sympathizers—were watching, and there was some blushing among the females at sight of the flapping shirttails and bare legs.

A Union sergeant in marching order.

Not that any of this mattered to Babcock. His message included all the information that was needed. At last Hooker was aware that Lee was bent upon a full-scale invasion of the North.

History, in its fickleness, would fail to give Babcock and his men proper credit for this important contribution to the campaign. They would be relegated to obscure mention in its official records.

Hooker reacted to Babcock's news at once, promulgating orders for his army to cross the Potomac into Maryland with a view to staying on Lee's "inside track."

And so it happened that the entire Fairfax-Manassas area was beginning to teem with Union activity when, on June 25, Jeb Stuart passed eastward through the Bull Run Mountains to launch his southerly encirclement. He found Federal troops on the very first road he planned to use.

Instead of accepting this as a bad situation and turning back, Stuart shelled the Yankees until they deployed to defend themselves; then he slipped away and expanded his southerly arc, thus increasing the distance he would have to cover to reach the Potomac, which Lee had expected him to cross quickly. (He did try to inform Lee of the Federal activity, but the courier failed to get through.)

In effect, Stuart now undertook an independent mission, one with little bearing on the needs of Lee's campaign. Compounding the mistake was that the troopers, after their series of clashes with Pleasonton's men, were not in the best of condition for so uncertain a venture. The horses, too, were tired, and there was no guarantee that the route of the raid would provide them sufficient forage.

On Friday, June 26, while Stuart's troopers were feeling their way to the southeast, behind them the infantry columns of both sides were in determined motion.

Employing pontoon bridges, Hooker's units were crossing the Potomac into central Maryland at Edward's Ferry, with the general looking toward Frederick as the site of his headquarters during the movement's next pause.

Their transfer from the desolation of Virginia to a state only lightly touched by the war impressed the bluecoats as a unique experience. In the words of one: "The rolling hills of Maryland, with fair and fertile valleys intervening, abounded with teeming orchards, exuberant grain fields, green and glorious meadows, abundant gardens; and, dotted with smiling towns and happy hamlets, appeared in all their beauty before the eyes of the soldiers of the Army of the Potomac like a vision in fairyland."

The columns were warmly welcomed by Maryland's loyalists, who gathered in crowds along the routes of march. Hurrahs rang out, hats were swung, and the Union flag was flourished. Children stood outside country schoolhouses and sang patriotic songs. Small girls with colorful bouquets approached some of the mounted officers, who paused to reach down and accept the tributes with smiles and words of thanks. On a more practical side, wooden buckets of cool water, each with a dipper, were provided for the use of all who thirsted.

Morale soared. An officer said later: "We were no longer the defeated of yesterday. We were predestined conquerors of tomorrow."

To be sure, there were shadows in the picture. Lee was rumored to have superior numbers, and few of the bluecoats had full confidence in

A break in a Union march.

Joe Hooker's leadership, however much they liked his style. But these were familiar shadows. The troops had been contending with their like since the war's beginning. What was different this time was that the foe had penetrated the North and they were marching to its defense. The issue seemed to be moving toward a showdown.

More than one man expressed himself in this vein: "If we get whipped this time and I survive, I'm heading for home!"

It was expected the battle would occur in Pennsylvania, and there were many Pennsylvanians in the army. The men from the other Northern states promised them full support. "We'll be with you till hell freezes over—then, if necessary, we'll perish on the ice!"

Unaware that Hooker was coming north, news that would have altered his movements, Lee was pursuing his original plan of march. Ewell was well into Pennsylvania, having passed through Chambersburg, the scene of Albert Jenkins' cavalry raid. The columns of A. P. Hill and Longstreet were stretched through western Maryland and into Pennsylvania, their orders to halt at Chambersburg.

Though Lee had authorized the destruction of public property related to the Union war effort, he had issued orders that private prop-

Invaders marching into Pennsylvania.

erty, aside from official levies, be respected; and the orders were generally followed, aside from minor infringements.

On one occasion, a swarm of Confederates who were raiding a farmer's raspberry patch were surprised when he came out of the house with a shotgun, berated them violently, and demanded their instant departure. They reacted with a burst of laughter, followed by a hearty cheer for the farmer's courage. Then they returned to eating his raspberries. The man had little choice but to go back inside.

The cherry season was at its height, and laden branches were broken off, the fruit eaten even as the men marched, branches bristling everywhere.

A great joke was made of stealing the felt hats of elderly men who stood along the roadway as spectators. The offender sometimes made an exchange, lifting the victim's hat and dropping his own battered hat on the bared head.

Eggs were stolen from chicken coops, milk was dipped from crocks in springhouses, and rail fences were used for campfires. But wanton destruction was rare.

The soldiers were intrigued by the Pennsylvania Dutch people who inhabited numbers of the farms. Some of these people spoke only German, and of a curious dialect. Those who spoke English did so with a broad accent the Southerners found amusing. Most of the Pennsylvania Dutch were oblivious to the genesis of the war, were concerned only with the security of their property. In an attempt to ward off entry, plump, red-cheeked women stood at gateways behind tables laden with fresh-baked bread and crocks of a brown spread known as applebutter. The ruse was often successful, for most of the graycoats found the "cut and smear" delicious.

A lieutenant and his men who lingered with a Dutch couple at one of the farms were given food for which they paid a dollar in silver. The couple were only the farm's caretakers, with a salary of a mere one hundred dollars a year, so the dollar made them beam.

"By chimminy," exclaimed the husband, "dis var iss big luck for some peebles!"

In another case, a Dutchman who'd lost a mare to the Confederates

A view of Gettysburg.

came lamenting to an officer that the animal was his favorite possession. He'd had "t'ree vifes," he said; then added, "I vood not giff dot
mare for all dose vomans." This testimonial was irresistible, and the
mare was found and returned.

Dick Ewell's corps, in the fore of the invasion, was making an easterly swing from Chambersburg toward the Susquehanna River, the
purpose to draw Hooker's attention in that direction, away from Lee's
communications corridor. Ewell's troops were in two columns, with
Ewell himself leading the northernmost toward Carlisle, and Jubal
Early taking the other through the South Mountains toward York. In a
valley in Old Jube's path lay the town of Gettysburg.

Some seventy miles northwest of Washington, Gettysburg had a
population of about 2,500. It was surrounded by low hills and ridges
that were part of a broad expanse of rich farmlands dotted with large
red barns. The view west toward the South Mountains was known for
its gorgeous sunsets. Though pleasantly rural in its flavor, the town
was anything but sleepy. It was a county seat, had railway communications, and there were roads stretching in all directions from its center.
The shrill sound of its train whistles was mingled with the creak and
clop of busy wagon traffic. In addition to its county courthouse, the
town boasted a college and a theological seminary.

Ever since the Battle of Winchester and Jenkins' raid on Chambersburg, days during which the cavalry chief had been perpetrating lesser

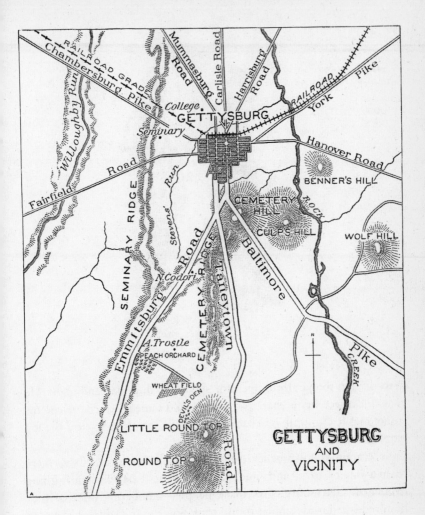

GETTYSBURG
AND
VICINITY

depredations in the Maryland-Pennsylvania border regions, Gettysburg had been in a state of agitation and uncertainty. Conceptions of Lee's plans were shaped largely by information—a mixture of facts and rumors—provided by the groups of refugees that passed through the town.

Gettysburg had a telegraph office, but little was learned that way,

Drilling a raw recruit.

even though the youthful operator stayed on duty day and night. He often fell asleep in his chair, and people who came in to send telegrams sometimes had to walk him back and forth in the office to clear the fog from his mind.

Several times it was believed that the Rebels were near. Horses were rushed out of town and hidden, then brought back when nothing happened. Gettysburg's free black people—numbering three or four hundred—had made similar round trips. Some of the whites had sealed up their houses and joined the refugees. Most of the town's merchants, taking no chances, had just about emptied their stores and sent the goods away by rail. There was so little merchandise left to sell that the citizens were almost in want.

Anger arose over the fact that Hooker had not forestalled Lee's advance. A Gettysburg diarist wrote: "Where is our army, that they let the enemy scour the country and do as they please?"

Harrisburg, the state capital, was trying to help with some of the new troops put under arms there. As early as June 23 the 26th Regiment, Pennsylvania Militia Volunteers—which included a company of youths brought from Gettysburg—had left the capital by rail to act in the town's defense. While chugging through the countryside, the engine slammed into a cow that failed to heed its whistle, and the train was derailed. Except for the unfortunate cow, there were no casualties, but the mission was delayed for two days.

When the troops, no more than 750 in number, reached Gettysburg early in the morning on the 26th, a cloudy day, the people who turned out to see them were more dismayed than encouraged. However smart the soldiers looked in their new uniforms, and however resplendent their weaponry, what could this single regiment achieve, especially since most of its members were woefully young and inexperienced? Some of the mothers of the Gettysburg boys remonstrated about the unit's assignment, but to no avail.

Ignoring a light rain, the regiment, with a group of local horsemen scouting ahead, marched westward at once. But the column was only a

John B. Gordon

few miles out when its horsemen drew up in astonishment. A brigade of Early's division of Ewell's corps was approaching, cavalry in the van and infantry stretching afar.

This happened to be the brigade commanded by John Brown Gordon, one of the South's most remarkable citizen-soldiers. A thirty-one-year-old college-educated Georgian, Gordon was six feet tall, slender, superbly erect in the saddle, stentorian-voiced when issuing orders, seemingly fearless under fire. One of his men termed him "the prettiest thing you ever did see on a field of fight."

Off the field Gordon was a man of gracious manners and courtliness toward women. He was a good public speaker and a dexterous writer.

A captain at the outset of the war, Gordon became a major during his first year of service. During his second he rose to colonel and then to brigadier general. All of the promotions were based on combat performance.

At Antietam Gordon was wounded five times, relinquishing his command only when a fifth bullet smashed through his face, knocked him off his feet, and deprived him of his senses. He fell facedown in his cap, and he might have drowned in his own blood, but a Yankee bullet had supplied the cap with a drain hole.

Gordon's wife, Fanny, who followed him through the war (sometimes with him in camp and sometimes staying in a nearby village), nursed him in this crisis, and he credited her with saving his life. He liked to call his facial scar his "dimple of Antietam."

It is just as well the raw Union militiamen did not know they were facing the redoubtable John Gordon. The situation was bad enough as it was. But the militia commander, Colonel William W. Jennings, was a veteran officer, and he quickly arranged a retreat. The regiment's mounted escort raced back along the road to Gettysburg, and the unit's supply wagons followed; but the colonel took the troops themselves on a northerly trot across an expanse of fields for a swing around the town toward Harrisburg.

The rear guard was captured almost at once by a group of jeering troopers who called the natty Yankees "bandbox boys." Numbers of other captures were made during the pursuit; but the major part of the regiment, after making a stand during which John Gordon was shown that at least some of these callow soldiers could shoot their burnished weapons, managed to escape.

The day saw only one Union fatality, and it was not an infantryman. One of the fleeing horsemen was obliged to turn and defend himself against a Confederate trooper coming up close behind. The bluecoat fired at the pursuer, who told his Confederate comrades later: "He did not hit me, and I shot at him and blowed him down like nothing, and here I got his horse, and he lays down the pike."

Largely forgotten by history, the 26th Pennsylvania Militia and its cavalry escort had the distinction of being the first Federal troops to encounter Lee's army in the Gettysburg area.

Word of Jubal Early's approach to Gettysburg was carried to the town by the horsemen, who shouted the news as they galloped through the streets on their way to safer territory. Emphasizing the alarm were the militia's supply wagons, which came thundering in the cavalry's wake and also kept going.

But the word did not reach everyone at once, and many people continued with what they were doing. Even some of those who heard the commotion of the retreat were unaware what it meant. Commotion was a common thing in Gettysburg these days. A few people even refused to credit the information.

The undulating column of graycoats approached the town from the

The Lutheran Seminary

west, with cavalry trotting in the lead. Among the first citizens to descry the invaders were the members of a small group standing on the steps of the outlying Lutheran Seminary. Their alarm was not assuaged by the multitude's ragged and filthy appearance. The image was surprising, since these soldiers were supposed to be the flower of Southern manhood.

Apprehension mounted when a squad from the column came to check the building for Yankee soldiers. The Confederates were damp from the day's intermittent rains, and the emanations from their unwashed bodies and long-worn clothing were decidedly unpleasant. They were civil enough, however, and respectful of the religious ground. Finding no Yankees, they posted a guard to protect the place, and left. From then on, the people connected with the Seminary felt perfectly safe.

Not everyone in Gettysburg got by with so light a spell of alarm. Among the badly frightened were a number of teenaged girls attending a private school at the western edge of town. They were engaged in their regular "Friday afternoon literary exercises" when they heard someone in the street shouting, "The Rebels are coming! The Rebels are coming!"

The girls and their teacher rushed from the room out onto a portico and beheld the approach of "a dense, dark mass."

"Children, run home as quickly as you can!" cried the teacher, and the portico was cleared in an instant, the girls fairly flying toward various points eastward, fearful of being caught as they ran.

Living in the same western area that held the private school were Mr. and Mrs. Charles Tyson, newlyweds who were laying carpet in an upstairs room of their recently purchased home. (Charles Tyson was Gettysburg's first commercial photographer.) The two were drawn to a window by noises made by the Confederates, who were now entering the town.

The vanguard of troopers, at a gallop, were giving shrill hoots, some flourishing their swords, others firing carbines or pistols into the air. The foot soldiers, their exultant voices making a lively medley, poured in behind, filling the streets from side to side and soon coming to a halt.

The gate to the Tyson place was locked, as was its front door. Quick work was made of the gate by a group that proceeded to the stoop. The couple upstairs heard one of the men spelling the door's nameplate: "T-Y-S-O-N. Wonder who the devil he is?" then there were sounds of one of them trying to force an entry.

"There's no use trying to keep them out if they want to get in," said Tyson to his wife. "I'll go down and open the door."

As he threw the door wide, Tyson told the men they looked warm and thirsty. "We have a well of good cool water. Come in and refresh yourselves."

The men crowded in, asking for bread and butter to go with the promised water. When Tyson told them the house was very short of these things, they accepted his word. He found them "polite and gentlemanly."

As they left the house, their thirst satisfied, one of them told Tyson they were after Joe Hooker and planned to chase him all the way to Philadelphia.

To the consternation of the citizens, most of whom at first shut themselves up in their houses, the Confederates were soon spread through the town, investigating the stores and the taprooms, entering yards to pump well water, and banging on doors to ask for food. Some began setting up camps for the night in the town and in the fields at its edges, the largest camp in the northeast along the pike to York, Old Jube's next goal.

The people's alarm began to diminish when it became clear that these Southerners—some of whom, in their rags, looked more pitiful than dangerous—had no intention of doing them drastic harm. To be sure, there were the usual minor violations of Lee's orders to respect private property, largely motivated by hunger and thirst and the need for clothing.

Many of the citizens soon began to show themselves, taking the sensible course of providing food as freely as their meager supplies permitted. This helped keep forcible searches at a minimum.

The conversational exchanges were mostly civil, often even friendly. There was mollification for the townspeople in that many of the Southerners marveled at the richness of the North.

It was obviously difficult for some of the soldiers to understand the logic behind their orders not to steal anything, when they knew that one of the reasons Lee had come north was to steal things in a big way.

This work, they'd been told, was all supposed to be done by requisition carried out by designated officers. Random stealing was unacceptable. Stealing had to be authorized. The difference seemed slight.

Jubal Early's authorized attempt to make a levy on Gettysburg that evening did not avail him much. He met with town officials at the courthouse and demanded 1,200 pounds of sugar, 600 pounds of coffee, 60 barrels of flour, 1,000 pounds of salt, 7,000 pounds of bacon, 10 barrels of whiskey, 10 barrels of onions, 1,000 pairs of shoes, and 500 hats, or—in lieu of these things—$5,000 in cash.

The officials, explaining that most of the town's money and goods had been sent away, said they could not comply. Old Jube had the stores searched and got what he could. A requisition might have been made on the people themselves, but Early did not have time for this. He wanted to leave for York first thing in the morning.

It was now dark. The rains had ended and the thinning clouds permitted some periods of moonlight. The temperature was mild.

Never in its history had Gettysburg seen such a night as this. Nor did anyone dream that this was only the most miniature sample of what was to come.

Those among the citizens who had lost their fear of the Confederates were sitting on their stoops conversing with groups of them. People still dubious stood in dark rooms and peeped from the sides of drawn shades.

There were campfires in the streets fueled by wood from the backyard sheds, and red-tinged figures were cooking their evening meal. Other soldiers had invaded houses—mostly by permission—to use their kitchen facilities for the task. The open kitchen windows were yellow with light, and out of them came the sound of mirthful voices.

A Confederate band was playing "Dixie" and other tunes in the town square.

When the houses of the northernmost residents began reflecting the light of fires attending the destruction of some railroad property, the citizens to the southward had to be assured by the invaders that the town was not being burnt.

The few black people who hadn't managed to flee were in hiding, prepared to feign limps or illness if they were caught, in this way making themselves seem poor material for sending south.

There were whites in hiding too—young, able-bodied men who feared being taken captive because of their potential as Union soldiers.

In one of the churches, under guard, were the 200 youths of the 26th Pennsylvania Militia who had been captured that day. The townswomen were permitted to bring them food, but the young men wondered apprehensively what was to happen to them. They shrank at the thought of their being sent to a Southern prison, which seemed to be a distinct possibility.

It was late before the town became quiet, and it was early when the commotion resumed as the Confederates began their march toward York.

Old Jube, departing with one of the first units, left word with a subordinate officer for the young militiamen to be paroled and sent home to their mothers.

Early's able brigade commander, John Gordon, rode from the town with a curious feeling about it. What he'd seen of the terrain to the south, with its two nearly parallel ridges, one higher than the other, gave him the impression that Gettysburg would be a good place to fight a battle, and that the side that held the higher ground would probably win.

8

A Weekend of Telling Events

IT WAS NOW Saturday, June 27. While Jubal Early was making his easterly swing toward York, the northern wing of Dick Ewell's probe, commanded by the general himself, marched into Carlisle without resistance. Camps were set up, one of the choice spots being the campus of Dickinson College.

Years before, Ewell had been a Federal officer stationed at the town's well-known military barracks. Now he hoisted a Confederate flag over the barracks and stripped the place of the government property that hadn't been sent to safer spots, the best discovery being a large store of grain. The town itself was made to give up many horses, and outlying areas were denuded of cattle. An abundance of flour was appropriated.

The citizens were careful not to antagonize Ewell. A group of church members approached him and asked whether he had any objection to their continuing their usual public prayers for the President of the United States.

"Certainly not," said Ewell. "Pray for him. I'm sure he needs it."

The general dispatched elements of his cavalry to investigate the defenses of Harrisburg, now only a day's march to the east. Ewell knew that Pennsylvania's capital was garrisoned chiefly by raw troops, and he believed he could take it. Apprehending his intentions, the town became a bedlam.

At this late moment, Pennsylvania's governor, Andrew G. Curtin, is-

Andrew G. Curtin

sued a call for additional militia volunteers, but there was a curious hitch in the proceedings. Washington had committed the Federal Quartermaster Department to arming and supplying new militia units raised in the state, but had somehow neglected to include the provision of uniforms.

Governor Curtin fired off a telegram to Abraham Lincoln urging that the oversight be taken care of at once, explaining that if he had to buy the uniforms himself he would have to go through the Pennsylvania Legislature, which would delay the mobilization.

Republican political luminary Simon Cameron was in Harrisburg that day, and he added a telegram of his own, in which he said to Lincoln: "I cannot use language strong enough to impress upon you my belief in the necessity of immediate action in this matter. The rebels are now in Carlisle, eighteen miles from the capital."

(One is left to wonder why, in so great an emergency, the troops could not be mobilized in civilian attire.)

It was Secretary of War Edwin Stanton who rectified the situation by authorizing the immediate provision of uniforms by the Quartermaster Department.

There really wasn't much else Washington could do for Harrisburg at this point. The national capital was looking to its own security. Not that the city felt critically threatened. Hooker's army was now well across the Potomac, with the general headquartered at Frederick, Maryland. He was interposing the army between Lee and Washington. Moreover, the city's defenses were strong and they held nearly 40,000 troops, many of them regulars.

However, at this time when the North needed every man it could get, the enlistment period of many short-termers was ending. In spite of pleas that they stay on, even if only for a few days, large numbers were going home. Washington was profaned with the sight of one New England regiment, 900 strong, making its way to the railway depot in parade formation, band playing and banners flying, not the least ashamed of its dereliction.

It was on June 27 that the contention between Hooker and the administration culminated. Lincoln had continued to mistrust the general's fitness for another confrontation with Lee, especially one so crucial as this one promised to be. Hooker, though presently handling the army with skill, had continued to entertain a like apprehension.

But Hooker could not simply step down for no apparent reason; his career would have been ruined. And Lincoln could not replace him with abruptness; the general had the strong support of a faction of the Republican Party the President could not afford to offend.

The impasse was resolved in this way: Hooker requested reinforcements from Washington. The administration did not comply. Then Hooker moved to attach the Harpers Ferry garrison and was stopped by a wire from his enemy, General Halleck, who argued that the troops must stay because the heights at the Ferry "have always been regarded as an important place to be held by us, and much expense and labor incurred in fortifying them."

This must have sounded silly even to Halleck.

Hooker shot back the rebuttal that the troops were of no use where they were and could be used to good advantage elsewhere. As for the precious fortifications, they would still be there if the troops were removed. The general closed by asking Halleck to refer the matter to the secretary of war and the President.

But Hooker did not wait for a response to this wire. It was hardly sent before he decided to use the moment to shed his burden. He said in a second wire to Halleck: "My original instructions require me to cover Harpers Ferry and Washington. I have now imposed on me, in addition, an enemy in my front of more than my number. [Not true; Hooker remained the stronger.] I beg to be understood, respectfully but firmly, that I am unable to comply with this condition with the means at my disposal, and earnestly request that I may at once be relieved from the position I occupy."

This telegram reached Washington at 3 P.M. In the evening Lincoln and Stanton met at the War Department and decided to replace Hooker with Major General George G. Meade, one of Hooker's senior corps commanders. Meade was not a spur-of-the-moment choice. He had been on the list of possible replacements for Hooker since the Battle of Chancellorsville.

Meade was forty-seven, about six feet tall, spare-fleshed and sinewy. A receding hairline was generally covered by a low-brimmed hat, the bridge of a Roman nose often held wire-rimmed glasses, and he wore a tousled beard that was brown with invasions of gray. Nervous-mannered

George G. Meade

and short-fused, Meade was known to his subordinates as "the old snapping-turtle." But he was basically a very decent and fair-minded man. He had no special political backing, nor did he seek any. His regard for the pomp of war was minimal, and he spurned self-promotion, his reputation based entirely on notable deeds. Under fire, his judgment was firm and his courage unshakable.

Though a West Pointer, Meade hadn't excelled there. His grades were mediocre, and he received many demerits—almost enough to wash him out—for things like not keeping his jacket buttoned properly. In the end, he managed to graduate sixteenth in a class of fifty-six. Service against the Seminole Indians in 1835 was cut short by malaria, but he forged a good career as an engineer in the war with Mexico. Back home he became involved in engineering projects that helped further the growth of the nation.

Told that Meade was a Pennsylvanian, Lincoln is supposed to have said he would most likely "fight well on his own dunghill." Had the President known Meade in depth he would have found interest in the fact that the general was about as different from Joe Hooker as it was possible for him to be.

Henry Halleck concurred with Lincoln and Stanton on the change of commanders, and the general-in-chief was happy to write the orders. It is worthy of special note that they gave Meade the unconditional use of the troops at Harpers Ferry.

Chosen to deliver the orders was Assistant Adjutant General James A. Hardie, who happened to be a friend to both Hooker and Meade. When Hardie told Lincoln this was going to be a very painful mission for him, the President averred he was taking personal responsibility for all wounded feelings—including Hardie's.

The adjutant general was soon aboard a special night train for Frederick, Maryland.

During that same afternoon and evening, General Lee was bringing the corps of Longstreet and Hill together in encampments to the north and east of Chambersburg, Pennsylvania. That town had seen a lot of Confederate activity lately, starting with the Jenkins raid in middle June, and many of the people were more exasperated than cowed, some even going so far as to jeer at the tattered marchers.

As a column passed her house, one woman was heard to say, "Look at Pharaoh's army going to the Red Sea."

This taunt and the others were countered with cheers and laughter.

Spotting a woman with the Stars and Stripes pinned across her bosom, a soldier warned her to be careful, that his unit was great for charging breastworks with the Union colors on them.

James Longstreet had a stock answer for the people he met who complained about the goods they had lost to requisition and theft: "Yes, it's very sad, very sad. And this sort of thing has been going on in Virginia for more than two years. Very sad."

Longstreet felt that the Yankees were being treated too leniently, that there was justification for putting their homes to the torch, but that this was not an option because it would destroy Confederate discipline by creating a general wantonness.

Lee established his headquarters camp at Shetters' Woods, a charming grove about a mile east of Chambersburg on the road to Cashtown and Gettysburg. The camp was marked by a Confederate flag but manifested no ostentation. There were half a dozen wall tents and as many

Longstreet's wartime servant.

supply wagons, while grazing in grassy spots or secured to trees were numerous horses and mules.

There was probably a lone chicken scratching and clucking about. Lee seems to have had a pet hen along on this campaign who laid her eggs under his cot.

Included in the picture was a comfortable private carriage (said to have been captured from Union General John Pope) that Lee never used. He preferred the image he displayed on his gray horse, Traveller, knowing it had a positive effect on his troops.

Not that the commander wouldn't have found the comforts of a carriage welcome at times. In addition to the residual effects of his heart-related illness, he was presently being nagged by sciatica. There were days when he found it difficult to maintain the aspect of a stalwart horseman.

Lee's campaign stresses were beginning to build. He'd had no word from Jeb Stuart and had no idea where he was. This meant that he knew nothing of the Yankee army either. He believed it was still in Virginia.

Lee had planned to order the consolidation of his troops as soon as the enemy's columns started north; and, by rapid maneuvering as they entered southern Pennsylvania, fall upon them in detail, his aim to create panic and virtually destroy the army, thus putting the North at his mercy.

The general did not know that his plan was no longer feasible. Hooker was fifty miles farther northward than he supposed.

By this time Lee was asking every officer who came to his camp, "Have you heard any news of Stuart?"

It was only during that night of June 27–28 that the errant cavalier and his men finally crossed the Potomac, the last segment of either army to do so.

After his encounter with elements of Hooker's army east of the Bull Run Mountains, Stuart had consumed two and a half days making his southeasterly detour to a Potomac crossing he could use. A brush with a party of Yankee cavalry scouts had not expedited matters. Nor had the need to stop several times to graze the horses and allow them to rest.

As for the elegant dinner with a wealthy family of Stuart admirers—

yes, of course there were lovely young ladies present—who could blame the general for fitting that in?

The crossing was made at Rowser's Ford, hardly more than fifteen miles northwest of Washington. Because of the darkness, the depth of the water, and tricky currents, the crossing was an extremely difficult one. The artillery shells had to be taken from their chests and carried across in the arms of the horsemen, and they themselves were up to their knees in water. The artillery pieces and their caissons were completely submerged, which put an extra strain on the horses.

Three o'clock in the morning found the entire command on the Maryland bank, the rear guard still dripping. There was much jubilation over the feat, and some singing of cavalry ditties. Then the need for sleep began asserting itself, and the need, for most of the men, was soon gratified.

During these same early morning hours of Sunday, June 28, Union General George Meade, sleeping partly dressed on a cot in his wall tent near Frederick, was awakened by a hand shaking his shoulder. In the light of a turned-down lamp he beheld the face of his friend from the War Department, James Hardie, who told him, smiling archly, that he'd been relieved of the command of his corps. In his stupor, Meade believed for a moment that, for some reason, he was being arrested to be taken to Washington.

When the general learned the true nature of Hardie's visit, he came wide awake, reacting with protests that could be heard by aides in nearby tents. In the first place, he said, the order wasn't fair to John Reynolds, a corps commander senior to himself. In the second place, a major battle seemed imminent, and he knew little of Hooker's dispositions and even less of Lee's maneuvers.

Hardie reacted by telling the general he had no choice in the matter, then compounded his friend's anguish by telling him he must now go along to Hooker's headquarters to obtain the command.

"Well," Meade finally said, "I've been tried and condemned without a hearing, and I suppose I'll have to go to the execution."

Aides were summoned, and horses saddled. The ride in the dark was a long one, the party reaching Hooker's tent at dawn. All were surprised to find the flaps thrown back and the general standing beside the pole in full uniform, sword included. Meade was relieved to see that Hooker had somehow discovered what was afoot.

But Hooker was not as pleased as he should have been. It was hard on his ego that his resignation had been accepted without the slightest protest.

There was friction in the tent while the two generals pored over maps and Hooker explained the things that Meade must know. One of the aides said later: "Hooker's chagrin and Meade's overstrung nerves made the lengthy but indispensable conference rather trying to the whole party."

But when the generals went public in Frederick that morning, with the church bells seeming to herald the moment, and with newsmen present, matters were amicable enough. The two men praised one another, and the sentiments seemed sincere.

Hooker cried as he shook hands with his top officers before departing for Baltimore in accord with his orders. Meade, characteristically, issued a statement informing the troops he had accepted this unsought command only as a duty, that he had "no pledges or promises to make." Their mission remained the same; they must rescue the North "from the devastation and disgrace of a hostile invasion."

To a group of friends who came to congratulate him the general said, "I don't know whether I'm an object of congratulation or commiseration."

By and large, the troops were not enthusiastic about the change. Most of them knew little of Meade.

"Why him?" they asked. "What has *he* ever done?"

Actually, the general had an outstanding combat record in this war, but only his own men knew it. Some of the others who got a glimpse of him at this time decided he looked more like a wagoner than a high commander.

Many were sorry to see Hooker go simply because he had kept a sharp eye on commissary affairs. The army had never been so rich in equipment and rations.

But there was little real bitterness over the new order of things. After so many switches at the head of the army, it hardly seemed to matter anymore who was in charge. The men were proficient veterans now, and they had come to depend a lot on their own initiative. In the end, most shrugged their shoulders over the situation and applied themselves to the northward march.

There was another place on Sunday morning, June 28, where the sound of church bells accompanied a campaign event: York, Pennsylvania.

Jubal Early's approach met no militia resistance. A committee of officials came forward and surrendered the town to John Gordon's brigade, marching in the lead.

The picture made by Gordon's troops was in striking contrast to that of the well-dressed citizens on their way to church, and many of these people were appalled at the sight of this horde of seeming ruffians.

Intending to say a few words to relieve the minds of one group of young women, the mounted Gordon approached them and doffed his hat. He did not realize that, because of the heavy dust of the march, he looked little better than his foot troops. Shrieks of alarm went up.

In a few moments, however, the general's rich, cultured tones had the desired effect.

"I assured these ladies," Gordon wrote later, "that the troops behind me, though ill-clad and travel-stained, were good men and brave; that beneath their rough exteriors were hearts as loyal to women as ever beat in the breasts of honorable men."

Gordon's brigade passed on through the town, the general's orders to continue to Wrightsville, on the Susquehanna River. Jubal Early's other brigades occupied York, the unit in the lead commanded by General William "Extra Billy" Smith, governor-elect of Virginia, sixty-seven years old, still sturdy in the saddle, and known for his beaming joviality.

To tranquilize the watching citizens, Billy had a band play "Yankee Doodle" while he rode at the head of his column, hat in hand, smiling and bowing left and right.

When this resulted in swelling the crowd and even eliciting a few cheers, Smith halted his unit and began making a speech. He explained that his troops had no hostile intent. "It was getting a little warm down our way, and we needed a summer outing, and thought we would take it at the North instead of patronizing the Virginia springs, as we generally do."

In the midst of a lot of similar nonsense that was drawing laughs from the crowd, the speaker was interrupted by a burst of profanity from Old Jube, who had, with much difficulty, pushed his horse up from the rear through the halted troops. Early demanded to know what the devil Smith was doing. Not the least bit ruffled, Billy explained that he was just having a little fun.

Old Jube, who liked the buoyant Smith, made no more of this; but he put a crimp in the townspeople's good humor by presenting York with a stiff requisition list. He was given a considerable measure of what he asked for, including $28,000 in cash.

James Gall, a Northern visitor to York during Early's tenancy, was surprised at the spareness of the Confederate camps. The officers had few tents, and the enlisted men had none.

Gall asked a soldier how he got along without a shelter-tent.

"First-rate," was the reply. "In the first place, I wouldn't tote one; and, in the second place, I feel just as well, if not better, without it."

"But how do you manage when it rains?" inquired Gall.

"Wall," said the soldier, "me and this other man has a gum blanket atween us. When it rains we spread one of our woolen blankets on the ground to lie on; then we spread the other woolen blanket over us, and the gum blanket over that, and the rain can't tech us."

Gall watched some troops make a meal of fresh beef, fried and well salted, and wheat griddle cakes raised with baking soda. Water was the only beverage.

An officer told the Northerner it was their Spartan life that made the Confederates superior soldiers. The Yankees, he said, "are too well fed, too well clothed, and have far too much to carry."

The salient events of that memorable last weekend in June were far from over. The next occurred to the south, at Rockville, Maryland, just northwest of Washington. It was about noon on Sunday when Jeb Stuart and his troopers, already four days out of touch with Lee, cantered into Rockville after scattering its small Union garrison.

As it happened, the town held a large academy for young females, most of whose members were Southern sympathizers and eager Stuart fans. The general and his staff were given a shrieking welcome, with some of the comely teenagers dancing about and clapping their hands while others slipped up to the men and scissored buttons from their uniforms. The horses were made to contribute snippets of mane.

After destroying Rockville's telegraph facilities, Stuart was preparing to resume his northward march when he got some thrilling news. A long mule-drawn supply train—about 150 wagons—had just left Washington and was coming through Rockville on its way to the Army of the Potomac in the Frederick area.

A detail of horsemen flew off toward the head of the train, whose drivers had just received word there were Rebels at Rockville. "And now," an observer said later, "commenced a scene of excitement and confusion which none but a maniac could properly describe."

Each of the wagons did an abrupt about-face, and the whole train started racing back toward Washington. Whips cracked above the ears of mules in a frenzy, and wagons careened. By the sides of the procession galloped civilians who had been en route to Rockville, and even some farmers on workhorses were part of the rush.

The pursuing Confederates were firing their carbines and pistols into the air and crying, "Halt! Halt!"

Many of the rearmost wagons were captured quickly. Those ahead were running a commendable race when, at a curve in the road, one of the wagons flipped over. There was a chain reaction that created a great tangle, with some of the wagons flipping like the first. Drivers cursed in bitter frustration, and many of the mules lay on their sides in their traces, kicking and braying wildly.

Up rode a laughing Jeb Stuart, who boomed to an aide, "Did you ever see such a sight in all your life?"

The uninvolved wagons at the head of the procession were run down and captured within sight of Washington. Stuart looked longingly toward the capital, for a moment toying with the idea of leading his troopers in and doing a little mischievous rapping on the outer defenses.

No one came out to challenge the impetuous raider. He lingered near Washington long enough to burn the ruined wagons, heedless that the smoke drew additional attention in his direction. When he returned to Rockville he was the exhilarated possessor of 400 prisoners and 125 wagons in beautiful condition, each with a six-mule team, and each laden with supplies. Included were tons of oats, a godsend for Jeb's horses, who had been doing a lot of hard work on skimpy rations.

Outside of the oats, however, the capture was not a fortunate thing for Stuart. Quite the contrary. The wagons were so attractive a prize that the general decided to adjust his march to the pace of carrying the whole train along north to present to Lee. Of milder detriment, though not negligible, was that the paroling of the prisoners made for an added delay in the Rockville area.

There was great excitement in Washington over Stuart's proximity, but the ranks of the fearful did not include Abraham Lincoln. When the War Department provided him with a cavalry escort for his personal carriage, he protested to Henry Halleck.

All of that jangling of spurs and clanking of swords, he said, made it hard for him and his wife Mary to hold a decent conversation. Moreover, the troopers looked so young and awkward he was more afraid of being shot by the accidental discharge of one of their carbines or pistols than he was of being shot or captured by Jeb Stuart.

(Lincoln was always casual about his security, and he even discouraged extra measures to protect him from assassination. "If there is such a plot, and they wanted to get at me, no vigilance could keep them out. . . . To betray fear of this, by placing guards and so forth, would only be to put the idea into their heads and perhaps lead to the very result it was intended to prevent." At another time, the President said: "I feel a presentiment that I shall not outlast the rebellion. When it is over, my work will be done.")

While Jeb Stuart was delighting in his 125 captured wagons at Rockville that Sunday afternoon, June 28, seventy-five miles to the north Confederate General John Gordon was making his march from York to the Susquehanna River town of Wrightsville.

Before leaving York for the dozen-mile northeasterly trip, the general had been approached by a girl about twelve years old and handed a bouquet of roses, in the midst of which he found a note from a Southern sympathizer, perhaps the girl's mother. The note bore the correct information that the approaches to the mile-long covered bridge over the river from Wrightsville to Columbia were guarded by a reinforced regiment of Yankees.

This unit, the 27th Pennsylvania Volunteer Militia, commanded by Colonel Jacob Frick, was made up largely of recruits but included a backbone of veterans home on convalescent leave, some wearing bandages over wounds. Among the recruits were about fifty very tired young foot soldiers and some of the horsemen who had been with that part of the 26th Pennsylvania Militia that had managed to escape John Gordon's pursuit at Gettysburg.

Also with Colonel Frick was a company of black volunteers from Columbia, just across the bridge. These were fighting men, not work

Civilian refugees on Columbia side of burning bridge.

troops, although they, like the other members of the regiment, had helped construct the earthworks that covered the bridge's Wrightsville approaches.

This bridge had been very busy of late. It was a combination railway crossing and toll crossing for wagon traffic, and it even had accommodations for pulling canal boats over, for the route of a canal crossed the river at this point. The wagon traffic of the refugees fleeing before the Confederate advance had become so heavy that the collection of tolls had been temporarily abandoned.

Jacob Frick's defenses were on the York side of Wrightsville, about half a mile from the bridge entrance. The defenses straddled the turnpike leading into town.

But the colonel and his reinforced regiment were no match for Gordon's battle-wise brigade, which launched its attack with artillery fire, some of the shells screeching over the defenses and crashing in the town, where many of the citizens had remained. (The record is unclear as to the damage the town sustained, but it was probably light.)

After putting up a lively defense with small arms for more than an hour, Colonel Frick and his men fell back and crossed the bridge to the Columbia side. The regiment had suffered nine wounded and eighteen captured.

Frick had been given orders to deny use of the bridge to the Confederates. Earlier, foreseeing the probability of a retreat, he had made provisions to blow one of the spans with powder as soon as he'd made his crossing. The charge failed to do its job, so the colonel at once resorted to fire.

Though constructed on a series of masonry piers, the roofed bridge was composed wholly of well-seasoned wood. The fire took a strong hold as darkness was falling, the flames and sparks shooting high, a sight visible for miles.

John Gordon and his men tried to fight the fire from the Wrightsville side, and the general called upon the town to provide utensils for carrying water. But, because of their reluctance to see the bridge saved for Confederate use, the citizens claimed that such utensils were in very short supply.

Presently the entire mile-long structure was fiercely ablaze. Then a lumber yard at the Wrightsville entrance was ignited. And soon the flames spread to some nearby houses.

The Confederates went to work on the house fires, and suddenly the citizens were able to find so many tubs, buckets, pots, and pans that Gordon believed he'd have been able to make firefighters out of Lee's whole army, had it been present.

It was by means of a bucket brigade that the struggle was waged. A long line of men anchored on the river passed the water containers hand-to-hand to the flames. The soldiers were already weary from their marching and skirmishing, but they persisted well into the night and were finally victorious.

Suddenly these enemy troops were friends and heroes, and Wrightsville was grateful. Few Confederates went without a good breakfast the next morning. John Gordon himself was part of a group given a special invitation to the table of a woman whose house had been saved. She told her guests frankly that she was a strong Unionist, had a husband in the army, and prayed daily for the North to win, but felt she owed them a token of appreciation.

Gordon and the others left the house with the deepest admiration and respect for this "brave and worthy woman."

9

Buford Makes a Decision

BREAKFAST ON THAT Monday, June 29, was not a happy meal for Robert E. Lee in his camp at Shetters' Woods, east of Chambersburg.

The general had spent the whole of Sunday there, receiving no news of the Army of the Potomac and having no reason, in spite of some uncertainty, to alter the development of his invasion. If there had been a change in the status of the enemy's columns, which he believed to be still in Virginia under Joe Hooker, Jeb Stuart should have found some way to let him know. Stuart's whereabouts, of course, was still a nagging mystery.

It had been on Sunday night that Lee finally learned some solid intelligence about the Federals. Harrison, the spy Longstreet had sent to Washington with a pocket full of gold, came to the Chambersburg camps and reported that the Army of the Potomac was now in Maryland under a new commander. Lee was skeptical until Longstreet assured him that Harrison had a reputation for reliability.

The Confederate leader was now in a deeply worrisome spot. The enemy's columns, spreading from Frederick toward the Pennsylvania border, were much too close for him to consider an offensive reaction. Now he must concentrate his army, and quickly, for his own protection. Ewell must be summoned southward from the Susquehanna, with Hill and Longstreet moving eastward from Chambersburg to meet him.

Adding to the seriousness of the situation was the enemy's switch in leadership. Lee had once said that Washington's penchant for changing commanders might sometime result in his facing one he'd have trouble handling. He knew George Meade from days they'd spent together in the Federal service, and had a high regard for his abilities, a regard that was presently coupling itself with apprehension. Lee found himself hoping that Meade's sudden promotion at so crucial a time would throw him off balance.

If Jeb Stuart would only surface! Lee's need for the trooper's intelligence-gathering skills was becoming desperate.

On that Monday morning a citizen of Chambersburg who came to Shetters' Woods to complain about the theft of a horse found Lee pacing his camp with his nerves in turmoil.

"Never have I seen so much emotion depicted upon a human countenance. With his hand at times clutching his hair, and with contracted brow, he would walk with rapid strides for a few rods, and then, as if he bethought himself of his actions, he would, with a sudden jerk, produce an entire change in his features and demeanor, and cast an inquiring gaze on me, only to follow this in a moment with the same contortions of face and agitation of person."

Lee, of course, was soon in complete control of himself again, prepared to deal with the crisis in a deliberate manner.

It was on that late-June day that the crossroads town of Gettysburg began to assume a critical importance to the campaign. The place was like the center of a spiderweb, the many roads leading there including those from Chambersburg, Carlisle, York, and Frederick.

Neither Meade nor Lee had a view to fighting at Gettysburg. Meade had his eye on Pipe Creek at Taneytown, Maryland, just below the Pennsylvania border. This spot would enable him to cover both Baltimore and Washington. Lee's thoughts turned to Cashtown, eight miles west of Gettysburg on the Chambersburg Pike. There he would have his back to a pass through the South Mountains. His flanks would be safe, and a withdrawal, if one became necessary, could be made with little hindrance.

But matters were developing in such a way that neither commander could handle his army wholly as he wished. Neither knew enough about the other's dispositions or intentions. They must probe toward each other and adjust their tactics to whatever happened.

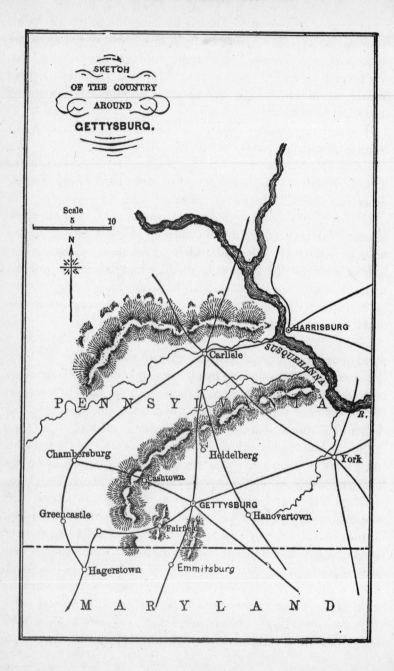

SKETCH
OF THE COUNTRY
AROUND
GETTYSBURG.

Scale
5   10

N

HARRISBURG

SUSQUEHANNA

Carlisle

PENNSYLVANIA

R.

Chambersburg

Heidelberg

York

Cashtown

Greencastle

GETTYSBURG

Hanovertown

Fairfield

Hagerstown   Emmitsburg

MARYLAND

General Meade, contrary to Lee's vision of his disorientation, had managed to take a quick, firm, and able hold on the Army of the Potomac's seven corps of infantry and one of cavalry. The new commander was not awed by his illustrious opponent, but he had a great deal of respect for him, and planned to proceed against him with consummate caution.

A noteworthy sidelight of Meade's assumption of the army's top command was that one of his first messages to Henry Halleck in Washington, an important one citing his plans, had a troublous journey. Thanks to Jeb Stuart's work, Meade was temporarily out of telegraphic contact with the capital, so he gave the message to a mounted courier, telling him to find an uncut line as quickly as possible.

While making his search, the courier was shot dead by a farmer who mistook him for one of Stuart's raiders. The farmer was devastated by remorse, but the message was taken from the body at once, and a line found to make the transmission.

The unfortunate courier was buried near the scene of the tragedy, but his father soon came to claim the remains and take them to the family plot in the North.

By the evening of Monday, June 29, Meade had deployed his columns so as to occupy a northeasterly-facing front, an irregular twenty-five-mile arc, the left at Emmitsburg, Maryland, southwest of Gettysburg, the right at New Windsor, Maryland, northeast of Frederick.

There was a blot, however, on this picture of efficient management. Each corps left a trail of stragglers, morally weak men who had found the Frederick area to be abundant with alcoholic beverages and had chosen to linger at the fountain.

These drunken soldiers, according to a newsman who saw them, were "worthless vagabonds," a lot of them cowards who had enlisted in the army not out of patriotism but to pocket thirteen dollars a month. They were swaggering about, many boisterously profane, some making a show of their weapons and intimidating the people into giving them more liquor and choice things to eat, with a few even stealing horses.

After the battle, a good number of these stragglers, worried about being shot for desertion, would rejoin their units with trumped-up excuses for their absence. And the day would doubtless come when some told their grandchildren they'd been heroes at Gettysburg!

"Of course," the newsman summed up, "these scoundrels are not types of the army. The good soldiers never straggle. These men are the debris, the offscourings from nearly a hundred thousand soldiers."

John Buford's division of cavalry was on the left flank of Meade's army, moving toward the Pennsylvania border and Gettysburg, while Judson Kilpatrick was on the right, spurring northeast toward Hanover, Pennsylvania, a diagonal route that would carry him across the front of Jeb Stuart's march. Meade knew that Stuart was moving northward in a false position, and he intended to block him from reaching Lee as long as he could.

In seizing personal control of the cavalry, Meade, in effect, demoted that dandified little braggart, Alfred Pleasonton, to the role of a head-

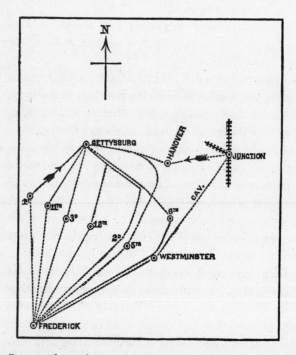

Routes of Meade's units from Frederick to Gettysburg.

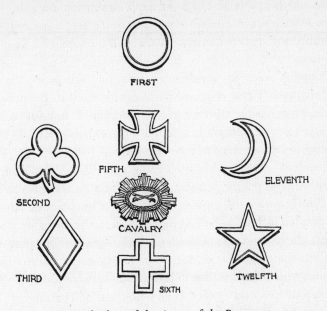

FIRST

FIFTH

ELEVENTH

SECOND

CAVALRY

THIRD

SIXTH

TWELFTH

Corps badges of the Army of the Potomac.

quarters staff officer. [Of course, if we listen to Pleasonton's postwar version of what happened, we learn that the commanding general wanted him handy as his chief advisor, at the same time allowing him to control the cavalry, exactly as he wished, from headquarters; and that it was mainly through Pleasonton's efforts, both as advisor to Meade and leader of the cavalry, that the Battle of Gettysburg was won.]

On the Confederate side, the waning of Monday the 29th found Lee's couriers seeking out Dick Ewell's columns with orders for their immediate withdrawal from the Susquehanna. Though Lee was keeping Longstreet, for the moment, at Chambersburg, A. P. Hill's corps had begun moving eastward from that town on the pike to Gettysburg. Henry Heth's division, in the lead, passed through the South Mountains and drew up at Cashtown, eight miles west of the fated community.

These were the same hours during which the Union troopers under John Buford were reconnoitering toward Gettysburg from the south.

Late that afternoon (the 29th), Jeb Stuart, still in northern Maryland, met some resistance at the town of Westminster. But Meade had nothing to do with this. Two companies of the 1st Delaware Cavalry, about ninety-five men, had come out from Baltimore, which lay to the southeast.

Making a brave but injudicious stand, the little party was overwhelmed, only a few of its members getting back to Baltimore, the dead and wounded being left in the hands of the Westminster civilians.

Stuart lost two officers killed, and a party of sympathetic townswomen insisted on seeing to their interment.

Stuart and his raiders had been doing a good job of damaging Federal railway and telegraph communications and spreading alarm to the east. But they were still moving at the pace set by the captured wagon train that Jeb insisted upon keeping. Food was a problem for men and mounts, the latter having made short work of the oats bonanza. Worst of all was the fatigue factor. Men were falling asleep in their saddles. One man who did this, unable to maintain his seat, slipped off his horse. He happened to land against a rail fence, and he continued to sleep while draped over it.

It is probable that Stuart's judgment during this latter period of his march was dulled by fatigue. He was showing little concern for his long separation from Lee's army, and did not seem worried that the Federal columns on his left were moving in such a way that he was denied knowledge of the army's whereabouts.

Lee's orders had specified that as soon as Jeb had crossed the Potomac he must start feeling for the right of Ewell's column, which was leading the invasion. Since the trooper had known from the start that Ewell would be heading for the Susquehanna, he decided to look for him in that region. The plan might have succeeded, but Stuart was moving too slowly. Most illogically, he seemed to think that nothing important was going to happen to the army until he had resumed contact with it.

Late in the morning on Tuesday, June 30, Stuart met Kilpatrick at Hanover, Pennsylvania, which happened to be only a dozen miles east of Gettysburg. The engagement was not a major one, but it was marked by some hot skirmishes.

During an encounter in the streets of the town, the Confederates

Scene of the fighting in Hanover.

were surprised to find a number of citizens with muskets and shotguns shooting at them from upstairs windows. In the out-of-town fighting, Stuart once had to turn and flee at a gallop to avoid capture, winning the race only by jumping his splendid mare, Virginia, over a fifteen-foot ditch the Yankees were unable to negotiate.

Jeb may have been tired these days, but he had retained much of his customary ebullience. The men of one of his regiments, while awaiting orders, began climbing the trees in a cherry orchard to pick the fruit. The general was watching as a line of approaching bluecoats spotted the pickers and began clipping the limbs about them with carbine bullets, and he laughed as they clambered down with all possible haste.

"What's the matter, boys?" he taunted. "Are those cherries sour?"

Especially active on the Union side were two very young brigadier generals who matched each other in fighting spirit: George Armstrong Custer and Elon J. Farnsworth.

Custer, demerited for slovenly dress at West Point—where he graduated at the bottom of his class but was later honored with a statue—was one of the war's most strikingly costumed officers. He wore a uniform of black velveteen, a blue shirt, and a scarlet tie, and he glistened with gold trim. Custer's hair was blond and his facial features were suggestive of weakness, but there was nothing weak about his will.

George A. Custer

The tall and slender Elon Farnsworth was not a West Pointer but a university student who volunteered at the start of the war. He learned how to fight by fighting, having managed to get himself into some forty encounters during the past two years.

For several hours after the guns fell silent at Hanover, the opposing lines faced each other watchfully at a distance. Kilpatrick was content to block the road to Gettysburg, while Stuart, unaware that all other units of both armies were gravitating toward that town, wanted only to continue his march toward the Susquehanna.

The Confederate troopers at last drew off to the northeast. Thus it was that Stuart, still dragging his caravan of captured wagons and encumbered also with 400 prisoners taken since the first 400 were paroled after the Rockville affair, began a plodding march in the opposite direction from Lee's position.

That Tuesday, June 30, was a day of rising excitement among the people of Gettysburg. During the previous evening, those in positions offering views to the west had seen scores of tiny red spots appear along the base of the South Mountains at Cashtown—the campfires of Henry Heth's division of Hill's corps. There were no Union soldiers in

Elon J. Farnsworth

Gettysburg at that time. John Buford's 5,000 troopers were still feeling their way up from the south.

Buford knew he was approaching a hornet's nest of superior numbers, but he knew also that a few miles behind him, easily reachable by courier, was the left wing of Meade's army—the First, Third, and Eleventh Corps—under one of the army's ablest leaders, Major General John Reynolds.

The forty-two-year-old Reynolds, known for his fine soldierly appearance and his flashing dark eyes, was the man Meade had fretted about displacing as the rightful heir to Hooker's command. Actually, the worry was a needless one. Reynolds did not want the job, feeling it was too strongly supervised by the people in Washington. Having faith in Meade's competence, Reynolds had no problem with taking orders from him.

Right now Meade, headquartered at Taneytown, Maryland, about twelve miles south of Gettysburg, was counting upon Reynolds to work with Buford and transform a highly uncertain situation into something amenable to control.

John F. Reynolds

The Confederates, of course, were in a similar state of perplexity.

It was they, in the end, who brought matters to a head—in a curious way. On the morning of the 30th, General Heth ordered James Johnston Pettigrew to take his brigade into Gettysburg to look for a supply of shoes that Jubal Early was believed to have missed during his visit of the 26th.

Pettigrew, aware that Yankee troopers were somewhere in the area, moved cautiously, his advance drawing up on a rise some distance west of town so that its streets and its approaches could be studied with field glasses.

At about ten o'clock some mounted bluecoats were seen entering Gettysburg from the south. This was Buford's advance, not a great many men, but enough to impel Pettigrew to turn back toward Cashtown for a consultation with Heth.

As Buford occupied Gettysburg in force, the citizens reacted with joy, many hurrying from their houses to welcome the dusty horsemen with cheers and brandished flags. Patriotic songs were added by groups of children, their manner poignantly appealing as they sang such lines as "The Union forever! Hurrah, boys! Hurrah!"

Food was provided, with some of the women launching baking marathons, producing not only bread but also pies and cakes.

Buford was viewed as Gettysburg's savior and protector, but he was actually neither. He was about to afflict the town with great trouble, this because he understood its military significance. His plans, however, were not centered upon making it the site of a showdown battle. Having learned that enemy columns were approaching it not only from the west but also from the north, he believed that Lee saw the place, as he himself did, as a convenient point for an army to concentrate; and he determined to try to deny the place to Lee, to try to hold it until John Reynolds came up, then leave it to Reynolds to decide what to do next.

Buford's aides noted that the general's mien was one of unusual anxiety as he prepared his defense. His main lines were set up west of the town, with his pickets about four miles from those of the enemy. Sent to the north and northeast of Gettysburg were pickets only, their mission to watch for the approach of Ewell's columns from the Susquehanna. Everywhere, Buford's lines were pathetically thin for the kind of task they were facing.

On the Confederate side, oddly enough, Henry Heth was still thinking in terms of shoes. When Johnston Pettigrew returned from Gettysburg without having pressed in for a search, Heth was unhappy, convinced that the town held no Federals beyond a few troopers on a scout.

When Corps Commander A. P. Hill, arriving from Chambersburg, was consulted about the matter, he agreed with Heth. The latter at once volunteered to take his whole division in the next morning to look for the shoes. Had Hill any objections?

"None in the world," said the commander, who, always ready for a fight, was not greatly concerned about the kind of resistance Heth might encounter.

That evening (June 30) the Confederate campfires were again visible to high-positioned people in Gettysburg, but this time the town's westerly woods and fields showed their own red patches. Around these latter fires the Union troopers wrote letters, talked, sang a variety of sad-melodied pieces, and held earnest prayer meetings.

Sitting at one of the fires, his companionable pipe in hand, was John Buford, and near him was Colonel Thomas C. Devin, commander of the right wing of the general's western defenses. Devin was inclined to discount Buford's view of the situation's gravity, feeling that no major work was pending. The colonel assured the general he'd be able to handle anything that developed in his front during the next twenty-four hours.

"No, you won't," said Buford. "They will attack you in the morning, and they will come *booming*—skirmishers three deep. You will have to fight like the devil to hold your own until supports arrive. The enemy must know the importance of this position, and will strain every nerve to secure it, and if we are able to hold it we will do well."

While the troops of John Buford and Henry Heth were sleeping around the embers of their campfires, Jeb Stuart's column was proceeding toward the Susquehanna. At midnight the general and a few aides stopped in the town of Jefferson at a tavern whose burly proprietor served them "cut and smear" with ale and coffee. (Stuart never drank alcoholic beverages, but he was a coffee lover.)

From Jefferson the column moved due north toward Dover, a few miles northwest of York. Stuart wrote later: "The night's march over a very dark road was one of peculiar hardship, owing to loss of rest to both man and horse."

The general might have elaborated on this. Out of hunger and thirst, the mules pulling the captured wagons were growing unruly, which further tired the weary drivers. Now and then one would fall asleep with the reins in his hands, his wagon drifting to a stop—which, of course, compelled all of those behind him to draw up.

The prisoners, too, were hungry and tired, and many pierced the night with profane protests. Some were bouncing along in the captured wagons, which were now diminished in stock, their edibles consumed and most of the other materials either put to use or claimed as booty by individual troopers. Principally, Stuart was keeping the wagons for Lee to load with requisitioned goods for transport back to Virginia.

Dover was reached at dawn on Wednesday, July 1, but nothing was learned of Dick Ewell's forces, except that Jubal Early was no longer at York. Information was hard to come by in this hostile region. The situation was a lot different from that in Virginia, where the citizens were always a good source of intelligence.

Jeb was unable to think of any other plan but to give the column a brief rest, then turn it toward Carlisle, about twenty-five miles to the northwest.

The trooper was continuing doggedly on a route *away* from Gettysburg.

Whereas that town was now the goal of all of Lee's infantry units, Meade's right wing—comprising the Second, Fifth, Sixth, and Twelfth Corps—was flung on a fanlike course to the east, the purpose to keep Baltimore covered. The Sixth Corps, under a sturdy, well-liked New Englander, Major General John "Uncle John" Sedgwick (already twice wounded in this war and destined to die at Spotsylvania), was on the extreme right, about twenty miles southeast of Gettysburg.

Some of the army's units had marched as much as 100 miles during the past four days, at times in the rain, at other times under a blistering sun.

Morale, however, was generally good, especially among the army's Pennsylvanians. As one said later: "Every heart beat warm with the thought we should soon press the soil of our Mother State, to whose defense we were marching."

At this time General Meade had not yet abandoned his vision of Pipe Creek, Maryland, as a good place to do battle. All of his units were under tentative orders to fall back upon this line if Lee came on aggressively, threatening them in detail. The Northern commander had no personal knowledge of the topography of the Gettysburg area.

10

The Battle Opens

THE FIRST SHOTS of the Battle of Gettysburg rang out at daybreak on Wednesday, July 1. But this was merely a picket exchange on the Chambersburg Pike west of a north-south stream known as Willoughby Run, a mile from the town. Confederate General Henry Heth's main forces were only now beginning to stir from their Cashtown camps to form for their march. The picket firing soon died away.

Lying quiet in the Gettysburg dawn were the two north-south ridges that were soon to be crowned with thunder, bathed in blood, and made eternally famous.

Just west of Gettysburg was Seminary Ridge, the southern segment of which, modest in elevation, extended three or four miles below the town. Roughly a mile east of this eminence and due south of Gettysburg, across a valley made up largely of farmlands, was Cemetery Ridge, a more commanding height. This was bounded in the south by Little Round Top and Big Round Top, while in the north, at Cemetery Hill, it made an easterly arc to join with Culp's Hill. The whole, running for about four miles, resembled a fishhook, with Culp's Hill the barb and Big Round Top the eye.

John Buford had established his lines between the Lutheran Seminary, just west of Gettysburg, and Willoughby Run. His troopers stood in the way of Confederate access not only to the town but also to both ridges.

These early morning hours at Gettysburg were marked by mixed

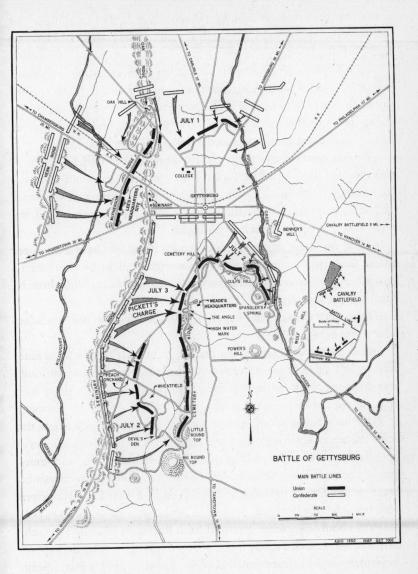

BATTLE OF GETTYSBURG

MAIN BATTLE LINES

Union
Confederate

SCALE
0   1/4   1/2   3/4   1 MILE

April 1959   NMP   GET 7000

feelings and varied activities among the townspeople. Many had not grasped the fact that a cataclysm was looming.

Youthful Anna Mary Young would later say in a letter: "The next time I hear the rebels are coming I'll believe, instead of laughing at the idea of such a thing; and I'll leave this region of the country, if I have to walk."

Lydia Ziegler, a teenager who lived at the Lutheran Seminary, where her father was steward, was uneasy at sight of Buford's battle formations but was able to marvel at the glory of the sunrise and the splendor it brought the town and countryside. Lydia and others in her family carried breakfast treats to the troopers in the lines.

The Zieglers were able to use the cupola of the seminary for observations toward the South Mountains. People of area farms, not so fortunate, sought information by wandering country byways with westward outlooks. Some of those in the town climbed out their attic windows and took up precarious rooftop positions.

Below, on street corners, stood groups of people engaged in animated discussions aimed at determining what might be expected to happen. At the same time, the town held many citizens who chose to take up the usual pursuits of the day.

There were women who baked bread—and this probably included Mary Virginia "Jennie" Wade.

In the backyard of one of the houses, eighteen-year-old Anna Garlach picked a pan of green beans from the family garden and sat in the sun stringing them for her mother, who planned to cook them with ham for the family's midday meal.

At Pennsylvania College, some of the professors began arriving with the aim of teaching their usual eight o'clock classes.

Charles Tyson, the photographer, opened his studio, and found himself doing a brisk business among those of Buford's troopers who were not on duty in the lines. Some of these men were having their picture taken for the last time.

In the home of seventy-year-old John Burns, an infantry veteran of the War of 1812, there was friction that morning. The small, peppery Scotsman—a sometime farmer, cobbler, and constable, a man fond of his "wee drop," and a claimant to kinship with the famous Robert Burns—was having trouble with his wife.

Ever since the present war's beginning, John Burns had been trying to volunteer, his age always against him. Even now, with the war at his

Pennsylvania College

doorstep, his services remained unwanted. A venture toward Buford's cavalry lines the preceding day had been turned back.

But the little Scotsman had been a foot soldier, and he knew that Meade's infantry was drawing near. There was still a chance for his participation. So that morning he took his War of 1812 musket from over his fireplace mantel.

"Burns," asked his wife, "what in the world are you going to do?"

The Scotsman hedged in a way that wouldn't have deceived anyone. "I thought some of the boys might want the old gun, and I am getting it ready for them."

Though charged with being a fool, Burns went on to secure a supply of ammunition. He also took from a closet his "Sunday best," which happened to represent a style about forty years in the past. Over a dark vest and dark trousers he donned a blue swallowtail coat with brass buttons, and on his head he placed a high-crowned hat veneered with black silk now worn and faded.

Then, to the tune of his wife's continuing protests, Burns took up his musket and ammunition, went out on his porch, and sat down in

John Burns

the morning sunlight to await the start of the fighting and the coming of the Union infantry.

No civilians in the Gettysburg area that morning were in a more pre-carious spot than schoolgirl Amelia Harmon and her aunt (name ob-scure), who lived in The Old McLean Place, a fine colonial-style brick house something over a mile from town on the west side of Willoughby Run. The southern flank of Buford's lines, on the east side of the run, faced this mansion. From their eastern windows, the two females could look into the mouths of a section of Buford's artillery pieces.

Most of the people in the few houses scattered west of Gettysburg had departed for safer locations, but Amelia and her aunt had chosen to remain. They knew that the mansion, filled with beautiful things, comprised a special target for looters.

With its eighteen-inch walls and its heavy wooden shutters, the place seemed a virtual fortress. Surely, the two believed, they'd be perfectly safe, whatever happened.

Confederate General Henry Heth, still thinking in terms of searching Gettysburg for shoes, was beginning his approach. Heth continued in his notion that the town held but few Yankees.

Lee himself believed that the enemy's leading infantry units were still well to the south, and he was only now advancing his headquarters to Cashtown. The commander would have been astonished to know that so formidable a Yankee as John Reynolds was only a few miles below Gettysburg, moving up rapidly.

This is something, of course, that Lee should have known through Jeb Stuart. That general, still ignorant of Lee's whereabouts, was presently starting his briefly rested column on the road from Dover to Carlisle.

James Longstreet's corps was on the Chambersburg Pike beginning to follow the rearmost division of A. P. Hill's corps. Longstreet had left one of his divisions—that of Major General George E. Pickett—encamped, for the time being, at Chambersburg as the army's rear guard. Dick Ewell's two columns, pushing down from the Susquehanna, were still several hours from Gettysburg.

It was soon after 8 A.M. that John Buford received word from his pickets that the Confederate column from Cashtown was in sight on the Chambersburg Pike, its van preceded by three rows of skirmishers spread through the fields to the right and the left. The cavalry lines were alerted, and by nine o'clock the two sides were exchanging a desultory artillery fire, with Henry Heth still unaware he was facing a major challenge.

The civilians in spots providing them westerly views knew at once what was happening, and many abandoned their observation posts for less exposed places. In other parts of Gettysburg, people who heard the firing began running about and shouting questions to one another:

"What's happening?"

"Are they shelling the town?"

"What shall we do?"

Numbers of children, shaken not only by the gunfire but also by the consternation among the adults, began crying.

Entrance to the cemetery.

After the first shock, and at the urging of troopers riding the streets, most of the frightened citizens returned to their houses to wait things out and to prepare their cellars for emergency occupation.

Some of the westernmost people, however, began hurrying eastward with valuables transported in various ways: borne by hand, stowed on horses or mules, thrown into carriages, even piled on wheelbarrows. One man was seen driving a wagon carrying a mound of trunks being used as a seat by his mother-in-law.

A safe place, at least temporarily, for refugees and observers alike was Cemetery Hill, south of town. In the very best spot for observation was Mrs. Peter Thorn, caretaker of Evergreen Cemetery, a woman with three children and a fourth on the way, whose husband was absent with the Union forces. Mrs. Thorn lived in the cemetery's novel arched gatehouse—near which, incidentally, stood this sign: ALL PERSONS FOUND USING FIREARMS IN THESE GROUNDS WILL BE PROSECUTED WITH THE UTMOST RIGOR OF THE LAW.

From an upstairs window of the gatehouse, Mrs. Thorn looked northwestward across the sea of fields below the town and beheld some scores of tiny figures begin the first encounter of the developing battle. She saw a spread of Confederate skirmishers appear over a rise beyond The Old McLean Place; and also saw, on the nearer side of the mansion, a party of Buford's horsemen ford Willoughby Run to oppose the advance. Mrs. Thorn was unaware, however, that the moment marked the beginning of a terrifying adventure for the two female occupants of the mansion, Amelia Harmon and her aunt, caught between the lines.

From an eastern window, the pair saw Buford's bluecoats coming up the slope from the stream. Spurring their mounts and shouting to one another, the men passed the house and its scattered outbuildings, and made for a woods a short distance westward. From the woods came several Confederate musket shots, and the troopers drew back in haste and began returning the fire from around the sides of the barn and the sheds and from behind solitary trees. One man, Amelia noted, seemed to think himself sheltered when he placed his mount behind the hand pump atop the property's well.

As the tumult increased, Amelia and her aunt locked all their doors and ran to an upstairs window that offered a better view westward. A Confederate minie ball shortly slammed into the shutter beside which the older female was standing. But the pair remained at the window, fascinated by what they saw. A field of timothy in front of the woods

Buford's cavalry at Willoughby Run.

was laced with Confederates crouching low as they advanced, with one and another of them rising erect from time to time to loose a quick shot at the Yankees.

Just below the window a horse fell dead. As its rider jumped clear, he heard a cry from above: "Look! The field is full of Rebels!"

The trooper shouted back, "Leave the window or you will be killed!"

This time the pair rushed up to the mansion's cupola, from which they could see still farther westward, and astonishment seized them as they became aware of the magnitude of the Confederate threat.

"It seemed as though the fields and woods had been sown with dragon's teeth," Amelia wrote later, "for everywhere had sprung up armed men where about an hour ago only grass and flowers grew."

The Confederates advancing through the timothy soon compelled the party of Union troopers to fall back across Willoughby Run. As the skirmish subsided, Amelia and her aunt, locked in their fortress, found themselves surrounded by the enemy, who established a line on the property. The two were not molested. But the lull in the fighting in that area marked only the end of the first act in the drama involving The Old McLean Place.

There was sharp skirmishing at other points along Buford's front while Henry Heth completed his deployments. The artillery exchanges continued, the gun muzzles producing drifts of smoke and the impact points marked by fierce puffs of dust and debris. A few deaths and maimings resulted, but the work had the effect of retarding progress toward heavy fighting at close range, a boon for the Union leader, who had a desperate need to keep things on modest terms until John Reynolds reached the field.

Buford had put a signal crew in the cupola of the Lutheran Seminary, in rear of his lines, its job to keep him informed of the enemy's maneuvers and of the effectiveness of the defense activities. These anxious-faced men were also turning to make surveys southward along the Emmitsburg Road, straining for a glimpse of the cloud of dust that would mark the approach of Reynolds' van.

It was perhaps nine-thirty when, far down the road, the prayed-for cloud began to show itself. One of the lookouts called the inspiring

Heth's troops on the Chambersburg Pike.

news to Buford, standing below. The general hurried up into the cupola, and, using his field glasses, soon made out the First Corps flag bobbing at the head of a winding column. The distance was too great for Buford to hear the drummers and fifers who had begun playing their tunes of inspiration.

Galloping a mile in front of the troops, John Reynolds himself, guided by the booming of the guns and one of Buford's scouts, shortly arrived at the Seminary. Buford hailed him from the cupola, and he responded by asking what was afoot.

Buford shouted back, "The devil's to pay!"

The trooper was soon on the ground conferring with Reynolds, who asked him whether his lines were strong enough to sustain themselves until the approaching infantry was up and deployed. Buford said he believed they were.

The leading First Corps troops turned leftward from the road into the fields south of town and began trotting toward the Seminary, their fixed bayonets flashing in the sun. Running some distance ahead of the column was a party of axe-armed pioneers who made short work of the fences that stood in the way.

Only one division was arriving at this time, that of elderly, snowy-haired, but still vigorous James S. Wadsworth, a well-to-do New Yorker whose civilian pursuits included farming and mixing into politics. The sword the old general brandished as he deployed his men as relief for Buford's mile-long line was a family heirloom that had seen service in the American Revolution.

Wadsworth's division held only two brigades, but, fortunately for the Union cause, they were first-rate. One, indeed, was Solomon Meredith's proud and confident "Iron Brigade," a composite of volunteers from Wisconsin, Michigan, and Indiana who were veterans of many fights and had won a reputation for firmness and capability under fire, and who wore black felt hats as their badge of honor.

One of Solomon Meredith's aides that morning was the librarian of Congress, John G. Stephenson, who had stolen away from Washington for a stint in the field.

John Reynolds hurried a courier off to Taneytown with word for Meade that he had joined Buford, that the Confederates were approaching Gettysburg in strong numbers, and that he intended to resist them "inch by inch." Reynolds also dispatched orders for the rest of the First Corps and the other units of his left-wing command to come up fast. The general assumed that Meade would respond by turning his right-wing columns toward Gettysburg and would come there personally.

Thus it was that John Reynolds, with his decision to support Buford, became the chief figure in the selection of Gettysburg as the site for the Meade-Lee showdown.

Confederate General Henry Heth had begun pushing forth vigorously, even recklessly. He knew he was facing foot troops now, but he supposed them to be militia, easy prey for the two brigades he'd placed in the fore, those of James J. Archer and Joseph R. Davis, the latter a nephew of the Confederate president.

It's true that Joseph Davis, attacking on Heth's left against the brigade of Lysander Cutler on the Union right, got a potent start. James Hall's 2nd Maine Artillery was mauled, and 450 killed or wounded

Hall's 2nd Maine Artillery.

were quickly inflicted on three infantry regiments: the 76th New York, the 147th New York, and the 56th Pennsylvania.

But James Archer, on the Confederate right facing the Iron Brigade on the Union left, was less successful. The point of contention here was McPherson's Woods, a stand that both sides saw as a key vantage area. Both began to enter the woods at the same time, Archer's Confederate brigade from the west and the Iron Brigade from the east.

On the Union side, the mounted Reynolds was leading in person. He shouted, "Forward, men, forward, for God's sake, and drive those fellows from the woods!"

As the general turned in the saddle to look back for reassurance that enough troops were coming, a Confederate bullet thudded into the back of his head and emerged near an eye. He gave an involuntary jerk on the reins that startled his horse, then went limp and fell to the ground without a sound. An observer said later: "I never saw a man die more quickly."

As explained by one of the general's aides: "It is striking proof of the discipline he had taught his own corps that the news of his death, although it spread rapidly, and that at a time when the inequality of numbers became apparent, produced no ill effect, led to no disorder, changed no disposition that he had directed, and in itself made the men only the more eager to carry out his orders."

Second-in-command to Reynolds was New Yorker Abner Doubleday, who had served as an artillerist in Mexico; and, stationed at Fort

Death of Reynolds.

Sumter, South Carolina, in April 1861, was in charge of the crew that fired the first shot aimed at the besieging Confederates. Lacking in color and dash, Doubleday was not an inspirational leader, but he had won trust through an earnest proficiency. He now assumed responsibility for the defense.

The Iron Brigade was moving on its own. Its men swept into McPherson's Woods, and one of James Archer's surprised graycoats was heard to exclaim: "There are those damned black-hatted fellows again! 'Taint no militia. It's the Army of the Potomac!"

The Confederates were driven back, with many being surrounded and captured. General Archer himself was seized physically by a big, rambunctious Irish private, the contact compounding the officer's feeling of disgrace. When he was taken to Doubleday, who had known him at West Point, Doubleday stepped forward with his hand extended and said, "Good morning, Archer! How are you? I'm glad to see you!" The Southerner ignored the proffered hand and replied, "Well, I'm not glad to see you, by a damned sight!"

As Archer's men were marched to the Union rear under guard, the procession passed the body of General Reynolds being borne from the field. Aware of the general's record in the war, the Confederates removed their hats out of respect for his remains.

Abner Doubleday's first serious command concern was the situation on the Union right. Lysander Cutler's decimated brigade was retiring toward the town, and Joseph Davis's elated Confederates were pressing after. In their confidence, however, these troops made the careless mistake of exposing their southern flank, the one facing Doubleday's personal location behind the Union left, and the general sent a reserve regiment—

Abner Doubleday

Rufus R. Dawes

Colonel Rufus R. Dawes' 6th Wisconsin, which was soon joined by the 95th New York and the 14th New York State Militia—against this flank.

The bluecoats had the advantage of position, but their numbers were none too strong, and as the enemy faced southward to meet them they found themselves involved in a savage fight. The Confederates soon fell back, but only to jump into a long east-west railroad cut that gave them excellent cover.

The Federals continued their northerly advance. Their commander, Rufus Dawes, explained later:

"Any correct picture of this charge would represent a V-shaped crowd of men with the colors at the advance point, moving firmly and hurriedly forward, while the whole field behind is streaming with men who had been shot and who are struggling to the rear or sinking in death upon the ground."

The colors went down several times, but each time rose quickly in the hands of a new bearer. Every man of the color guard was killed or wounded.

As the railroad cut was neared, several of the bluecoats ran forward and jumped in and began a hand-to-hand fight in an effort to take the Confederate colors, those of the 2nd Mississippi Volunteers. First to lunge for the staff was a mere youngster, and he was shot dead. An angry comrade brained the slayer with his musket butt. Then another Federal put his hands on the staff and was wounded. A third man finally seized the prize and kept it, coming to no harm as he bore it away.

By this time a party of the bluecoats had positioned themselves across the cut just east of the long Confederate line and were pouring in an enfilading fire. The cut had become a trap.

The Federals of the main force began shouting, "Throw down your muskets! Throw down your muskets!"

Hundreds of muskets clattered to the floor of the cut. Though a good many of the disarmed Confederates escaped by running out the west end, some two or three hundred were captured. The victory had cost the Federals at least 200 killed or wounded.

As both Abner Doubleday and Henry Heth turned to restoring the integrity of their lines, with the Federals exhilarated over their success, the action lulled at about 11 A.M. Triumphal music sounded from Gettysburg's town square, where several regimental bands had assembled.

Few of Gettysburg's citizens were reassured. Something horrendous was obviously developing, and there seemed little doubt it was going to engulf them. Already some of the public buildings and private homes were being made into hospitals for the wounded. Entryways were marked by trails of blood, and carpets were becoming stained. To the credit of the town's women, many at once adjusted to the horrors of the situation and offered themselves as nurses.

It was only now that wiry old John Burns left his house with his War of 1812 musket and directed his short legs toward the Seminary. What Burns had been doing during the first hour of the fighting can only be guessed at. Perhaps his wife, with continued scolding, had put a temporary crimp in his martial ardor.

Soon meeting a Union staff officer who was coming into town, Burns asked, "Which way are the Rebels? Where are our troops?"

He was told that he need only keep going and he'd shortly reach the

Union lines. As he hurried away, Burns proclaimed to the smiling officer, "I know how to fight. I've fit before."

The little Scotsman ended up with the Iron Brigade, then resting in McPherson's Woods, and he became the butt of many a joke about his age and quaint appearance. By a coincidence, he was wearing a black hat. It wasn't felt; it was silk over shaped cardboard; but it was black.

By this time both armies were receiving fresh troops—if "fresh" is the right word for men who had been pounding along dusty roads for several hours under a hot sun.

This was the lay of things as the morning waned:

The Confederate division of William D. Pender was moving in behind Henry Heth. A. P. Hill's remaining division, that of Richard H. Anderson, had reached Cashtown; and Longstreet's corps—still minus Pickett, on rear-guard duty at Chambersburg—was moving in Anderson's wake.

Dick Ewell's columns from the Susquehanna were closing upon Gettysburg, their participation imminent. The only Federals standing in their way were elements of Buford's cavalry.

Richard H. Anderson

Jeb Stuart and his troopers were trudging toward Carlisle.

Union General Abner Doubleday was being joined by the remaining divisions of the First Corps, those of John C. Robinson and Thomas A. Rowley. And Oliver O. Howard's Eleventh Corps was nearing the field. But the Army of the Potomac would remain overmatched, for none of its other units were close enough to help with the first day's fighting.

As for General Meade, he had no immediate plans to come forward from Taneytown, Maryland.

11

Lee's Afternoon Offensive

IT WAS ABOUT noon when the battlefield sounds began building again. Robert E. Lee was leaving Cashtown, moving eastward with Richard Anderson's division, and he reined up and began listening intently. Obviously deeply troubled, the general said at last, seemingly talking to himself: "I cannot think what has become of Stuart. I ought to have heard from him long before now. He may have met with disaster, but I hope not. In the absence of reports from him, I am in ignorance of what we have in front of us. It may be the whole Federal army, or it may be only a detachment. If it is the whole Federal force, we must fight a battle here. If we do not gain a victory, those defiles and gorges which we passed this morning will shelter us from disaster."

It was unlike Lee to express himself in terms of defeat. The measure of hope he'd harbored for achieving a great success in the North seemed to be fading.

Even while the commander was meditating, the fighting at Gettysburg was rising to a new level. The first units of Dick Ewell's corps, those of Robert E. Rodes' division, down from Carlisle, were coming in north of town, an approach that would unite their western flank with Heth and Pender's northern flank and thus transform the Confederate front into a great right angle.

During this development, Union General Oliver Howard's Eleventh Corps was arriving from the south, many of the perspiring men pausing by the cemetery gatehouse to drink from tubs of water set out by Mrs. Thorn, whose small sons blistered their fingers manipulating the pump from which the tubs were filled.

Oliver Howard was senior in rank to Abner Doubleday, and was prepared to take over as top Union commander on the field.

Neither Howard nor his corps were popular with the rest of the army. To be sure, the general had done his share of hard fighting in this war, had even given his right arm to the cause. This happened during the Peninsula Campaign.

(The misfortune gave birth to a memorable little story. General Philip Kearny, who had lost his left arm in Mexico, was present when Howard had his amputation, and sought to cheer him by saying, "I suggest, Howard, that you and I save money from now on by buying our gloves together." Unfortunately, the fates of war soon canceled Kearny's need for even one glove. He died during the Union retreat from Second Bull Run.)

Oliver Howard's popularity problem stemmed from the fact he was

Oliver O. Howard

stiffly self-righteous in his Christianity, and was too fervent an abolitionist to please the average bluecoat.

About half of Howard's men were German immigrants, and they
gave the corps its character. These men were not Pennsylvania Dutch—
they were of a more recent immigration period. But they fractured the
English language in much the same way; and this, coupled with habits
and mannerisms that seemed odd to the native-born soldiers, made
them objects of ridicule. Moreover, they had done poorly at Chancellorsville, putting the army in grave danger by folding under Stonewall
Jackson's flank attack.

All of this does not mean that Oliver Howard and his Dutchmen
were not welcome at Gettysburg. Abner Doubleday's First Corps
troops, threatened now from the north as well as from the west, greeted
the news of the column's arrival with a great round of cheering.

Howard allowed Doubleday to continue as he thought best with his
work on the western front, sending two Eleventh Corps divisions—
those of Francis C. Barlow and Carl Schurz—through the town to Doubleday's northern flank, where they began forming eastward against
Robert Rodes' Confederates from Carlisle.

Howard held his reserve division, that of Adolph von Steinwehr,
south of Gettysburg, for he had recognized the tactical importance of
Cemetery Hill. (It rose about eighty feet above the center of the town.)
Steinwehr's men were set digging in there.

Evergreen Cemetery's years of serenity were suddenly disrupted.
Tombstones were knocked over and the grass was rutted as the artillery rolled in, and guns were put in battery atop the graves.

On Abner Doubleday's front, meanwhile, new trouble had developed for Amelia Harmon and her aunt in The Old McLean Place,
which had become tactically important as marking the southern extremity of the battlefield. The graycoats who had been occupying the
property were suddenly driven away by a detachment of Federals, the
20th New York State Militia, who had been ordered to seize the brick
mansion and use it as cover for firing upon the Confederate flank.

From their position in the cupola, the two females watched the
enemy's flight with elation. But then a hammering on their locked
front door drew them downstairs, and they heard a Federal voice bel-

low: "Open, or we'll break down the door!" The attempt was already beginning as Amelia's aunt drew back the bolt.

Later, Amelia wrote colorfully: "In poured a stream of maddened, powder-blackened bluecoats who ordered us to the cellar while they dispersed to the various west windows throughout the house. From our cellar prison we could hear the tumult above, the constant crack of rifles, the hurried orders, and, outside, the mingled roar of heavy musketry, galloping horses, yelling troops, and the occasional boom of cannon."

Amelia may be forgiven for using dramatic license as she closed her account of this phase of her adventure: "We could hear the beating of our hearts above all the wild confusion."

By about 1:30 P.M., with the resumed contest in the west having settled into a series of isolated confrontations, the northern opponents, with a similar clatter, had begun skirmishing.

Both Union fronts were fairly stable. Doubleday was able to hold off A. P. Hill (Heth, supported by Pender); and Robert Rodes was not a mortal threat to Francis Barlow and Carl Schurz without the cooperation of Jubal Early, not yet arrived from York.

There was cool sniping by bluecoats and graycoats alike, and up and down the lines were heard such expressions as, "There he goes!" and "I brought my man!"

The Confederates under Rodes soon received a severe blow, not from Howard's Dutchmen but from troops to the west, on Doubleday's extreme northern flank. Lysander Cutler's brigade, badly hurt early in the day but still on the field, teamed up with elements of the newly arrived division of John Robinson against an ill-advised advance of Rodes' right-flank units.

During a round of confused fighting involving a good deal of maneuvering, Alfred Iverson's brigade of South Carolinians was nearly destroyed. Five hundred men were killed or wounded, scores by enfilading musket volleys, the bleeding figures falling in neat rows. Most of the survivors were demoralized, and many of them surrendered.

The northern fighting affected some houses on Gettysburg's outskirts. Union artillery pieces boomed in backyards whose fences had been knocked down, and the return fire chipped patches of bricks from walls, splintered wooden outbuildings, and scarred the trunks of shade trees. Powder smoke, with its acrid smell, found its way indoors.

Most of the involved residents huddled low in their cellars, but at least one young woman, Jane Smith, stood at the top of a set of cellar steps, both doors thrown back, and smilingly offered the Federals "cut and smear."

Robert E. Lee was nearing Gettysburg now, still trying to figure out what he was up against, still wishing that Jeb Stuart would make his appearance.

Not yet having reached Carlisle, Stuart heard the rumble of artillery fire drifting up from the south. He was unable to pinpoint the source, but this did not worry him. Convinced that Lee's Susquehanna plans were still in effect, he did not believe that anything important could be happening to the south.

One of the general's aides, however, was troubled by the development. He got out a map, and, noting the manner in which the various roads converged at Gettysburg, he suggested to Stuart that the noise might be coming from that area.

"I reckon not," said Stuart, retaining Carlisle as his objective.

It was sometime after 2 P.M. that the western Confederates facing Abner Doubleday made a thrust that involved The Old McLean Place on his southern flank. The Federals using it as a fortress were obliged to leave it and fall back, and this plunged Amelia Harmon and her aunt, still occupying the cellar, into a calamitous situation.

Looking through a grated cellar window, they beheld scores of gray-clad legs going by. The pair rushed up to the kitchen and were shocked to learn that their barn was in flames and that the house was full of Confederates who intended to burn it because of the trouble its Federal occupants had caused them. A fire had been kindled on the kitchen floor.

"We both jumped on the fire in hopes of extinguishing it, and pleaded with them in pity to spare our home. But there was no pity in those determined faces."

As the fire took hold, Amelia and her aunt had no choice but to run from the house. They turned toward the town, but drew up quickly. Their way was barred by a hot skirmish involving both musketry and artillery. Swinging about, with bullets snapping around their ears and shells bursting near them, the pair fled directly into the heart of the main Confederate lines.

There was less danger here, though the lines were busy enough, with officers shouting orders, with foot troops maneuvering on the run, and with artillery pieces either firing or being drawn by galloping horses toward likely positions. Farm crops were being flattened. Here and there, Federal shells were bursting.

Wounded Confederates were moving toward the rear, some walking, some being borne on stretchers, and some riding in ambulances, with numbers of the men stripped of much of their clothing and wearing bloodstained bandages.

Groups of Federal prisoners were being marched to the rear under guard, some with bandages over minor wounds. There appeared to be little ill will between the prisoners and their guards. The parties were humming with fraternal conversation.

Great surprise arose among the Confederates who saw Amelia and her aunt, and the two were urged to hurry along, which they did for about two miles, at last coming to a group of officers and newsmen gathered in the shade of a tree.

The officers were disinclined to believe that Confederates had burned their house, but one of the newsmen, an Englishman with the *London Times*, gave them his courteous attention and offered to assist them. He established them in an abandoned cottage, then went to report the matter to General Lee, who was not far away.

Soon returning, the newsman said he had seen Lee in person, that the general had ordered a guard placed at the cottage, and that food would be sent them.

They had lost their mansion and its treasures, but Amelia and her aunt were finally safe!

As for General Lee, he was on his way to the front. Thus far his army's efforts had been somewhat inhibited by orders he'd sent that an all-out battle be avoided until he was fully prepared for one.

Now the commander found a point from which, with the aid of his field glasses, he could survey the entire scene of operations, with its patches of smoke, its rumbling artillery fire, its dust-enveloped troop

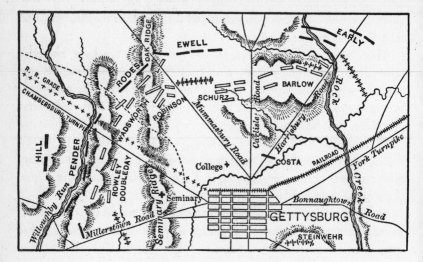

First day at Gettysburg, about 3 P.M.

movements, and its front-line formations delivering musket volleys, the strongest of which were still sounding from the northwestern angle where the Confederates under Robert Rodes remained in trouble after Alfred Iverson's disaster.

Lee continued in a state of uncertainty. He could only guess at the enemy's numbers, and he was worried about his own, since the corps led by his "old war horse," James Longstreet, was still a good distance from the field.

Then, even while the commander was pondering his options, Jubal Early arrived on the eastern flank of the two Union divisions north of town. Lee decided at once that, at least for the moment, he would strike as hard as he could with the troops he had at hand.

This decision boded ill for the Federals, with their lesser numbers; though, actually, the disparity at the front was not enormous. The day saw about 20,000 Federals brought into action, with the Confederates employing about 25,000.

It was Old Jube's division that, at about 3:30 P.M., brought things to a head, making a devastating flank attack on Francis Barlow, who, in his eagerness for battle, had pushed his division too far to the front on the Union right.

The twenty-eight-year-old Barlow, in civilian life a New York lawyer, had risen to his high command through the ranks, having enlisted as a private. The general's men, who included a good many of the German immigrants, sometimes resented the rigidness of his discipline. Perhaps it was his boyish looks, which he knew did not inspire respect, that prompted him to unusual sternness.

The attack on Barlow's exposed flank was led by the flamboyant John Gordon. The general was riding a splendid black stallion that afternoon. He stood erect in his stirrups, swinging his hat in his right hand, and issuing orders and exhortations in trumpetlike tones. His men gave shouts of their own as, supported by artillery, they rushed to the charge.

Barlow's forces made a valiant effort to stand, but this served only to increase their casualties. As Gordon said later: "Any troops that were ever marshalled would, under like conditions, have been as surely and swiftly shattered."

Francis C. Barlow

First to give way was Battery G, 4th United States Artillery, which Barlow had stationed in a vulnerable spot on his right flank. The battery's commander, eighteen-year-old Lieutenant Bayard Wilkeson, went down with a mortal wound.

The boy's father, noted war correspondent Samuel Wilkeson, was then on his way to Gettysburg, and he'd soon be lamenting in print: "How can I write the history of a battle when my eyes are immovably fastened upon ... the dead body of my oldest-born son, caused by a shell in a position where the battery he commanded should never have been sent, and abandoned to die in a building where surgeons dare not stay?"

Soon after young Wilkeson fell, Francis Barlow himself went down, a bullet piercing his trunk and brushing his spine, leaving him unable to move. John Gordon came upon him lying on his back in the sun amid a scattering of Union dead, and, noting his rank, dismounted to see what he could do for the seemingly dying man. Lifting Barlow's

Bayard Wilkeson

head, Gordon gave him a drink from his personal canteen. Barlow himself thought he was dying, and he spoke regretfully about leaving his wife. The sympathetic Gordon gave him what time he could spare, then had him carried to a shady spot and rejoined the attack.

[Barlow not only recovered but reentered the war. Soon he learned that one of the battles had claimed the life of a General J. B. Gordon. This happened to be a kinsman of the Gordon of Gettysburg, but Barlow naturally assumed it was the man he'd encountered. Years later, with each man thinking the other dead, the two met at a dinner in Washington, D.C. Gordon asked, "Are you related to the Barlow who was killed at Gettysburg?" Said Barlow, "I am the man, sir! Are you related to the Gordon who killed me?" Said Gordon, "I am the man, sir!" In telling of this incident in his memoirs, Gordon averred: "Nothing short of an actual resurrection from the dead could have amazed either of us more." The two became warm friends.]

While Gordon's brigade, assisted by other elements of Early's division, was pressing Barlow's men toward Gettysburg's northern environs, Union General Oliver Howard's remaining front-line division, that of Carl Schurz, strung from Barlow's left toward Doubleday's northern flank, began to reel under blows inflicted by Robert Rodes. That general's punishment by the units on Doubleday's right had ended as A. P. Hill renewed his attack from the west, with William Pender's fresh and aggressive troops in the fore.

As the Federals under Schurz began retreating southward in the manner of those of Barlow, Doubleday's right flank was left starkly exposed to Rodes. With Pender pressing his front and threatening to turn his southern flank, the Union general could hold no longer.

Soon all of the Federals, north and west, were in retreat, with Doubleday's wing, like the other, being forced toward the town. It was the intention of both wings to use the streets as routes to a junction with Oliver Howard's reserve division in its south-of-town position on Cemetery Hill.

More than a few Federal units gave ground only grudgingly. As one of Pender's Confederates put it: "The enemy did not fly readily." This was all the more remarkable on the part of Doubleday's troops because their numbers were already down almost 50 percent.

Final moments of Doubleday's defense.

Artillery sections made heroic stands. The sweating men served their pieces with their sleeves rolled up, some of them bareheaded; and the roaring muzzles belched sprays of canister that cut bloody alleys in the approaching formations. Supervising officers yelled such encouragements as, "Feed it to 'em, God damn it! Feed it to 'em!"

The Confederates managed to keep coming, with their own artillery at work, with their mounted leaders shouting orders and gesturing with their swords, and with some of the panting men throwing aside their blanket rolls to give them greater freedom of action. Numbers concentrated their musket fire on the Union gun sections. The minie balls, together with artillery bursts, performed harshly, exploding caissons, splintering wooden wheel spokes, killing or maiming many crewmen, and inflicting butchery among the artillery horses that were rearing and plunging in terror.

Stands made by the Union infantry units were equally costly. Among those that held the longest was Doubleday's Iron Brigade, which was finally shattered beyond reorganization.

During his participation in the fight as an honorary member of this brigade, citizen John Burns, whose work, some say, included the downing of a mounted Confederate officer, was wounded three times. The first two hits were minor, but the third damaged his ankle to the extent he was unable to walk. He was left west of town, sending word for his wife to bring a wagon to take him home.

Tradition has it that Mrs. Burns was so provoked with her mate that she threatened to leave him where he was. [She had no notion that, through praise in Doubleday's report of the battle, together with widespread newspaper notice and a poem in his honor by the famous Bret Harte, her troublesome husband would be raised to the status of a national hero, and would even become the subject of a monument on the battlefield.]

Union trooper John Buford supported Doubleday on his left as his lines were breaking with a large detachment of the horsemen deployed some distance south of the Seminary, their purpose to prevent William Pender from making his planned southeasterly swing around the harried general's rear.

The successful management of this task was the last of Buford's special contributions to the Union victory at Gettysburg. [The trooper fared little better than John Reynolds in the enjoyment of his fame. He died less than six months after the battle, drained of strength, a victim of the rigors of his job, his body apparently unable to sustain the demands of his will.]

Abner Doubleday's thinned units made their way through Gettysburg's southwesterly streets in tolerable formation, not long pursued. Confederate General A. P. Hill said later: "My two divisions exhausted by six hours' hard fighting, prudence led me to be content with what we had gained."

The relative order of Doubleday's retreat in the southwest contrasted signally with the late-afternoon developments in the town's northern areas. Oliver Howard's two divisions of Dutchmen, after making some close-range stands expensive to both sides, were being crowded, pell-mell, down into the streets and among the houses. A few men were still firing their muskets, and the Confederates were responding with both musketry and artillery fire, some of which damaged bricks and wooden siding, and also shattered windows.

Bluecoats fell by scores and soon began surrendering by hundreds. The confusion was titanic, and the noises—the shouts, the oaths, the shrieks and groans, the musket and artillery reports—merged into a sustained roar.

Most of the area's civilians were aghast. "All I could do," one woman said later, "was sit in the cellar corner and cry."

Anna Garlach, the girl who had begun the day stringing beans for her mother, summoned the courage to peep out as a throng of bluecoats went by in full retreat. "In front of our house the crowd was so great that I believe I could have walked across the street on the heads of the soldiers."

Some of the people in the cellars began to hear the stomping of feet in the rooms overhead as fleeing Federals rushed in and concealed themselves, some slipping into closets, some rolling under beds, some falling behind couches, and still others climbing to attics and pressing themselves into dark corners.

New footsteps, along with shouts, were soon heard as Confederate search parties bounded in, pulled the fugitives from their hiding places, and, with bayoneted muskets, prodded them back to the street and into the custody of prisoner guards.

Not all of the bluecoats who managed to find hiding places in the town were caught. Sneaked food and water by citizens, a few remained secreted during the entire Confederate occupation.

The best-known case was that of General Alexander Schimmelfennig. His horse shot from under him, the general managed to conceal himself in a narrow aisle between two stacked rows of wood, drawing some of the pieces over him to form a kind of hut. There was a pigpen nearby that the foe did not molest, and the woman of the house slipped some bread and water to the general on one of her trips to feed the pigs. The worst part of Schimmelfennig's three-day ordeal was his need to huddle in cramped positions.

Even during the retreat and pursuit, some of the town's houses were invaded by Confederates looking for food. Other houses were commandeered as hospitals for the wounded of both sides, with some of the civilians coming up from their cellars to give the unfortunates what help they could.

Though shells and bullets did considerable property damage that afternoon, few civilians were hit. One casualty was a student of the college who, according to a woman of the town, "was bound to witness the fight in the streets and was favored with a bullet which lodged in one of his limbs and kept him from further sightseeing."

Perhaps half the Federal foot troops who had taken part in the day's fighting made it to Cemetery Hill, the pursuers drawing up at the southern edge of town. The halt was a serious Confederate mistake, attributable to indecision on the part of Dick Ewell. Even when, at about 4:30 P.M., an order came from Lee, who had been watching the rout from Seminary Ridge, for Ewell to take the hill if he found it practicable, the general did not act. He had lost the impetus that had given him his great victory at Winchester. He was not, after all, a second Stonewall Jackson.

A group of Ewell's subordinates, including John Gordon, tried, within the bounds of military discipline, to prod Ewell into moving. Their argument was excellent. The Federals were presently weak and demoralized, whereas they would soon be reorganized and strongly reinforced. If Cemetery Hill was to be taken, now was the time to do it.

Ewell hedged with the statements that the last of his divisions, Edward Johnson's from Carlisle, was not yet on the field, that the men who had done the fighting needed rest, and that he was loath to risk bringing on a general engagement until Longstreet's corps arrived.

As the subordinates left Ewell's vicinity, their disgust barely concealed, one was heard to exclaim, "Oh, for the presence and inspiration of Old Jack for just one hour!"

Shortly afterward, Dick Ewell was nearly removed from the scene. He and John Gordon, together with some others, were riding along a southerly street when a party of Federals lingering below the town fired a fusillade at them. Several of the riders were hit, and Gordon thought he heard a bullet thud into Ewell.

"Are you hurt, sir?"

"No, no, I'm not hurt," said Ewell. "It don't hurt a bit to be shot in a wooden leg."

The Confederates were now in control of all sections of the town, many of the streets of which were strewn with debris of the fighting, most of it of Federal origin: dead men and dead and wounded horses; discarded muskets, knapsacks, and blanket rolls; hats and other items of clothing. Confederate soldiers were already going through the knapsacks in search of booty.

Street-ends facing the Federals were barricaded with stones from walls, fence rails, and materials taken from yards and outbuildings: carts, wheelbarrows, wooden buckets, odds and ends of furniture.

Most of the civilians, badly shaken, kept to their houses, quietly observing through windows and doorways. One six-year-old girl, however, thrust the top half her body through an open window and sang, with all the force she could muster, "We'll hang Jeff Davis on a sour apple tree!"

A Confederate straggler.

On the farms north of town the Confederate foragers were already at work, killing steers, sheep, and chickens. The farm women were obliged to bake for the intruders to keep them in a mood of moderation. The women had to provide food for stragglers, too, men who, when asked why they weren't with the front-line troops, laughed and said, "Oh, there are enough to whip the Yankees without us." Some of these stragglers would end up deserting and staying in the North.

Battle losses for the day were: Federals, about 10,000; Confederates, about 8,000. On both sides, prisoners accounted for a good part of the toll. On the Federal side, in fact, the portion was about 50 percent.

West of Gettysburg on Seminary Ridge at 5 P.M., James Longstreet, who had ridden well ahead of his corps, joined General Lee. The commander was studying the field with his glasses as the last of the routed Federals were mounting Cemetery Hill.

Longstreet, with his own glasses, made a long and thorough examination of the Federal position on the hill and of the ridge extending southward from the hill to the Round Tops.

He said at last: "If we could have chosen a point to meet our plans of operation I do not think we could have found a better one than that upon which they are now concentrating."

All the Army of Northern Virginia need do, the general averred, was to march around the Union army's southern flank and take up a defensive position between the army and Washington.

"The Federals will be sure to attack us. When they attack we shall beat them, and the probabilities are that the fruits of our success will be great."

With all of the day's vexations, Lee was in a sober mood; and his generals were a good part of the problem. Jeb Stuart's absence had become critical. Henry Heth's impulsiveness, encouraged by A. P. Hill, had brought on a battle Lee did not want. Dick Ewell, who had seemed to be working out splendidly as a replacement for Stonewall Jackson, had, just when the day was looking up, succumbed to indecision.

It is not likely that Longstreet's unsolicited advice made much of an impression on the commander. "No," he said, "the enemy is there, and I am going to attack him there."

This was not a rash decision. Lee had been drawn into a situation that gave him few choices.

The first consideration was his army's subsistence. He could feed the men off the country as long as they were in scattered columns making rapid marches and finding new sources of rations almost daily, but if the entire army was kept assembled in one area for more than a short time the yield would soon be depleted.

Then, too, the army's supply of artillery ammunition was limited. Lee could not go on indefinitely making piecemeal expenditures.

Even if there hadn't been a need for him to be regardful of food and ammunition, Lee probably would have been against moving toward Washington, for this would have placed his army between Meade and the considerable forces in the capital's defenses.

A retreat from Gettysburg might have been resorted to, but the work of disengaging would have been difficult and dangerous—and a retreat was hardly in keeping with the image of invincibility the commander was trying to project.

Lee saw that his best course was to proceed with his involvement at Gettysburg as it was developing, and to try to bring matters to a climax as soon as possible.

12

Meade Reaches the Field

WITH NIGHTFALL STILL three hours away, the 10,000 able-bodied Federals trying to reorganize on Cemetery Hill and its adjacent heights feared that Lee would renew his attack that evening; but, to their vast relief, things remained quiet. They were luckier than they knew, for Lee did consider doing something more; but even the aggressive A. P. Hill, who did not feel well that day, was opposed to the idea.

There was a good deal of grumbling among Abner Doubleday's First-Corps survivors that Oliver Howard's Dutchmen had let the army down again, had repeated their Chancellorsville performance. But little of the criticism was warranted. The units of the Eleventh Corps had done the best they could under the tremendous disadvantage of Jubal Early's flank attack.

For the moment, the Federals on the hill were being led by Winfield Scott Hancock, temporarily taken from his Second Corps command at Taneytown and sent forward to replace the fallen John Reynolds. Hancock had arrived during the retreat. Meade remained at Taneytown, not yet certain where he and Lee would fight it out. Hancock had orders not only to take over at Gettysburg but also to send word back as to the suitability of the place for a showdown battle.

One of Meade's foremost qualifications for the supreme command of the army was that he understood the abilities of his subordinate generals. He had been right about the team of Buford and Reynolds, and the choice of Hancock as successor to Reynolds was an excellent one.

Winfield S. Hancock

Nearly forty years old, Hancock had done some notable leading in this war, and his striking stance in battle had earned him the sobriquet "Hancock the Superb." His prewar record embraced service in Mexico and against the Indians of Florida and the West. He was brevetted for gallantry in Mexico. At Molino del Rey, Hancock took part in an assault that included Southerners James Longstreet, George Pickett, and Lewis A. Armistead, who were fated to be associated with him in another historic assault, but in a different manner.

For two months during the winter of 1858–59 Hancock had been part of a Washington, D.C., social circle that included Robert E. Lee himself. Lee was stationed there; Hancock was there on furlough before sailing for California, his post of the moment.

Upon learning that Mrs. Hancock did not plan to accompany her husband, Lee, who was about fifteen years older than the Hancocks, gave them some advice: "I consider it fatal to the future of young married people, upon small provocation, to live apart, either for a short or

Mrs. Winfield Hancock

long time. The result is that invariably they cease to be essential to each other."

He urged them to reconsider. They did, and they left for the West Coast together. Thus it was that Lee had a benign influence on Hancock's life.

The statuesque general's appearance on the field at Gettysburg was an inspiration to the defeated troops, but Oliver Howard, who was Hancock's senior in rank, was not pleased.

"Why, Hancock," he said, "you cannot command here!"

Hancock reached for his orders from Meade, but Howard declined to look at them, insisting upon his right of seniority. Hancock did not press the argument, but turned to deploying the battered regiments into a stable defense line, all the while issuing hearty words of encouragement, adeptly improving morale; and Howard made no objection, though he maintained the pose of command.

The two were in agreement that Cemetery Ridge was a good position.

Later, Howard would get the thanks of Congress for being first to see this. It was Hancock who dispatched Meade about it, but the message had little import. The commander had already decided to order all of his units to Cemetery Ridge. Like Lee, Meade had come to realize he'd been entrapped.

"We have so concentrated," he said, "that a battle at Gettysburg is now forced on us."

By early evening the roads into Gettysburg from the south were teeming with new Federal traffic, the Third Corps under the notorious Dan Sickles and the Twelfth Corps under small, dark-eyed, quick-moving Henry W. Slocum. Since Slocum outranked both Hancock and Howard, he assumed top command of the Union forces, pending the arrival of Meade from Taneytown.

The farms scattered south of Gettysburg were overrun with the new arrivals and their horse-drawn auxiliaries. Crops ready for the harvest were crushed into the earth. The wells and springs were hard taxed to keep up with the demands made upon them, the springs soon dropping to the point where dippers and cups brought up bottom sand. As thirsts were quenched, appeals for food were begun.

Among the civilians engulfed in the turbulence was fifteen-year-old Tillie Pierce, who was not a farm resident but a very recent visitor from Gettysburg. Tillie's story has an ironic twist. She was at her home in the town that afternoon when the fighting began to involve its streets. Fearing for her safety, her parents placed her in the custody of a neighbor who was taking her children down the Taneytown Road to the Jacob Weikert farm, just east of the Round Tops. As it turned out, this was not a spot of greater safety, but one of greater danger.

Tillie's introduction to violence was quick and brutal. She had just arrived and was watching some artillery pieces roll by, thrilled by the sight, when a caisson on which a man was perched exploded accidentally, throwing its passenger aloft and into a wheat field. As the man was carried to the house for care, Tillie saw that his eyes had been blown out and that he was powder-blackened from head to foot. He was heard to exclaim, "Oh, dear, I forgot to read my Bible today! What will my poor wife and children say?" (The man was not fatally wounded, so it would seem that his family soon received him home.)

This was only the beginning of Tillie's dismaying experiences. Next in the sequence was that the Weikert property became a refuge for many of the wounded Federals coming down the road. "Before night," Tillie wrote later, "the barn was filled with the shattered and dying heroes of this day's struggle."

When Tillie learned from the wounded that the Confederates were occupying the town, she became worried about her parents. There was reason enough for her to worry about her father, an independent-natured man in his late fifties. That afternoon he'd been shot at, and barely missed, while walking the streets in an unsuccessful search for liquor for a group of wounded Union soldiers who were begging for it.

In the evening Mr. Pierce sat on the front porch of his house at the southern edge of town and watched the Confederate traffic. A squad stopped by, and one of the men asked, "What are your proclivities?"

"I am an unconditional Union man!"

This was accepted with good grace, but the soldier told him he'd better go inside. "*We* won't shoot you, but you are in danger of being shot by your own men. The Union sharpshooters out by the cemetery are already sending their bullets this way pretty fast."

Mr. Pierce went inside.

There were numberless other encounters between Confederates and Gettysburg citizens that evening. The Southerners were filled with confidence in their ability to finish the fight the next day, and many made swaggering claims to that effect. Some even insisted that Lee's invasion would be carried all the way to Bunker Hill in Massachusetts, an idea that had its roots in the publicized boast of prominent Georgian Robert Toombs that he planned to count the roll of his slaves at the base of the Bunker Hill monument.

Catching up with his duties of the evening, Dick Ewell stomped into a northerly home on his crutches and asked for a meal, which he was served, albeit reluctantly. The house was filled with Union wounded, and the women tending them were not feeling kindly toward the authors of the misery.

One of the women came to the general and told him of an incident

Robert Toombs

that had left her deeply affected. The sufferings of a dying man she was looking after had become so great that he tried to sever an artery to hasten his end, and he had desisted only after much pleading on her part.

"Madam," said Ewell, "we become hardened to such things in war."

Robert E. Lee spent a part of the evening in the cupola of Pennsylvania College, which gave him a good view of the enemy's lines. (There were citizens who believed the commander was violating military principles by making this kind of use of a building designated as a hospital.) Lee noted that the troops on Cemetery Ridge were being reinforced, information that was accented at dusk by the appearance of hundreds of campfires extending southward from the cemetery.

It was probably about this time that Lee was approached by two bedraggled cavalry scouts who told him they'd been dispatched by Jeb Stuart on a search for the army. There was relief for Lee, it is said, in the knowledge that Stuart was safe; but this relief must have been accompanied by exasperation. The general must have demanded to know what in the world his cavalry chief had been doing for the past week.

In the end, however, all Lee could do was to send the scouts back to Stuart with orders for him to report to Gettysburg as soon as possible.

Jeb and his played-out command had made their approach to Carlisle, the foragers in the lead with instructions to requisition the town for rations and fodder.

At this point Stuart's ill-advised expedition began to assume the aspect of a comic opera.

Unknown to the general, Dick Ewell had been at Carlisle, found it undefended, and had got what he could from the residents. The town was very nearly bare of the things Jeb needed. But it wasn't bare of defenders. Now present were about 2,000 militiamen under an experienced general with a pugnacious nature, William F. "Baldy" Smith.

Stuart sent in a demand for the garrison's surrender and got back a flat refusal. In a second demand, the trooper threatened to burn Carlisle unless the surrender was made. The result was a second refusal.

Jeb next sent a few shells shrieking into the night-cloaked town, the fire causing turmoil among the citizens, some of whom fled their homes, according to a witness, "with outcries and terrified countenances."

When this measure did not bring about a surrender, shells were used to ignite one of the town's best-known landmarks, its military barracks, and the all-consuming fire created some grand pyrotechnics.

Not to be overlooked is that Dick Ewell had visited Carlisle with orders from Lee to spare the barracks, even though it was a military target. (There seems to have been some sentiment involved in this; many of the officers in the Confederate army had been stationed at the barracks during their Federal service in the prewar years.)

So here was Jeb Stuart, doing something Lee did not want done while trying to supply himself from a town already stripped!

Stuart was stayed from further shenanigans by the arrival of his scouts from Gettysburg. The historical record makes no mention of the general's reaction to word that Lee's army was in a position not compatible with his own conception of the campaign.

Jeb issued orders, of course, for a prompt turn southward, orders that were met with groans—at least among those troopers who were still wakeful enough to know what was going on.

A positive note, some of these men believed, was that this emergency march would surely prompt their general, at long last, to abandon the expedition's painfully burdensome train of captured wagons.

They should have known better.

A bright moon was shining, and down at Gettysburg the mellow light illuminated war scenes grown quieter but far from still. Union camps were expanding on the eastern slopes of Cemetery Ridge, and Confederate camps now formed a great northerly curving arc about the town, with some of the camps extending into the streets and among the houses.

Sleep was the resort of most of Gettysburg's visitors, but parties of looters—men of that element of the army that persisted in ignoring Lee's orders regarding private property—were busy investigating homes from which the occupants had fled.

The houses and public buildings taken as hospitals, now lighted by lamps and candles, were in full function, with ambulances and stretcher-bearers continuing to arrive with new cases.

There were still wounded among the dead lying on the day's battle-fields. A newly arrived Confederate soldier, looking over a scattering of dead Yankees, spotted a man wearing a fine set of boots. The Southerner took hold of one, only to let go quickly as a voice proclaimed, "Mister, I'm not dead yet!"

On Cemetery Hill, many of the Federals were sleeping, but some were occupied with building breastworks. The sounds of the chopping and digging reached the camp of Confederate General John Gordon, who was still in a fret about the afternoon's discontinued attack. Unable to sleep, Gordon sought out Ewell and Early, then settling into a big red barn just north of town, and suggested that a night attack be organized to interrupt the buildup and take the hill. He was told that Lee had other plans.

Overriding another plea by Longstreet for a march around Meade's southern flank, the commander had decided to make a general attack as soon as he could get one arranged in the morning.

In Mrs. Thorn's cemetery gatehouse there was an informal late-night meeting of Union generals, including Oliver Howard, Dan Sickles, Henry Slocum, and Carl Schurz. The party sat around an inverted barrel with a candle perched upon it, and Mrs. Thorn served them cold meat, buttered dough cakes, and coffee. The men discussed the day's fight and the prospects for the morrow. All hoped that George Meade, upon his arrival from Taneytown, would approve the defense they were establishing.

When the generals finally said goodnight to each other, according to Carl Schurz, there was little anxiety in evidence. "It was a rather commonplace, business-like 'goodnight,' as that of an ordinary occasion."

The generals would doubtless have been less relaxed had they known of the mood in the loyal North that night. Aware of the critical nature of this showdown battle, and fearing for their own security, the people were appalled by the telegraphic news that John Reynolds was dead and his forces routed. Untold thousands were unable to sleep, and the churches were thronged with beseechers to God.

As expressed by a Northerner of the time: "It was the most anxious night through which America ever passed. God grant that we shall never pass through another like it!"

It was about one o'clock in the morning on July 2 when General Meade and his staff—one of the members of which was his son, Colonel George Meade—reined up on Cemetery Ridge. A few camp-fires were still burning, and those men who got a glimpse of the commander's face under his broad-brimmed hat saw that it was sober and haggard.

In the company of Oliver Howard and the army's artillery chief, Henry J. Hunt, Meade made a moonlight tour that gave him a fair idea of the topography of the entire arena. Some of the advantages of the Union position and the disadvantages of the Confederate position were obvious, though the deployment picture was still in its developmental stages.

What it would come to was this: Meade's "fishhook," with its four-mile front, would give him the superiority of interior lines of communication. Culp's Hill, on his right, was only two miles from the Round Tops on his left. To oppose this deployment, Lee would be obliged to set up a six-mile front handicapped by exterior lines of communication.

This was a matter affecting not only courier traffic but also the shifting of troops.

Though aware of his defensive advantages, Meade considered making a morning attack. His subordinate generals disliked the idea, and it was abandoned.

The initiative remained with Lee.

13

Longstreet's Role Begins

BOTH SIDES WERE stirring before dawn on Thursday, July 2, with breakfast fires springing up everywhere, with the smell of brewing coffee pervading the damp air, and with orders coming down for the tactical shifting of troops and artillery batteries.

Bugles blared at daylight as the work began with the usual shouting of orders, rumbling and creaking of wheels, and clumping tread of men, horses, and mules. The usual complaints, accented with colorful swearing, resulted when mix-ups occurred.

In contrast with the turmoil in the ridge areas, the mile of farmlands and wood patches between was a picture of serenity under a lingering haze. Barnyard roosters crowed, cows grazed, and birds darted and sang in orchards and expanses of wildflowers.

Despite the gathering storm, some of the farm dwellers remained in their homes, most of which had strong-walled basements.

Lee was nearly up to his full strength now, with only Pickett, marching from Chambersburg, unavailable for use that day. As for Meade, he was heartened in the early morning hours by the drum-and-fife arrival of Hancock's Second Corps and George Sykes' Fifth. Only the troops of the Sixth under John Sedgwick were not present, but they were on their way, making the hardest march of their career.

Meade's "fishhook" was manned in this manner:

On the extreme right, facing eastward at Culp's Hill, was Slocum's Twelfth Corps. Joined with Slocum's left and forming a northerly arc that embraced Cemetery Hill were the remnants of the First Corps, now under John Newton, and the remnants of Howard's Eleventh. Howard's left ran southward on Cemetery Hill and joined with the right of Hancock's Second Corps.

This unit stretched down Cemetery Ridge, its left meeting with the right of Dan Sickles' Third Corps. Sickles' left reached toward Little Round Top, at present hosting only a Union signal station. Sickles had misconstrued Meade's orders that the knob be occupied. (Big Round Top, south of the smaller hill, was considered to be of minor tactical value because it was thickly covered with trees.) The Fifth Corps under George Sykes was in reserve.

Lee's army contained only three corps, but Confederate corps were larger than those of the Union. Even so, Lee's entire command probably did not exceed 70,000 men, while Meade's total was probably not less than 85,000.

Longstreet, not yet in position, would make up Lee's right, his southern wing. A. P. Hill was already occupying that part of Seminary Ridge that would be the army's center, which put him opposite Hancock and that part of Howard's corps facing west on Cemetery Hill. Dick Ewell's lines, starting on A. P. Hill's left, ran eastward through Gettysburg, passing the north face of Cemetery Hill and curving southeastward around Culp's Hill.

Sharpshooters were posted on second floors and attics of some of the town's southerly homes. Here and there a section of wall was chopped out to improve visibility. The street barricades were strengthened with heavy pieces of furniture carried from living rooms.

Gettysburg's residents were now in the peculiar position of being shut off from all communication with the outside world. Almost everyone in the nation, North and South, was receiving news from the battlefield through the telegraph, but the people of Gettysburg could only guess at what was happening, not sure how to interpret the maneuvers they could glimpse, in part, from high places, and getting only twisted reports from the boastful occupying army.

There was one Gettysburg citizen, however, who was able to keep abreast of things in a big way: fifteen-year-old Tillie Pierce, guest at the

Jacob Weikert farm east of the Round Tops. The area continued to teem with Union traffic.

Early that morning Tillie took up the task of giving the soldiers water, and she even had the honor of handing a cup to General Meade himself.

A little later she escorted a group of officers to the Weikert attic, where they opened a trapdoor in the roof and made a study with their glasses.

Soon Tillie was given a turn, and the panorama amazed her. "The country for miles around seemed to be filled with troops; artillery moving here and there as fast as they could go; long lines of infantry forming into position; officers on horseback galloping hither and thither. It was a grand and awful spectacle."

Not all of the troops who occupied the great arena were on the move. Some on both sides had already taken up their battle posts. These men had little to do but wait, and they had plenty of time to think. Many wrote letters home, knowing full well they might be doing this for the last time. Others searched for comforting verses in their battered pocket Bibles. Moments were also taken for looking at photos of family members and sweethearts.

The war correspondents of the period were fond of saying that troops were "eager for the fray," but this was never true of the great majority. Both sides at Gettysburg believed in their cause, and both sides revered battlefield courage, but very few men on either side looked forward to exposing themselves to a deadly storm of metal.

On the other hand, this field would see less than the usual amount of hesitation. The stakes were extremely high. The Southerners envisioned a win of great significance. The Northerners feared a major disaster. "We've got to fight our best today," announced a Union sergeant, "or have these Rebs for our masters."

Over on Seminary Ridge, Lee was having trouble getting his attack organized, and Longstreet's attitude wasn't helping. That general had renewed his argument for a maneuver around Meade's southern flank.

Longstreet was encouraged when the early morning hours produced no orders from Lee for an attack. But this meant only that the commander was obliged to make a thorough daylight study of the situation, with its many confusing aspects, before settling upon a course of action. Again, he was handicapped by Jeb Stuart's absence.

By 9 A.M. Longstreet had been informed that Lee's developing plan would require his corps to attack from a position to the south and that he should begin preparing for this. Lee spent the next two hours on Dick Ewell's part of the line. When he returned to Seminary Ridge he found that Longstreet hadn't begun his move southward. What he'd done was to sulk and to hope for a change of plan.

It was sometime after 11 A.M. that Lee's orders for the day were made definite. From a position southwest of Meade's left flank, Longstreet was to attack on a northeasterly oblique that would roll up the Cemetery Ridge line. Dick Ewell, upon hearing Longstreet's opening guns, was to make a diversionary attack on Culp's Hill, turning the diversion into a real attack if conditions seemed to invite success. A. P. Hill was to keep Meade's center occupied and to cooperate with Longstreet.

It was a grim-faced Longstreet who began a swing to the south with his two available divisions, those of Lafayette McLaws, a solidly built, forty-two-year-old Georgian, and thirty-two-year-old John Bell Hood, a daring Kentuckian who had gained fame leading a brigade of Texans, now a part of his division.

Though he knew that Lee was impatient to get his attack under way, the "old war horse" did not strain his traces. Delays arose, too, because of the need to find routes through the woods and fields that would keep the columns out of the enemy's sight, and the march developed into one of several hours.

During this period, nothing consequential happened between the armies, though the arena was restless with exchanges of picket fire, and occasionally resounded with brief artillery exchanges.

General Meade spent the time trying to fathom Lee's intentions and reconsidering his own decision to remain on the defensive. He had established his headquarters in a tiny farmhouse just behind the center of his lines, an ideal spot for communicating with his units but a highly dangerous spot in regard to Confederate artillery fire.

The general, of course, did not bind himself to headquarters. Much of the time he rode his lines on "Old Baldy," a horse with a habit of getting himself wounded—but, nevertheless, a survivor; he would manage to outlive his master, who was destined to die a few years after the war ended.

On this, Meade's first day at Gettysburg, many a soldier made a point of seeking out the new commander to observe him in action. Most turned away satisfied. Though there was nothing inspirational about the man, he projected an air of calm efficiency.

In mid-afternoon, while Longstreet was making his concealed approach from the southwest, and while Meade was occupied at his headquarters, Dan Sickles, on the left near the Round Tops, was in a fret over the likelihood of his becoming the target of an attack. A detachment he'd sent out on a scout had learned that the enemy was making a movement. Sickles did not like his corps' position on the southern section of Cemetery Ridge, which, along this stretch, was nearly flat. Out ahead a half mile, in the middle of the arena, was a slightly higher ridge, and the general decided to put his 10,000 men upon it.

The move created a colorful show. Bugles sounded, flags and guidons went aloft, and muskets and bayonets sparkled amid a rolling sea of blue uniforms. Aides galloped about transmitting orders. As Dan Sickles, a cigar in his mouth, rode forward with his staff, which included men in the brilliant Zouave costume, a cheer arose. Many of the troops admired this man with the checkered career. He had an inspiriting style in the field, and his courage was unshakable.

The Federals to the north who witnessed Sickles' advance were astonished. Some wondered whether Meade had ordered an attack they hadn't been told about.

Meade himself, drawn toward the commotion, galloped out to Sickles' side as he was making his new dispositions. Meade was not on Old Baldy but on a horse he'd borrowed for the moment.

The commander did not like Sickles. In the first place, Meade was too straitlaced to have any appreciation at all for Sickles as a colorful personality. In the second place, Sickles had what Meade considered to be too high a post in the army for a nonprofessional soldier. Right now the commander was appalled that Sickles had abandoned Little Round Top and had created a half-mile gap between the right of his corps and the left of Hancock's.

When Sickles explained that he was taking advantage of higher

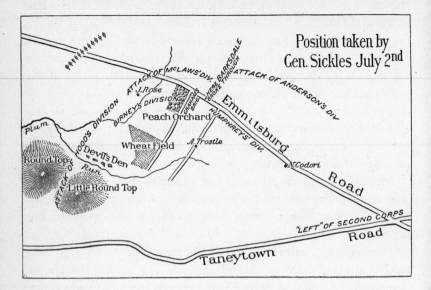

ground, Meade agreed that the spot was a little higher. "But," he added, "there is still higher ground in front of you, and if you keep on advancing you will find constantly higher ground all the way to the mountains."

When Sickles offered to withdraw to Cemetery Ridge, Meade said, "I wish to God you could, but the enemy will not permit it."

He was right, for Longstreet had completed his circuit. Still in a gloomy mood, the general showed little concern at finding the Federal position different from what he'd expected. His two divisions, totaling at least 15,000 men, began deploying to meet the situation, and their covering artillery started booming.

Meade at once had trouble with his borrowed horse. Alarmed at the sudden noise, the animal took the bit in its teeth and bolted for the rear. As it happened, the mount's move was militarily sound. Meade had to get to the rear as quickly as possible in order to repair his disrupted line and see that the imprudent Sickles was supported.

Sickles' new position, as more than one Federal observer noted, "stuck out like a sore thumb." His southern flank lay west of Little

Round Top in a scrubbily wooded area holding a jumble of boulders known as Devil's Den. From this point the line ran northwestward for nearly a mile through a wheatfield to a peach orchard on the Emmitsburg Road, this segment manned by David B. Birney's division. At the orchard the line turned northeastward and ran along the road for nearly another mile, with this front held by the division under Andrew A. Humphreys.

The chief weakness of Sickles' position was its salient at the Peach Orchard, where it invited pressure from three directions: against its point and both its sides.

For the first half hour the fighting consisted mainly of artillery exchanges, with the quaking battlefield displaying its earliest clouds of smoke. Some of the exchanges were duels that did grisly work among the crews and their horses.

Targeted accidentally by the Confederates was a herd of horned cattle trapped in the narrow valley between Devil's Den and Little Round Top. As the creatures stampeded about, bellowing in terror, one was torn to pieces and others were wounded.

East of the Round Tops, Tillie Pierce and the other civilians at the Jacob Weikert farm, though not under fire, found the noises and vibrations nerve-shattering. Their soldier friends advised them to go to a farmhouse a half mile across the fields to the east, and they took off on the run, the women leaving a batch of bread baking in the oven.

When the refugees reached their supposed haven, the soldiers there told them they had been safer where they came from, that any shells the Confederates lobbed over Cemetery Ridge would be likely to pass over the Weikert farm as well, perhaps to land at this spot. So the party ran back again, the women certain their batch of bread had burned to a crisp; but some of the soldiers had watched it carefully and had removed it from the oven in good time.

General Meade's first reaction to the crisis had been to send the army's chief engineer, Gouverneur K. Warren, to examine affairs at the Round Tops. At thirty-three, Warren had been an engineer for thirteen years and a husband for two weeks. Even during the army's northward march he had taken a brief leave for a wedding in Baltimore. Riding to the Round Tops, Warren had three aides with him. [One of these was

Gouverneur K. Warren

Washington A. Roebling, who survived the war and became the main figure in the construction of the Brooklyn Bridge, completed in 1883, and went down with the *Titanic* in 1912.]

When Gouverneur Warren mounted the bare and rocky Little Round Top and looked westward, he found he could see past the southernmost boulders of Devil's Den and over some patches of stubbly trees to the Emmitsburg Road, about a mile away. A woods on the far side of the road seemed a likely place for the enemy to deploy unobserved, and the resourceful engineer sent an aide to the captain of an artillery battery at Devil's Den—James E. Smith, 4th New York—with a request for him to fire a shot in that direction.

"He did so," Warren explained later, "and as the shot went whistling through the air the sound of it reached the enemy's troops and caused everyone to look in the direction of it. This motion revealed to me the glistening of gun barrels and bayonets of the enemy's line of battle, already formed and far outflanking the position of any of our troops, so that the line of his advance from his right to Little Round Top was unopposed."

Warren rushed a courier off to Meade with a scribbled note requesting that troops be sent to him at once. There was a need, he said, for at least a division.

The Confederates Warren had glimpsed were those of Longstreet's southern wing, his right, the division under John Hood. That general, actually, had no wish to move toward the Round Tops, for such an advance would carry his left flank into the southern segment of Dan Sickles' line, which lay in extremely rugged terrain. Hood wanted to make a wide southerly swing around Big Round Top and come in on the Union rear. But Longstreet had informed him, in glum tones, that Lee was opposed to turning the enemy's flank, that a frontal attack was mandatory.

It was about 4 P.M. when John Hood began his movement. As his lines poured from the woods and crossed the Emmitsburg Road, the men cut loose with the shrill yip of the Rebel Yell.

On Hood's left, Longstreet's northern wing—Lafayette McLaws' division—remained inactive in its position facing the Peach Orchard salient. Longstreet was with this wing, and he planned to throw it forward only after Hood's attack was well developed.

John B. Hood

Evander M. Law

This delay was a great frustration to General William Barksdale, a former U.S. congressman known for his passionate speeches in favor of states' rights, whose brigade had made a name for itself at Fredericksburg. The brigadier saw the present situation as offering him an opportunity to lead his Mississippians to greater glory. To begin with, there was a Federal battery operating in the Peach Orchard, and Barksdale believed he could take the guns in five minutes. He begged Longstreet to allow him to charge at once.

"Wait a little," said Longstreet. "We are all going in presently."

John Hood's leading troops had barely crossed the Emmitsburg Road before James Smith, the Union gun captain at Devil's Den, began assailing them with the rapid fire of four pieces. He was joined in this effort by a battery to his right rear, in the Wheatfield.

One of the first Confederates to get hit was Hood himself, who had an arm shattered. He was borne from the field on a litter, lamenting that he must leave his men to a fate he deemed unjustified.

[Two and a half months later, John Hood, his permanently crippled arm in a sling, fought at Chickamauga, where he lost a leg. Remarkably enough, Hood continued to play a leading role in the war to its end. Afterward he became a Southern businessman, and he kept siring children until the number reached eleven. Hood died in his late forties, perhaps the victim of too intense a life.]

Dan Sickles' southern wing caused the attacking division all of the trouble Hood had foreseen. The Confederates were now under Evander M. Law, a South Carolinian of fine appearance and graceful bearing. Law wrote later that the left wing of the division encountered "a most determined resistance" on the part of the Federals in the Devil's Den area.

These were the brigades of J. H. Hobart Ward, a wounded veteran of the Mexican War, and P. Regis DeTrobriand, a French-born intellectual whose men were amused by his accent and his mannerisms but found little fault with his qualities as a soldier.

Elements of these two brigades engaged Law's left in a largely disorganized way among brushy gullies and monstrous rocks.

Watching from Little Round Top was the famed war correspondent

Charles Carleton Coffin

for the *Boston Journal*, Charles Carleton Coffin. "From the woods," he noted, "came the prolonged yell of the Confederates, mingled with the hurrahs of the Union soldiers. White clouds suddenly burst into view. There was a whirring of jagged pieces of iron, mingled with the continuous singing of the leaden rain." Coffin shortly retired from his vantage point because "there were too many bullets in the air for the comfort of a noncombatant."

The fighting in this sector was bypassed by Evander Law's right wing, which bore directly toward Big Round Top, defended by Major Homer R. Stoughton's 2nd U.S. Sharpshooters, detached from Hobart Ward's brigade. Stoughton's men formed a thin line at the hill's western base. According to the major, they did "splendid execution" as the enemy charged.

The Confederate unit most active in this attack was the 15th Alabama under twenty-nine-year-old Colonel William C. Oates. A working-class Southerner who had done some school teaching, Oates was an ambitious and aggressive soldier. But right now he was also a *thirsty* soldier. John Hood's order to attack had come while the canteens of the 15th Alabama were in the hands of a detail assigned to filling them, and the attackers had been obliged to move out "dry," which gave them a serious handicap on this warm July afternoon.

But it didn't stop them. Reinforced by about 150 members of the 47th Alabama, they scattered Stoughton's sharpshooters, some of whom retreated up the craggy, wooded slopes of Big Round Top. Oates, with his 600 men, struggled in pursuit, sniped at by turning Federals but mostly overshot. By 5 P.M. the attackers had taken the summit.

As his panting and perspiring troops dropped for a rest, the colonel, facing northward, occupied himself with a study of the battle arena, all of which was within his sight.

Nearby, on his left, the fighting at Devil's Den continued, its sounds reaching him through its canopy of smoke.

Up at the Peach Orchard, there was still no infantry action. Longstreet had not yet ordered Lafayette McLaws to go in, though an acceleration of artillery fire in that region disclosed that the time was nearing.

North of McLaws, in the arena's center, Richard Anderson's divi-

The Devil's Den attack.

sion of A. P. Hill's corps, ordered to cooperate with Longstreet, was awaiting McLaws' movement.

In the Culp's Hill–Cemetery Hill sector, Dick Ewell's artillerists had just opened as the general began his demonstration, with the Federal gunners making an immediate response.

This firing came as a fearful shock to the residents of southeastern Gettysburg. "It was all so near us," one woman wrote later, "that we closed our ears, crouched into a corner, not knowing how to endure it. The ground trembled, on which our house stood, and the continuous roar was far worse than the heaviest thunder from heaven's artillery. To me, it was the most awful time of that awful battle."

His study of the arena convinced Confederate Colonel William Oates that Big Round Top could be made the key to Confederate victory. All that was needed, he believed, was for some long-range artillery pieces to be wrestled to the summit and for a few fire lanes to be cut through the trees. Cemetery Ridge could be swept with an enfilading bombardment that would make it untenable.

But the colonel's idea died aborning. One of Evander Law's aides arrived with orders for him to take his men down the slope and capture Little Round Top.

Oates was disappointed. To be sure, Little Round Top could be used for the kind of bombardment he envisioned. But he already *had* Big Round Top. The new assignment, however, looked like an easy one. Little Round Top, separated from the larger hill by a saddle only a few hundred yards in width, was obviously unoccupied. All Oates could see down there was a signal team.

But even as the 15th Alabama started its descent toward the saddle, Little Round Top's situation began to change. Union General Gouverneur Warren did not get the division he requested for the knob's defense, but a brigade was arriving, about 1,000 men of George Sykes' Fifth Corps under Colonel Strong Vincent, a Pennsylvania lawyer with a Harvard education who was presently finding a prideful satisfaction in upholding the Stars and Stripes on the soil of his native state.

A good tactician, Vincent did not place his troops in exposed positions atop the knob but amid the brush and rocks arcing its southwestern base. Because of his limited numbers, however, Vincent's right did not reach far enough northward to connect with Dan Sickles' left, the line under Hobart Ward and Regis DeTrobriand, and the gap invited exploitation.

The brigade's left wing arced far enough eastward to cover the saddle terrain stretching toward Big Round Top. On the extreme left was the 20th Maine under thirty-five-year-old Colonel Joshua L. Chamberlain, a college professor, a student of theology, a writer, and currently one of the North's most capable soldiers.

By the time Strong Vincent's arc was established, the Devil's Den sector had fallen to the Confederates, its defenders pulling back toward the Wheatfield. The attackers paid a heavy price for the win, but the Federal toll was also high. One of the worst-hit regiments was the 4th Maine of Hobart Ward's brigade, which took 144 dead or wounded and 31 holes in its colors.

Artillery Captain James Smith, expending 240 rounds in the whole of this fight, tried a last-ditch stand with canister, but the swarms of pellets did most of their damage to the trees and rocks. Three of the four guns had to be abandoned. Smith's casualties numbered twelve men and eleven horses.

As the victorious Confederates began forming to push their way toward Little Round Top, a brief period of relative quiet settled upon this part of the great arena.

Up at Culp's Hill, Dick Ewell was getting the worst of the artillery contest, since the Federal guns held commanding positions. Ewell had determined to turn his demonstration into a real attack, but the punishing shellfire was retarding the effort. This was a fortunate thing for Meade, since he had been drawing troops from that sector to bolster his imperiled southern wing.

In the arena's center, A. P. Hill was still doing little more than looking across the saucer of farmlands at Winfield Hancock's Second Corps lines. Richard Anderson's division remained inactive.

Also inactive in that area was Robert E. Lee, who was spending much of his time sitting on a stump at the edge of a woods, listening to the sounds of the conflict and trying to interpret them, a task not made easier by a regimental band somewhere off to his left that, for some strange reason, found this a good time to be playing a series of polkas and waltzes.

It was Lee's policy not to interfere with the battlefield work of his corps commanders once his master plan had been put into action. At Gettysburg, this seems to have been a mistake. Lee was too accustomed to working with Stonewall Jackson, who needed no further instructions once he understood the master plan. On this field, the commander would have done well to keep a closer eye on developments, making adjustments as they seemed necessary.

An interesting question arises. How good was Lee as an offensive commander without Stonewall Jackson? Some years after the war, Lee himself said: "If I had had Stonewall Jackson at Gettysburg, we should have won a great victory."

Lee was once asked how many of his offensive plans he owed to Jackson's suggestions, and he hedged with words to this effect: "I am sure you are aware who would have been blamed if the plans had failed."

Questions regarding Lee's offensive talents would never be answered beyond his showing at Gettysburg. For the rest of the war he would remain on the defensive—showing a superior talent for this kind of fighting, a talent that would sustain the rebellion, at the cost of many thousands of lives, long beyond the point where it should have folded.

It was during the time Lee was located at his "stump headquarters" that Jeb Stuart, following a brush with some Union horsemen north of Gettysburg, completed his trip from Carlisle. If Lee happened to be sitting when Jeb rode up, he was certainly on his feet by the time the trooper dismounted.

His face reddening, the commander exclaimed, "General Stuart, where have you been? I have not had a word from you for days, and you the eyes and ears of my army!"

Stuart countered with, "I have brought you a hundred and twenty-five wagons and teams, General Lee!"

When Lee frowned and declared that such an acquisition, at this point, was nothing more than an impediment to him, Jeb's face fell.

At once Lee softened and said, "We will not discuss this any longer. You must help me fight these people."

If Stuart was depressed by this interview, it was only for a brief time. Criticism directed at him was never analyzed; it was simply dismissed as groundless. In his own mind, his raid had no negative aspects. The report he wrote for headquarters glowed with personal satisfaction. The raid was the greatest of his career, and that was that!

Lee and Stuart probably had their talk at about 5:30 P.M., and it was very close to this time that the battle assumed a new dimension. From west of the Peach Orchard, there suddenly rose a medley of cheers as Lafayette McLaws started in. Longstreet went part of the way in person, a big figure on a white horse, urging the troops on with sweeps of his hat. William Barksdale's face was radiant as he prepared to take his brigade toward the Federal battery he had been watching so impatiently.

Dan Sickles' salient regiments were determined to defend themselves gamely, though the obvious insecurity of their position was a drag on their confidence.

The crisis in this sector, however, was only beginning to unfold. The one at the Round Tops was rapidly coming to a head.

Union Colonel Strong Vincent's sparsely manned arc, because it utilized the cover of the rocks and brush at Little Round Top's southwestern base, was passably firm in itself, but there were still no troops between Vincent's right flank and Dan Sickles' left. The gap had actually been widened by the Federal pullback from Devil's Den toward the Wheatfield.

When the Confederates, supported by sharpshooters they'd left at the Den, began attacking toward Little Round Top, their northern regiments approached the right wing of Vincent's arc while their southern regiments headed for the saddle between the Round Tops to link up with William Oates and the 15th Alabama, now down from Big Round Top and facing Joshua Chamberlain's 20th Maine on Vincent's extreme left.

The Confederates on the northernmost part of the line soon spied the undefended spot on Vincent's right, and their left began making for it.

Union General Gouverneur Warren, observing the foe's approach from Little Round Top, reacted to the new crisis by leaping on his horse and hastening down the hill's northeastern slope in search of available troops. Almost at once he came upon Colonel Patrick H.

Dead Confederate sharpshooter in Devil's Den.

O'Rorke's 140th New York Volunteers, of Stephen H. Weed's brigade, Sykes' Fifth Corps. The regiment was following other units of the brigade toward Dan Sickles' hard-pressed front.

Warren, who happened to be acquainted with O'Rorke, began shouting, while still a distance from him, "Paddy! Paddy! Turn your regiment this way!"

O'Rorke called back, "General Weed is ahead, and he expects me to follow him."

"Never mind that! Bring your regiment up here, and I will take the responsibility!"

O'Rorke hesitated no longer. He put his men on the run up the slope, formations abandoned. The troops were followed by Battery D, 5th United States Artillery, led by Charles E. Hazlett, the horses straining under the whip, and crew members manhandling the wheels.

Union guns on Little Round Top.

O'Rorke and his men did not have time to load. The patriotic Strong Vincent had been mortally wounded while giving encouragement to his exposed rightward troops, and the shouting foe was nearing that area.

Taking the lead with his sword held high, O'Rorke shouted, "Down this way, boys!"

While the surprised Confederates reacted with only a few random shots, the newcomers descended the rocky slope on Vincent's right and quickly formed an irregular front. There must have been further surprise for those watchers who could see the universal bobbing of ramrods as the regiment loaded.

In the ensuing series of firefights, here and southward along the lines, the Confederates, severely punished, made no sustainable progress up the slopes of Little Round Top. Their fire, however, was destructive enough. Among the many Union slain was the courageous Paddy O'Rorke.

On the knob itself, additional blood was spilled. Gouverneur Warren took a grazing wound in the neck. Brigade Commander Stephen Weed and artillerist Charles Hazlett were mortal cases, their fate intertwined.

After Gouverneur Warren had detached O'Rorke's regiment from the rear of Weed's column, the general had turned his other regiments back for placement on O'Rorke's right, and had personally joined Hazlett and his gunners in their exposed position on the knob. While Weed was standing beside one of the pieces, he was shot down, probably by a sharpshooter in Devil's Den. Hazlett, bending over the general trying to catch something he seemed to be saying, was shot through the head.

Weed, according to tradition, said something like this: "I would rather die here than that the Rebels should gain one inch of this ground."

The general did not die there. He was carried to the Jacob Weikert farm, where Tillie Pierce sat and talked with him while he was fading, his calm acceptance of his fate making her very sad.

On the Confederate side, the dead included a set of identical twins who were shot down at the same time.

While the Federals of the western wing of the Little Round Top defense sector were waging their successful fight to keep the foe at bay, those of the wing facing south were involved in work of equal difficulty. It was on the extreme eastern flank of the southern lines—the absolute flank of the battle itself—that a situation developed that was as unique as it was critical.

Here Union Colonel Joshua Chamberlain and his 386 men of the 20th Maine were standing against the reinforced 15th Alabama under colonel William Oates. The Southerners were numerically superior but were not in the best of shape because of those missing canteens.

Neither side had access to reinforcements, and both were fighting as though the outcome of the battle depended upon how warm they kept their muskets—and it probably did, for this was the showdown struggle for Little Round Top.

Many thousands were contending elsewhere that afternoon, but here an issue of great consequence was being settled by a few. The numbers on both sides, indeed, were getting fewer by the moment.

The slope, with its rocks and trees, was the scene of charges and countercharges; and the front, according to a participant, "surged backward and forward like a wave." Added to the musket blasts, another said later, were "cries, shouts, cheers, groans, prayers, curses."

Men's faces grew black with powder stains, their teeth gleaming as their lips curled back in their gasps for breath. Bayonets came into play, and the losers went down with punctures or gashes. Dead and wounded were scattered about, their blood staining the ground and standing in puddles on the rocks. One of the dying Confederates was William Oates' much-loved brother, Lieutenant John Oates.

In the end, the Federals prevailed. It was the oddest sort of coincidence that Oates gave the order for a rapid retreat at the very moment that Chamberlain, with his men running short of ammunition, ordered an all-out charge. Federal morale surged at the ease of the chase, and when Chamberlain shouted for the men to come back, one called over his shoulder, "We're on the road to Richmond!"

With the prisoners taken at this time, Confederate losses came to about half the 600 engaged.

The pursuers returned at last and formed on the site of their original front, sobered by the cost of their victory. Chamberlain, too, lamented the toll, which came to 136 killed or wounded. The colonel himself bore two wounds, but his work that afternoon won him the Congressional Medal of Honor.

[Chamberlain's notable service in this war would cost him a total of six wounds, three of them serious; but he would return to Maine to become its governor, afterward pursuing an illustrious academic career to the age of eighty-five.]

Thanks largely to the leadership of Gouverneur Warren—who earned a promotion and one of the battlefield's best-known statues—and to that of Joshua Chamberlain, Meade's leftward extremity was rendered secure.

During this same period, however, much of the rest of the line was being buffetted into disarray.

14

Fury at Dusk

THERE WERE TWO bright spots in the Union situation. First: John Sedgwick's Sixth Corps had arrived behind Cemetery Ridge, which meant that Meade's entire army was now on the field. Second: In the Culp's Hill sector Dick Ewell's infantry units, retarded not only by Federal shellfire but also by preparational difficulties, continued inactive.

It was a deep disappointment to Lee at Gettysburg that his plans were persistently frustrated by the inability of his generals to coordinate their movements. In the present case, Ewell was not providing the expected help for Longstreet, who, after a slow and ineffective start, was involved in promising work.

The opening of Lafayette McLaws' attack on Dan Sickles' Peach Orchard salient at about 5:30 P.M. was the beginning of grave trouble for Meade's Cemetery Ridge line.

McLaws employed a two-brigade front (reserves following), with James B. Kershaw's South Carolinians making up the southern wing and William Barksdale's Mississippians the northern. Through a communications snarl, however, there was a lag in Barksdale's advance, which occasioned more frustration for the impetuous brigadier.

James Kershaw was at first on his own. Moving just south of the Peach Orchard—which was Barksdale's target—he headed for the already-thinned lines in the woods in front of the Wheatfield, those of Regis DeTrobriand.

There was still a lot of fight in the Frenchman's brigade, and the

Southerners came under some well-aimed musket fire. At the same time, shells from a bypassed battery on their left, and also from a formidable row of guns on Cemetery Ridge, made disheartening gaps in their ranks.

The members of one regiment began to believe they were taking an especially heavy fire because their colors were being waved too conspicuously.

"Lower the colors!" the men began shouting. "Down with the colors!"

The color-bearer reacted by thrusting his staff still higher. "This flag," he said, "never goes down until I go down!"

The right flank of Kershaw's brigade was soon linked with those elements of Hood's division (under Evander Law) that had been fighting the Federals on Little Round Top, and the combination brought new trouble to the Federal brigade on DeTrobriand's left, that of Hobart Ward, which, during Law's advance, had been hit hard and forced back from Devil's Den.

But now substantial reinforcements for the Ward-DeTrobriand line were on the way south from Winfield Hancock's corps. Among these was the famed Irish Brigade, presently commanded by Colonel Patrick Kelly, a unit easily identified by its flag of green and gold. These 530 men, after forming, paused for a few moments of special religious preparation.

The brigade's chaplain, Father William Corby, a small, energetic man with a strong voice, mounted a rock in front of the unit, and the troops bowed their heads, some also dropping to their knees. Hancock and his staff, near the scene on horseback, drew up and watched.

Corby extended his right hand toward the heavens, and, in tones that could be heard above the sounds of the battle, asked that the men be granted the courage they needed to face their impending ordeal. Next he addressed the men themselves, reminding them of the sacredness of their cause and warning them that any man who failed in his duty would be denied a Christian burial. Then, after reciting the Latin words of the general absolution, Corby committed the brigade to its march toward the Wheatfield, where 135 would be killed or wounded.

The defense of this sector and that of the Round Tops now involved

David B. Birney

elements of three corps: the Second, Third, and Fifth. James Longstreet had thrown a large part of his powerful First Corps against these positions, since he was counting upon Anderson's division of Hill's corps to help him assail the Peach Orchard–Emmitsburg Road line.

The Wheatfield and its environs became a vast caldron of chaotic fighting marked by sheets of musket flashes, seas of smoke, sulfurous fumes, and a wild medley of sounds ranging from the boom of artillery to low moans from among the fallen. Scattered among the fallen, as was often the case in hot situations like this, were a few perfectly sound men of failing courage who feigned wounds in order to make smaller targets of themselves by hugging the earth.

Over at the Peach Orchard the Union troops of David Birney's division at the point of the Sickles salient, those of Charles K. Graham's brigade, were now under attack and were retrograding. William Barksdale's brigade had at last come charging in, with the eager-mannered general riding at the very front, his drawn sword reflecting the late afternoon sun, and his prematurely white hair, strung from a thinning pate, serving as a beacon for his cheering men.

It took longer than five minutes for Barksdale to silence the Peach Orchard battery he'd been watching, but the deed was done in good time.

Charles Graham's infantry regiments fired some determined volleys before succumbing to the hopelessness of their advanced position. As their lines broke, the brigadier was wounded and captured.

The shattering of Graham's brigade, following the extensive damage inflicted upon the brigades of Regis DeTrobriand and Hobart Ward, filled the division commander, David Birney, with the deepest gloom. "My poor men! My poor men!" he cried. "I wish I were dead!"

After routing Graham, William Barksdale cooperated with elements of Anderson's division of Hill's corps that had come in on his left (to his north) against the Emmitsburg Road line manned by Andrew Humphreys' division of Sickles' corps.

Looking northward across the battlefield from Little Round Top. Cemetery Hill is in background on right.

Humphreys was unable to hold, but he began a series of fighting withdrawals that cost his pursuers dearly.

It was now about 6 P.M. Only in the Culp's Hill sector was musketry still lacking. Dick Ewell was not yet ready! Elsewhere, the afternoon's action was fully developed, with that of the Wheatfield and Peach Orchard areas having melded.

According to a Union observer in the north: "The fields west of the Round Tops were alive with moving masses of infantry enveloped in flames and smoke; a dozen batteries in different positions were blazing and roaring; shells were bursting in every direction; buildings and haystacks were on fire here and there; pandemonium had broken loose generally."

As explained by a bluecoat who was part of the picture: "This almost incomparable death-grapple was marked by advances, rebuffs, hand-to-hand struggles, intervolutions of hostile lines, dreadful losses, and hundreds of captures on either side."

Some of the most significant events of the day occurred on the

Slain artillery horses at the Trostle House.

grounds occupied by the house and barn of Abraham Trostle, north of the Wheatfield and about halfway between the Peach Orchard and Cemetery Ridge.

It was in this area that Dan Sickles, while riding about making mettlesome efforts to pull things together, was hit by a round shot of artillery that shattered the bone just below his right knee, leaving his foot dangling.

Dismounting and dropping to the ground, the general yelled to an aide, "Quick! Quick! Get something to tie it up before I bleed to death!"

The job was done with a leather strap. Though beads of sweat stood on his brow, Sickles put on a game show. While borne away on a litter, he puffed a cigar with special animation, saying that he didn't want the troops to think he was dead. The useless appendage was soon amputated.

[Oddly enough, Sickles came out of Gettysburg with the Congressional Medal of Honor, a tribute to his "distinguished gallantry." He lived for another fifty years, his handicap not impeding a resumption of his political career, nor a continuance of his freewheeling ways, which swelled his notoriety. There was even a venture into diplomacy that carried him to Spain and into a scandalous relationship with a deposed queen.]

Another high-ranking casualty of the fighting in the Trostle House area was Confederate General William Barksdale. He insisted upon leading conspicuously, and at last he drew a whole volley of fire upon himself. Five of the balls hit him, and he fell from the saddle a dying man. Barksdale ended up in Yankee hands, still conscious and still strong-spirited. He advised the Union medical people not to waste their time trying to help him. He also presented them with a prediction: Lee was going to clear their army from its ridge.

It was on the Trostle property that Union artillery Captain John Bigelow and his 9th Massachusetts Battery made a do-or-die stand that checked the Confederates at a crucial time and helped save the day for the Union. The six-gun battery had begun its work at the Peach Orchard with seventy-one men and eighty-six horses. By the end of its half-hour stand at the Trostle House the battery was down to thirty-four

Guns of the Union center, July 2.

men and six horses. In all, the battery fired over three tons of ammunition, including ninety-two rounds of canister.

By this time the battle as a whole, after numberless maneuvers on both sides, was being fought on a line that formed a rough parallel with Cemetery Ridge and extended about a mile and a half northward from Little Round Top.

At the Wheatfield, James Longstreet rode with an attack launched by one of his fresher brigades, that of William T. Wofford. After wreaking some havoc, the attack was thrown back by Samuel Wiley Crawford's Pennsylvania Reserves, Sykes' Fifth Corps.

(That night Arthur Fremantle, a British officer traveling with the Confederate army as an observer, would record in his diary: "Everyone deplores that Longstreet *will* expose himself in such a reckless manner.")

Little more was achieved by the Confederates in the Wheatfield area, and their work was also faltering along the Trostle House front, a condition wrought by Andrew Humphreys' stubbornness and a powerful line of artillery behind him.

It was just to the north of Humphreys' position, on his right, that the greater number of the Confederate participants from Anderson's division of Hill's corps came across the valley from Seminary Ridge. The move carried them toward that part of Cemetery Ridge held by Hancock's corps, now a line with weaknesses because of the transfer of troops to the south.

Fortunately for Hancock, and perhaps for the Union cause, Anderson's efforts were not coordinated. The three brigades that came across—those of Cadmus Wilcox, David Lang, and Ambrose R. Wright—did not sustain one another. Through a misunderstanding of their orders, they fought individually.

This is not to say they were impotent. On the contrary, they struck strongly.

The exploitation of a gap in Hancock's line was thwarted only through the sacrifice of a regiment, the 1st Minnesota, ordered to hold the spot until reinforced. The work cost the unit more than three-fourths of its number, seemingly a record for the war.

Ambrose Wright's brigade actually penetrated Hancock's line, and had to be met with a quick concentration of troops. General Meade himself went under heavy fire to lead some of these forward, distressing his staff and subjecting poor Old Baldy to another wound.

Dusk was nearing when Wright fell back, and the fighting along Cemetery Ridge was ending. The Federals occupied their original line between Cemetery Hill and the Round Tops, with the smaller knob now well fortified and the larger hosting a Union detachment. Longstreet had

Ewell's attack on east slope of Cemetery Hill.

driven the Yankees in, but he had won nothing worthwhile but the high ground at the Peach Orchard, which was a good spot for the emplacement of Confederate artillery.

As for Dick Ewell, he was finally ready—with the late-evening shadows falling over his formations—to launch the Culp's Hill attack that was supposed to have coincided with Longstreet's work.

The attack's opening shots, together with the usual round of cheering, rang out while the battle-weary Federals on Cemetery Ridge were beginning to reorganize and were feeling a great relief at the foe's withdrawal from their front.

The listeners grew apprehensive. What now? They had saved the Cemetery Ridge position from being rolled up from the south. Could the weakened line survive an assault from the other flank?

It could. But the Culp's Hill sector saw some desperate close-range fighting, marked not only by the customary mixture of earsplitting sounds but also by dazzling flashes amid clouds of smoke turned gray by the gathering darkness.

Ewell's troops struck both at Culp's Hill and at the saddle between that eminence and Cemetery Hill. Some real damage might have been done, for the Federals were thin at these places because of the troops withdrawn to help meet the southerly crisis. But, in the Confederate style of the day, the attacks were made disjointedly. Moreover, the

Group of Union dead.

Federals had the heights studded with breastworks of earth, stones, and felled trees. And reinforcements soon arrived.

When the Confederates fell back down the slopes, one brigade, that of George E. Steuart, Johnson's division, was left in a lodgment it had won on Culp's Hill in the region of Spangler's Spring. This was Meade's extreme right flank, and the situation portended Confederate exploitation the next day.

The fighting of the afternoon and evening of Thursday, July 2, was finally over. Casualties now stood at about 19,000 for Meade and about 15,000 for Lee, a staggering 34,000 in all. July 1 and 2 had become the worst two days the war had seen, and the Gettysburg issue was far from resolved.

But—and this was important—the Confederates had lost some of their psychological edge. Although the Yankees had been driven on both days, their hold on their position had obviously become a very strong one. Lee's men were less sure of themselves now, and doubt among soldiers affects their performance.

There was no corresponding rise in Union morale. Meade himself was depressed over the heavy losses suffered in the unnecessary fighting at the Wheatfield and Peach Orchard, especially since this disastrous punishment compounded that of the first day.

Later, when the general was accused of having been overcautious at Gettysburg and during his pursuit of Lee after the battle, he said: "These losses of the first and second day affected greatly the efficiency and morale of the army and prevented my having the audacity in the offense that I might otherwise have had."

It was about 9 P.M. when quiet settled over Thursday's field. As the smoke dissipated, the moon looked down on a vast area of woodlands and farmlands whose long-standing beauty had undergone a hideous transformation.

Shells had scarred the woods, pocked the fields, and damaged or destroyed the buildings. Some of the last had been reduced to smoldering ashes. Fences were down, and crops were crushed. Places where the ground was soft held harsh networks of wheel and hoof marks. Scattered everywhere, amid odds and ends of discarded military equipment, were mutilated men and horses, many alive, the men awaiting help, and the horses, unknowingly, awaiting a mercy bullet through the brain at the battle's end, if they lived that long.

Help for hundreds of the wounded was slow in coming, the situation being especially bad for those lying halfway between the lines, where most of the stretcher-bearers, because of the peril posed by the fire of indiscriminate pickets, dreaded going in the dark. These casualties, interminglings of Federals and Confederates, did what they could for one another, with the groups usually sharing the little water they had at hand. Few animosities survived the general misery.

Numbers of these waiting wounded on both sides could look toward the cheerful campfires of the troops who had made it through the day. Conversely, a good many of those at the fires, after consuming their late meal of meat, hardtack, and coffee, went out in the moonlit arena to search for missing friends.

That night a Pennsylvania lieutenant lying wounded amid a scattering of dead had an experience of unparalleled horror. A number of stray hogs approached the spot and, with rapturous grunts, began feeding among the corpses. At length one of the larger animals came grunting toward the lieutenant. By a great piece of good luck, the man had a sword. As the hog reached him he plunged the point deep into its side, and it drew off with a prolonged squeal. But the lieutenant had to stay awake all night in order to defend himself against other members of the ravenous pack.

By this stage of the battle, there were impromptu hospitals everywhere, the Confederates having the better facilities, since they held the town. The Federals were using farm buildings, ambulance corps tents, and spots in the open air, most of the stations located along the Taneytown Road.

Circulating among the Federal hospitals, distributing supplies, were civilians of the Sanitary Commission. Among the welcome items these people dispensed were bandages, towels, blankets, shirts, underwear, stockings, brandy, concentrated beef soup, crackers, concentrated coffee, condensed milk, corn starch, and farina.

A Union soldier who had occasion to ride the Taneytown Road that night had the experience burned in his mind.

Union ambulance camp.

He saw "innumerable groups of wounded in all stages of misery; groaning, crying, swearing, begging for water or whiskey, or for food; entreating the surgeons and attendants to come to them; some in delirium, calling for their friends at home; some even begging someone to shoot them to escape from their present pangs; and the whole scene fitfully lighted up by the flaring lanterns of the hospital forces, or the flickering fires of rails and boards here and there; the fields toward the front full of flitting lights from the lanterns of the stretcher parties busy bringing fresh additions to the wretched mass."

Since the medical people were deplorably overworked, there wasn't time for measured attention to individual cases, and amputations were performed too freely. Chloroform was administered, but it wasn't always effective, and some of the men had to be strapped or held down, and they tensed and shrieked as the knife and saw were applied.

Each hospital area accumulated a great pile of bloody human parts:

legs, feet, toes, arms, hands, and fingers—refuse slated for burial en masse.

The Jacob Weikert property east of the Round Tops had expanded as a hospital, with victims now occupying not only the house and barn but also the ground around the buildings and a nearby orchard. Many of the red-splotched figures were awaiting their turn at the amputation bench.

Tillie Pierce, kept busy that night providing the sufferers servings of bread and beef tea, said later, "The scene had become terrible beyond description."

Tillie continued to worry about her family in Gettysburg, and there would have been no consolation for her in the knowledge that the Pierce house now held about a dozen bullet holes. The Confederates had been right the previous evening when they warned Mr. Pierce he was in danger from Yankee sharpshooters on Cemetery Hill. The fire, of course, was being drawn by Confederate sharpshooting from that area of town.

Gettysburg's citizens had endured a day in which fright, gloom, and uncertainty were intermixed. No one knew what was happening. Those who had access to good observation posts tried to appraise the situation, but the smoke thwarted them. And nothing reliable could be learned from the few Confederates who had remained in the town for the day.

Things got a little better around 10 P.M. when some of the participants in Dick Ewell's work came into the town to make their supper. The change in the general attitude was noted.

It's true there was some optimistic talk about the Vicksburg Campaign. Someone started a rumor that Ulysses Grant had retreated. Actually, he was about to accept John Pemberton's surrender.

The supposed good news did not offset Confederate concerns about the fighting at Gettysburg. Citizens heard Ewell's men say such things as, "The Yankees have a good position. We must drive them out of it tomorrow."

All, it was clear, was not lost. But deep apprehension remained. That night a townswoman penned in her diary: "I cannot sleep, and as I sit down to write to while away the time, my husband sleeps as soundly

Meade's headquarters.

as though nothing was wrong. I wish I could rest so easily, but it is out of the question for me either to eat or sleep under such terrible excitement and such painful suspense. We know not what the morrow will bring forth."

Even as the woman was writing, the morrow was being planned.

George Meade held a council of war at his headquarters cottage, a dozen generals gathering in a small room containing a bed, a pine table, and a few straight-backed chairs. In the soft, shadowy light of a single candle, glued with its own tallow to the bare tabletop, and in a haze of pipe and cigar smoke, the council made the unanimous decision that the lines be kept positioned as they were and made ready for Lee's next move. Meade believed that this move would be an attack on his center.

The star-crossed Confederate commander was plagued by a new ailment that night, having been smitten with diarrhea. But he began developing his plan for the next day, and it would evolve into something very much like Meade had calculated.

Longstreet was to hit the Union center with a 15,000-man force built around the 5,000 fresh troops of Pickett's division (now closing in from Chambersburg), while Dick Ewell resumed his attack on the Union right, the composite effort to be heavily supported with artillery fire.

In addition, Jeb Stuart was to position his troopers, currently about 6,000 in number, on Ewell's left in rear of the Union center, his mission to cooperate with Lee's attack, first engaging in harassment tactics, then helping to turn the expected Confederate infantry success into a rout.

All that was needed for victory, Lee believed, was "a proper concert of action."

But that, to be sure, was exactly the rub!

15

Movements Toward a Climax

ALREADY AT EARLIEST dawn on Friday, July 3, Lee's plans began going awry. Dick Ewell was not allowed the time he needed to develop a co-operation with Longstreet. The Federal guns bearing on George Steuart's lodgment at Culp's Hill opened the moment the crews could see to aim, and the infantry—units of Henry Slocum's reinforced Twelfth Corps—soon joined the effort.

Ewell had sworn to break Meade's right, and he tried hard enough, but it was uphill work against troops in strong positions. The Confederates got much the worst of things.

One large formation of Ewell's attackers was met with a volley so devastating that only a single man was left on his feet. For a brief time the stunned survivor stood and looked at the dead and wounded around him. Then he faced the Federals and raised his musket to fire. At that moment a fusillade laid him among his comrades.

The morning's fighting saw a point along its front where the men on both sides were from the same part of the border state of Maryland, with some of the adversaries well known to one another. This occasioned no failure of purpose.

A former Gettysburg citizen was among the Confederates who died on Culp's Hill. He was Wesley Culp, who was living in Virginia when the war came, and had embraced the Southern cause. He fell on the site of his grandfather's farm, which had given the hill its name.

Federals forming on Culp's Hill.

Wesley's last moments were spent among scenes he'd known well as a boy, scenes he was helping to desecrate on behalf of his family's enemies.

The damage done to sections of the woods on Culp's Hill was tremendous. A popular picnic grove was shot to shreds. Even a number of its sturdiest oaks were fatally damaged, their trunks bearing scores of holes and jagged furrows. Later some of these oaks would be sawed into pieces for display in Northern historical societies.

Fierce as it was, the prolonged struggle on Culp's Hill had no great importance. Lee was not deeply disturbed by this miscarriage of his master plan. His main intent was to smash through the Union center. If this effort succeeded, Dick Ewell would function as the tong of a vise that would help crush the enemy's northern wing. As for Meade's view of the Culp's Hill fighting: he had strengthened these lines and he

Meade studying Lee's lines from Little Round Top.

deemed them safe. He was giving most of his attention to his center and his left.

In significance, then, the deadly storm on Culp's Hill that morning amounted to little more than a noisy accompaniment for the arena's other developments.

A civilian facet of special note was the shooting of twenty-year-old Jennie Wade, who was living in one of Gettysburg's southernmost homes. For the past two days bullets aplenty had been flying around the place, but it was constructed of brick, and Jennie felt safe inside it. During quiet times she ventured out to help with the nearby wounded. On the morning of July 3, Jennie was in the house when a group of Federals from Cemetery Hill sought to drive some troublesome sharpshooters from the area. During the firefight a stray Confederate bullet winged toward the house. Avoiding contact with the brick walls, the missile pierced both an outer door and an inner one, finding Jennie in the kitchen, where she was preparing to bake bread. Struck in the back, the young woman died at once. Among the several civilians hit during the battle, she was the only fatality.

The morning hours saw another event involving Confederate sharp-shooters, this one on the battlefield, in its northern zone, where a determined group occupied a house and barn between the lines. There was a stiff little fight here, with even the artillery joining in. The issue was finally settled when a Union regiment, the 14th Connecticut, drove the Confederates from the buildings and set them afire.

Both Meade and Lee spent many moments of the morning looking through field glasses. Lee had the clearer view. The terrain on Cemetery Ridge was mostly open, while the Confederates were largely concealed by woods running along Seminary Ridge. One thing that Meade could see plainly was that Lee was establishing a line of artillery extending from the Peach Orchard to Gettysburg. The array was becoming highly formidable, but Meade could take comfort in that his own ridge was appointed in a like way.

Lee was still having trouble with Longstreet. At their first meeting early that morning Longstreet had said: "I have had my scouts out all night, and I find that you still have an excellent opportunity to move around Meade's army and maneuver him into attacking us."

When Lee was adamant about his plan to hit the Union center, Longstreet stated: "It is my opinion that no 15,000 men ever arrayed for battle can take that position." But the corps commander set about preparing the desired attack.

Longstreet's attitude apparently instilled a measure of doubt in Lee, for an aide heard him mutter, "The attack *must* succeed. The attack *must* succeed."

To support the three brigades of Pickett's division of Longstreet's corps, Lee chose eight brigades from A. P. Hill's corps. (The preponderance of Longstreet's corps, under Evander Law and Lafayette Mc-Laws, was to remain in the south as security for that flank.)

Unfortunately for the attack plan, Henry Heth's division made up about half the supports Lee selected. Though it was true this unit had done no fighting on the previous day and was well rested, it had been severely hurt during the fighting of July 1. Heth himself was down with a head wound, and his second-in-command, Johnston Pettigrew,

George E. Pickett

had taken over. To bolster his strength the general had ordered such people as cooks and clerks into the ranks.

Strangely enough, Lee was unaware of the division's decimation, and he did not learn of it until he rode past the unit while it was preparing for its new task. Some of the men, the commander noted with concern, were wearing bandages.

Another error on Lee's part was that he failed to make sure there was enough artillery ammunition at the front for the kind of effort he was planning.

There was a plus for the commander in that Jeb Stuart would be playing a part in the attack, but Stuart's men and their mounts were still overfatigued. And even while the expedition was making its way around Dick Ewell's lines toward the rear of the Union center that morning, vigorous units of Alfred Pleasonton's troopers were preparing themselves for opposition to just such a threat.

There is little room for speculation regarding Lee's choice of Pickett's division as the foundation for his attack plan: the unit was the freshest on the field. Perhaps there was some extra meaning for the general in that these troops were all fellow Virginians, men for whom he had a special affinity.

George Pickett was thirty-eight years old, of medium height and well formed, an officer who drew second looks because of his sleek black horse, his spruce way of dressing, and his wavy beard and shoulder-length ringlets.

As a youth, Pickett had become acquainted with Abraham Lincoln, whose lawyerly skills had helped him gain admission to West Point. He disappointed Lincoln by graduating at the very bottom of his class, but redeemed himself by becoming a publicized hero in the Mexican War and then doing well with his peacetime duties. He met Longstreet while both were still in the Union army, and "Old Peter" had become very fond of him.

Pickett was presently in a torment of love with a woman half his age. He had met LaSalle Corbell, his "Sally of the Sunset Eyes," on a Virginia beach while she was still a small child, and he had waited for her to grow up. Now the two were engaged to be married, and Pickett favored Sally with an adoring letter at every opportunity.

The enamored general had every reason for wanting to stay alive, but he viewed his Gettysburg assignment as a splendid chance for him to further his reputation. Thus far the war had not been generous to him in this respect. Of course, he believed that his breakthrough attempt would be solidly supported and would have a good chance of succeeding.

The fighting on Culp's Hill ended at about 10:30 A.M., with Dick Ewell's troops drawing back. Henry Slocum's defenders reacted with a round of cheering that told the bluecoats on Cemetery Ridge that all was well on the right flank.

Between the northern segments of Cemetery and Seminary Ridges the farm buildings still burned, a tower of smoke marking the spot. But all of the related shooting had stopped.

It was about eleven o'clock when a profound silence settled over the entire battle arena. Troop movements continued, but only in a minor way. Between the lines, stretcher-bearers persevered at bringing in the helpless wounded of the previous day's strife. Most of the dead of both sides still lay where they fell, somewhat less conspicuous than the dead and dying horses around them. Wounded horses on their feet, some limping, had taken to grazing, numbers of them intermingled with grazing farm animals.

The day was growing oppressively warm, and the Confederates were grateful for their generous woodland shade. Those many Federals in the open had to contend with the heat as best they could, some finding ways to put up tarps.

One bluecoat said later: "The air, surcharged with the smoke and vapor of two days of battle, held a sort of murky haze which was almost sedative in its effect on the senses."

In both armies, thousands dozed. Others overcame their lethargy to work at improving their makeshift barriers against shells and bullets. There was also the usual letter-writing and Bible-reading, and even some card-playing. On both sides, officers stood about in small groups reflecting quietly on what might be expected to happen.

There was one young Federal officer, however, whose mind was on something entirely different. We'll let Lieutenant Ziba Graham speak for himself: "All being quiet in our front, I received permission to go back to the hospital to get an ugly tooth extracted that had kept me dancing all the night before. Our surgeon, Doctor Everett, who had been hard at work all night at the amputation table, made but short work and little ado about one tooth. He laid me on the ground, straddled me, and with a formidable pair of nippers pulled and yanked me around until either the tooth had to come out, or my head off. I was glad when the head conquered."

Though the operation was successful and his source of trouble gone, Graham decided he'd made a mistake: "I saw the boys who were wounded from the fight of the day before, poor fellows. . . . My heart sickened and I turned away. It unmans one for the bloody work before him to witness the sufferings of the field hospital. No soldier but of iron nerves should ever leave the front to see the sufferers."

On the Confederate side of the arena, a strange situation was developing. Unable to reconcile himself to taking the responsibility for Pickett's attack, James Longstreet was trying to pass the buck to the commander of his artillery.

This was Colonel E. Porter Alexander, an alert Georgian in his late twenties, a man of pleasing presence who shunned military posturing. His mount was an ordinary looking animal chosen for its dependability; and he was armed with a clumsy old horse pistol loaded with buckshot, an instrument intended not so much for use against the Yankees as for shooting game for his table, game cooked for him by "Charlie," his indispensable servant.

All of the supporting guns, about 130 in number (80 belonging to Longstreet's corps, the rest to Hill's and Ewell's), were now in position along Seminary Ridge. George Pickett's attack force, to the accompaniment of band music, was forming just behind the ridge in open fields and fringes of woods.

The plan was for Pickett to notify Longstreet when he was ready to move, at which time Longstreet would order two guns to fire single shots in quick succession as a signal for the batteries to begin their bombardment. From then on, it was to be Porter Alexander's game. He was expected to watch the effect of the shelling, and, when conditions seemed right, was to order Pickett to advance.

Even while the colonel was pondering the magnitude of his role with apprehension he received the following note from Longstreet (who, after sending it, had lain down in the woods for a nap!): "If the artillery fire does not have the effect to drive off the enemy or greatly demoralize him so as to make our efforts pretty certain, I would prefer that you should not advise General Pickett to make the charge. I shall rely a great deal on your good judgment to determine the matter, and shall expect you to let General Pickett know when the moment offers."

This was too much! Alexander wrote back: "I will only be able to judge of the effect of our fire on the enemy by his return fire, for his infantry is but little exposed to view and the smoke will obscure the whole field. If, as I infer from your note, there is any alternative to this attack, it should be carefully considered before opening our fire, for it will take all the artillery ammunition we have left to test this one thoroughly, and, if the result is unfavorable, we will have none left for another effort. And even if this is entirely successful, it can only be so at a very bloody cost."

Longstreet, back on his feet by this time, countered: "The intention is to advance the infantry if the artillery has the desired effect of driving the enemy's off, or having other effect such as to warrant us in making the attack. When the moment arrives, advise General Pickett, and of course advance such artillery as you can use in aiding the attack."

This did nothing to assuage Alexander's anxiety. When the note came, he happened to be viewing the Federal lines in the company of Ambrose Wright, whose brigade had reached Cemetery Ridge during the previous day's fighting. The problem, Wright told the colonel, was not so much a matter of *getting* there as of *staying* there.

Alexander next sought out George Pickett to get his opinion of the situation. The general was found to be aware of the hazards involved, yet eager to make the attack.

The colonel now decided to accept his fate. He'd spread word among the artillerists for the bombardment to open at the sound of Longstreet's signal guns; and he'd proceed from there. Longstreet was sent this brief dispatch: "When our artillery fire is at its best, I shall order Pickett to charge."

On the Union side, there was rising wonderment about Lee's intentions, with the row of guns remaining the only clue. But even as the situation tautened, the troops turned to their noonday rations, modest enough for most of those at the front, with hardtack the staple. Fires were not permitted here at this critical time, so coffee was lacking. Warm canteen water was the general beverage. In the rear, however, there was both coffee and even some decent meals, mostly for officers, provided by black headquarters servants (some of them "contrabands" from the South), who were good foragers.

The resumption of the interrupted activities, front and rear, was accompanied by a widespread resort to cigars, pipes, and "chaws," those companions of digestion and palliatives for nervousness.

The stillness was now broken for a time by artillery sounds drifting from the east, from a point about two miles from the rear of the Union center. This was sparring by the horse artillery of Jeb Stuart and David Gregg, of small significance in itself, but an indication that something bigger was pending in that region.

It was exactly seven minutes past 1 P.M., according to a Gettysburg citizen who also noted that the temperature was creeping toward the high eighties, when the main arena's unnatural silence was shattered by James Longstreet's first signal gun, with a second shot soon following.

Even as the attention of those on both sides was sharply arrested, the Confederate batteries all along the line—variously employing fused shells, a few percussion shells, and round shot—began flashing and booming, the medley assuming a constancy that made it sound like an endless roll of thunder—though some of the bluecoats said later that comparing the firing with thunder was to give it less than its due. All agreed, however, that the shot and shell arrived as a storm.

Some of the Union guns—there were about eighty in bearing positions—soon began replying, but only at a moderate fire. Their commander, Brigadier General Henry Hunt, one of the nation's finest artillerists, wanted to conserve his ammunition for the expected infantry assault.

The noise, however, now rose to such a volume as to be heard at points nearly 150 miles away. The Western Hemisphere had never known anything like it. For days afterward, there would be troops on both sides who suffered from dulled hearing, prompting newly arrived observers to wonder why so many conversations were carried on at a shout.

Fortunately for the people of Gettysburg, the work of the previous two days had rendered them somewhat accustomed to artillery fire that shook their homes, else those with weak nerves might have rushed out in panic. Once again, there was a general resort to the cellars.

In her diary, Sallie Broadhead said of the noise: "More terrible never greeted human ears."

Union General Henry Hunt's arsenal actually included a good many more than eighty guns, but the configuration of Meade's lines provided spots for the placement of only eighty at a time. This fact, plus Hunt's orders for restraint, gave the Confederates a powerful superiority in the weight of metal thrown. They also had better fields of fire. Much of the Federal position was starkly exposed, while their own was largely blended with woodlands. Consequently, the Federals took the greater damage.

The infantrymen at the front kept their casualties moderate by lying prone, but the artillerymen and their horses had no such recourse, and some of the positions were devastated. Men and animals were blown to pieces, caissons were exploded, guns were dismounted. The great flashes that marked the exploding caissons thrilled the Confederate gunners, but their ecstatic cheering was lost in the general uproar.

Many of the Confederate shells were aimed too high, and these did their brutal work behind Cemetery Ridge amid the reserves, the support personnel, the stragglers, the camp followers—and the hapless wounded. The unexpected assault spawned terror and confusion. Hastily hitched supply trains went lurching from the area, and they tangled with clamoring throngs on the run.

Down at the Jacob Weikert farm there were moments when shells crashed about, but Tillie Pierce and the other civilians were not present. Their military friends had provided them carriage transportation to a safer location.

General Meade was forced from his headquarters cottage when shells began piercing it and killing the horses tethered in its yard. The commander made his departure with the utmost coolness, smiling at the concern for his safety shown by his aides, and even taking the time to tell them a little story about a shelling he'd known in the Mexican War.

The careless dispersion of some of the Confederate fire surprised the Union's Henry Hunt. He'd been an artillery instructor during the prewar years, and one of his students was A. L. Long, now a colonel on Lee's staff. As such, Hunt assumed, Long was doubtless involved in the bombardment. Later, when the two met on friendly terms at Appomattox, Hunt mentioned that the Confederate shelling at Gettysburg hadn't been done according to the principles Long had been taught. Long smiled and said, "I remembered my teachings. When the fire became so scattered, I wondered what you would think about it."

During their passage through the arena's ceiling of smoke, the shells made a variety of sounds: howls, growls, whistles, whizzes, wails, sputters, hisses. There were even missiles, some men said later, that seemed to ponder their choice of victims, with one type shrieking, "Who? Who?" and another type asking hoarsely, "Which one? Which one?"

On Cemetery Hill, Union Brigade Commander Carl Schurz noted that some of his ground-hugging troops were showing signs of breaking under the strain. Lighting a cigar, the general began walking back and forth in front of the position in complete disregard of the danger, and the performance had the desired effect.

"I could not speak to them, for the incessant roar of the cannonade would not let them hear me. But I noticed that many of them returned my smile in a sort of confidential way when I happened to catch their eyes, as if to say: 'It is not jolly, but *we two* will not be frightened by it.'"

Other Union commanders on the ridge performed in much the same manner as Schurz. Winfield Hancock, accompanied by his staff, made a slow ride along the entire half mile of his Second Corps front, the unit's colors on prominent display. Hancock was on a borrowed horse. His regular mount, a veteran of several battles, had found the present bombardment to be unbearable and had refused to function.

Officers on the Confederate side put on shows of equal boldness, none rising above those of Lee, Longstreet, and Pickett. Some of the graycoats cheered these promenades, while others protested. During one of Longstreet's rides, a private shouted, "Go to the rear! You'll get your fool head blown off!"

And there was more anguish than inspiration for the troops who saw Lee, with a single aide, ride over a section of ground being heavily shelled. When begged to get out of the area, the commander responded by doffing his hat and urging Traveller to a slightly faster pace.

These were discouraging moments for Longstreet's artillery chief, Porter Alexander. He had hoped for a quick crippling of the Union batteries so that Pickett could be called forward while the Confederate guns still had enough ammunition to do a good job of covering the advance. Now, well over an hour into the cannonade, the measured fire of Henry Hunt's pieces continued as in the beginning. Moreover, Alexander had learned, the shells were doing considerable damage among Pickett's troops as they waited in the rear.

The colonel at last wrote Pickett that, even though the Federal fire hadn't slackened, he'd better come forward at once if he was coming at all. Then, a few minutes later, Henry Hunt ordered his batteries to begin winding down their effort, lest they run short of ammunition for use against the expected attack. The desperate Alexander interpreted this as an indication that Hunt had been bested, at least for the moment, and word was rushed to Pickett: "For God's sake, come quick!"

Already after receiving the first message, Pickett had ridden to the front to clear the matter with Longstreet, apparently unwilling to make so critical a move at the order of a colonel.

Longstreet's attempt to pass the buck had failed.

Pickett was standing with Longstreet when the bearer of Alexander's second note found him. He read the message and passed it to Longstreet to read, then asked whether he should proceed with the attack.

Longstreet gave him an intent look, then held out his hand. As Pickett extended his own, Longstreet took it and placed his other hand upon it. He tried to speak, but nothing came forth, and he issued the affirmation that duty demanded by dropping his bearded chin to his breast.

"Then, General," said Pickett, "I shall lead my division on."

As Pickett mounted his black horse and turned toward the rear, he remembered that he had in his pocket a letter to Sally that he wanted Longstreet to mail for him. Drawing up, Pickett took out the letter and scribbled across a corner of the envelope, "If Old Peter's nod means death, then good-bye and God bless you, little one."

As he reached down and handed the letter to Longstreet, Pickett saw tears on the commander's cheeks and in his beard. In a later report to Sally, Pickett said: "The stern old war horse, God bless him, was weeping for his men."

At this point, Pickett himself was still confident he could lead the attack's survivors to victory.

While Pickett was going back to order up his troops, Longstreet rode forward to the line of guns, now at a slow fire, to consult with Porter Alexander. The colonel told the general that he had grown more optimistic with the slackening of the enemy's fire, but that he feared there wasn't enough ammunition left in the Confederate chests to give a full support to Pickett's advance.

Longstreet snapped, "Stop Pickett immediately and replenish your ammunition!"

Alexander explained that this would take too long, that it would give the Federals time to recover from the effects of the bombardment. Moreover, he said, there was very little ammunition to replenish with.

"I don't want to make this attack," Longstreet lamented. "I would stop it now, but General Lee has ordered it and expects it to go on. I don't see how it can succeed."

Even while the two were talking, the men of Pickett's division, in multiple ranks covering a wide front, guiding on their blue Virginia flags and showing also the red banner of the Confederacy, began sweeping from the woods and forming in the fields behind the line of guns. The sun sparkled on the burnished metal of their muskets, bayonets, and swords as they dressed their lines.

The greater part of the supports from A. P. Hill's corps—men from various parts of the South, with North Carolina strongly represented—formed on Pickett's left, toward Gettysburg, while the rest were located on his right, toward the Peach Orchard; and the whole made up a front of about a mile.

This was old-style military pageantry at its best, and, with the arena's smoke dissipating, it was admired even by the troops over on Cemetery Ridge.

Admiration, however, was not Henry Hunt's reason for withholding his artillery fire. He was saving his ammunition for blasting these magnificent formations at closer range.

Among the observers on the Confederate side was a Richmond war correspondent who had seen Ambrose Wright's regiments make the three-quarter-mile trip across the shallow valley the day before. "I had witnessed their death struggle with the foe on the opposite heights. I had observed their return with shattered ranks, a bleeding mass.... Now I saw their valiant comrades prepare for the same bloody trial, and already felt that their efforts would be vain unless their supports should be as true as steel and brave as lions."

Completion of the formations was followed by inspirational talks by company commanders, prayers led by regimental chaplains, and scattered hymn-singing. Brigade commanders rode up and down the lines shouting cheerful encouragements. Color-bearers were challenged: "Are you going to put that flag in the enemy's works?"

It was about 3:30 P.M. when the mounted George Pickett, looking splendidly martial in front of the center of his Virginians, ordered the units brought to attention. Then he called out, "Forward!"

The order was repeated along the lines and was greeted with cheers. Some of the men yelled, "We'll follow you, Marse George! We'll follow you!"

As the advance began at "common step" with muskets carried "at will," Pickett's northerly supports, their numbers actually exceeding his own, were also activated; and soon the broad fronts were passing through the now-silent line of guns, with the crews swinging their hats and urging the men on.

Then the formations were in the open, their skirmishers out ahead. Orders to dispense with all cheering were issued, but they were scarcely needed. The sight of the gun-studded ridge across the valley, its troops indistinct but known to be there in heavy numbers, was grimly sobering.

In many spots in the ranks a new cry arose:

"Good-bye, boys! Good-bye, boys!"

16

The Charge

HANDILY FOR LEE'S purposes, the point in Meade's center that Pickett was supposed to hit was marked by a small clump of trees that could be guided upon. Located on the forward slope of the ridge, this happened to be the approximate center of the half-mile front of Winfield Hancock's Second Corps, about 6,000 men in two divisions. Alexander Hays' division was on the right, to the north, while that of John Gibbon made up the southerly left.

Running northward on the side of the grove toward the valley was a low stone wall. A short distance past the grove the wall turned sharply eastward for about seventy-five yards, then angled back to its northerly course. This barrier, generally about thigh-high, gave passable protection to a good part of Hancock's front-line troops. It did little, however, for his artillery batteries, some of which had been severely handled during the cannonade.

Hancock's secondary lines were tiered up the slope to the crest of the ridge. Out ahead of his front, forming a northeast-southwest diagonal, was the Emmitsburg Road, which bisected his skirmish line, some of the men of which were strung along the road's rail fences.

The long-range sight of the Confederate advance, with its scintillating steel and vividly colored banners, produced a combination of apprehension and fascination among the Federals. Exclamations went up: "Here they come! Here comes the infantry!"

Hancock rode along the slope behind his front, radiating the best of cheer as he called out encouragements and admonitions. "Steady, boys! Steady! Hold your fire until they're in close."

The general's manner was casual as he drew up now and again to make a field-glass study of the formations.

Had he known exactly where to look, Hancock would have seen an officer moving along on foot with his black felt hat held aloft on the tip of his sword, a guide for the men behind him. This was Lewis Armistead, commander of a brigade of Pickett's division, one of Hancock's closest friends in the old Union army.

The two were serving together in California when the war broke out. At an evening farewell party, one of the ladies present, Mrs. Albert Sydney Johnston, played the piano and sang that sad song of parting in the gray dawn, "Kathleen Mavourneen," which includes the line, "It may be for years, and it may be forever."

Lewis A. Armistead

Lewis Armistead cried as he gripped Hancock's shoulders and bade him good-bye.

The Southerner had taken great pride and satisfaction in serving the Union, and had agonized over his decision to go against it. Now Fate was carrying him toward a critical showdown with his old friend's Union guns.

The bluecoats had orders to keep low, but, with both sides still holding their fire, some of the men stood up to get a better view of the grand show.

The commander of Hancock's northern wing, the tall, dynamic, and bluff Alexander Hays, was riding his lines when he saw a man rise.

"Lie down!" Hays roared. Then, pointing at a prone figure, he added, "Lie down like that man!"

"That man is dead, General."

"I wish *you* were!" snapped Hays. "Be quiet!"

The Confederate advance had shaped itself into two wings. Pickett's division was on the right, in the south, and Henry Heth's division, under Johnston Pettigrew, comprised the left, or northern, wing. Behind Pettigrew were two brigades of William Pender's division led by Isaac R. Trimble. Pickett's southerly supports, two brigades of Richard Anderson's division under Cadmus Wilcox, were not advancing; they were standing in reserve, to be used as needed to protect the attack's right flank.

Unfortunately for Pickett's effort, this array that looked so handsome to the Federals was tactically faulty.

Johnston Pettigrew's weakest brigades were on his northern flank, his left, which was his most vulnerable spot. Isaac Trimble was behind Pettigrew's right when he should have been following that weak left. Cadmus Wilcox, on Pickett's right, had no specific instructions as the division's flank protector.

Both Lee and Longstreet were guilty of negligence in arranging the attack, Longstreet through lack of faith in such an effort, and Lee through an overconfidence in his army's striking power, coupled, no doubt, with a dulling of his judgment by health problems: the fatigue associated with his still-mending heart, his nagging sciatica, his siege of diarrhea.

Cadmus Wilcox

One thing Lee had done that was precisely correct was to send Jeb Stuart's troopers eastward around Meade's position. This might have led to important results, for it was Stuart's intention to make a diversion against the Union rear at the same time Pickett was attacking in front. Even though many of the horsemen were not at their best, they comprised a powerful strike force.

But while Pickett was making his advance, the Union troopers of David Gregg's division moved to frustrate Stuart.

The resulting battle, much of it hand-to-hand, was signally fierce, with the bluecoats of George Custer's brigade, his Michigan "Wolverines," giving a notable account of themselves in crashing charges. During the course of these encounters, Southerner Wade Hampton was badly hurt, sabered on the scalp and hit in the side by a piece of shrapnel.

In the end, Stuart was obliged to desist, not having made the slightest contribution to Pickett's effort. (In his report, of course, the trooper managed to make the failure seem like another Stuart success!)

George Pickett's formations were about halfway across the broad, sunlit valley when the Union artillery opened, not only batteries in the center but also on Cemetery Hill in the north and Little Round Top in the south. The concentration produced a cruel deluge.

"Through our field glasses," the Union's Carl Schurz said later, "we could distinctly see the gaps torn in their ranks and the ground dotted with dark spots—their dead and wounded."

The hits drew cheers from the Federal gunners. In the stricken ranks, cries of anguish arose. But the gaps were closed and the advance continued.

Some of the Confederate batteries were soon replying, firing over the heads of the attackers, who found hope in the aid. Porter Alexander personally gathered fifteen or twenty guns with fair supplies of ammunition and followed the attack, looking for targets of opportunity.

The usual battlefield smoke began to gather, and the enveloping patches provided some of the marchers brief respites from their stark exposure.

As the Confederate skirmishers approached the Emmitsburg Road, they began nearing their Federal counterparts. White puffs marked the resulting musket exchanges. Here and there, on both sides, men went

Custer leading the fight against Stuart.

down. Then the Confederate skirmishers were absorbed by the gray wave rolling up behind them, while the Federals, at the sound of Second Corps buglers blowing "recall," ran in and joined their comrades along the line of the stone wall.

Experiencing a few moments of trouble with the roadway fences, the Confederates, once across, paused to dress their lines. Then they renewed their advance at an increased pace. Soon, for the first time, the Rebel Yell rang out.

Almost at once the sound was lost amid the roar of a great volley of musketry from Hancock's position.

Scores of graycoats in the front ranks went down, along with numbers of the regimental banners. Many of the felled men lay still, but all of the flags went up again in new hands.

The Federal fire was returned, and now began a sustained flashing and crashing of thousands of muskets, with a new pall of smoke forming as the weapons wreaked their carnage.

George Pickett had interrupted his personal advance at a barn just east of the Emmitsburg Road. The spot was within musket range of the enemy's lines, and he found it to be a good one from which to observe and control his forces. Very soon, however, the general was doing a lot more observing than controlling. The fight was developing a will of its own.

By this time the Confederates were in serious trouble on both flanks. In the south, Pickett's division had advanced in such a way as to expose its right (which Cadmus Wilcox had not moved to cover) to an enfilading fire not only from Henry Hunt's southerly artillery batteries but also from the musketry of George J. Stannard's brigade of Vermonters, along with some New Yorkers and Pennsylvanians, who had swung down the slope on Hancock's left.

During these same moments, something of a like nature was happening in the north. A single Union regiment, the 8th Ohio, under a man of exceptional daring, Colonel Franklin Sawyer, had taken up a position down in front of Hancock's extreme right and was pouring enfilading volleys into Johnston Pettigrew's left. This work, too, was accompanied by artillery fire.

With the attack force now being hit from three sides, at least one of the Confederates got the impression that Hancock was being reinforced by "all creation." The man claimed later that he heard a Yankee officer boom: "Attention, universe! Nations into line! By kingdoms, right wheel, march!"

The truth was that Hancock, at this time, was not being bolstered at all. As this long day had progressed, Meade had become uncertain of his belief that Lee would attack his center, feeling that another attempt on his left, which could be flanked, was a distinct possibility. Now that Lee's intent was at last clear, Meade was on a hurried search for reinforcements to meet the threat. The commander was not with Hancock's corps for the culmination of Pickett's charge.

It was Franklin Sawyer's Ohio regiment, down in front of Hancock's right, together with artillery cooperation from the main line, that dealt the attackers a blow that portended the frustration of their effort. Sawyer's musketry was deadly enough, but the artillery's canister was even worse. Johnston Pettigrew's leftmost brigade was enveloped by clouds of dust and smoke, and, according to a Federal observer, "arms, heads, blankets, guns, and knapsacks were tossed in the air."

A moan swept the brigade, and those troops still on their feet became frantic. As Franklin Sawyer explained in his report: "The whole mass gave way, some fleeing to the front, some to the rear, and some through our lines, until the whole plain was covered with unarmed rebels, waving coats, hats, and handkerchiefs in token of a wish to surrender."

The 8th Ohio took about 200 prisoners and three sets of colors.

George Pickett galloped toward the scene, soon recognized the situation as hopeless, and returned to his post at the barn.

Observing from the edge of the woods across the valley, his big frame perched on a rail fence, was James Longstreet. Despite his reluctance to make the attack, the general was prepared to send Pickett extra support if it seemed he was about to breach Meade's line. Lee had placed the whole of Anderson's division at Longstreet's call. But the sight of the left-flank rout convinced Longstreet that the attack was going to fail, and he believed that supplying more troops would only compound the disaster. He did, however, allow Cadmus Wilcox, one of Pickett's original supports, to start forward on the right.

Lee was apparently of the same mind as Longstreet, for he gave no orders for increasing Pickett's supports. A. P. Hill would have been quite willing to advance with the troops still under his control, but Lee wanted these kept in reserve against the possibility of a counterattack.

But Pickett's failure was not yet written in stone. To be sure, the troops on both his flanks were now entirely on the defensive, simply trying to hold on. But the pressure they were getting resulted in a crowding toward the center; and this, coupled with Isaac Trimble's support from the rear, increased the strength of the attack toward the breakthrough target, the clump of trees.

The spearhead of this attack was approaching the stone wall at the spot where it formed its angle in front of the clump, the station of Alexander S. Webb's "Philadelphia Brigade" of Gibbon's division. (John Gibbon, incidentally, was a Southerner who had chosen to fight for the Union. He had three brothers in the Confederate service, all of whom had disowned him.)

Alexander S. Webb

Commanding the battery of guns at the angle, not more than three of them still operational, was Lieutenant Alonzo H. Cushing, a soft-faced youth with the heart of a lion. Already bearing two wounds, one of them a groin injury that required him to hold the mutilated parts in place with a hand, Cushing kept his guns firing as the foe closed in.

"I'll give them one more shot, Webb!" he cried, then fell dead as a bullet entered his mouth.

The bluecoats of the regiment holding the angle, the 71st Pennsylvania, lost their nerve as the shouting attackers, many times their number, swarmed toward them. Except for two companies on the right flank, the 71st broke from the wall and ran up the slope behind it toward the position of the reinforced 72nd Pennsylvania on the crest of the ridge. Having no intention of stopping there, the dismayed men swung around the unit's right. Webb, their brigade commander, was on foot with the 72nd, and he howled for the rush to stop, but was heeded by few.

At this moment one of John Gibbon's aides, thirty-five-year-old Lieutenant Frank Aretas Haskell, a citizen soldier—a Dartmouth graduate of outstanding brilliance—happened to come riding from the rear on Dick, a mount whose reputation for calmness and dependability under fire was to be harshly tested during the next half hour.

Haskell found himself approaching the head of the stream of shirkers. Recognizing this as an emergency situation, knowing that battlefield panic can easily escalate, the lieutenant drew his sword as a symbol of command and pushed Dick into the throng, shouting for the men to face about, and using the flat of his weapon as a manual persuader.

The rout was stopped, and Webb was able to re-form the 71st on the crest with the 72nd, now busy pouring its musket fire into the Confederates down at the wall, where, Frank Haskell noted, "the damned red flags of the rebellion began to thicken and flaunt."

Haskell would have been mightily surprised to know that one of the Confederates under those flags was a young woman. She had been posing as the son of an older man who was really her husband. Both died at this spot, and the Yankees would later bury them near it, listing her in their records as, "One female private in rebel uniform."

Confederate General Lewis Armistead, Winfield Hancock's old friend, had begun the charge in a reserve position, but now he pushed his way through the tangle of troops and up to the wall.

"We can't stay here!" he called out. "Who will follow me?"

His black hat still aloft on the tip of his sword, the general stepped over the wall and started up the slope toward the abandoned wreckage of Alonzo Cushing's battery, with its bloody scattering of felled men and horses.

Armistead's goal was Webb's line of Pennsylvanians on the crest directly above. Perhaps 200 Confederates, including several color-bearers, leaped the wall in the general's wake, and he shouted, "Give them the cold steel, boys!"

But Webb and his men were having none of this. They loosed a blast of fire that stopped the advance, and many of the Confederates who remained on their feet drew back to the wall.

Lewis Armistead had just placed a hand on one of Alonzo Cushing's abandoned guns when he was shot down, the wound mortal. The general was still a few hours from death, however. He remained aware of events about him, and he seems to have pondered, with deep regret, his role in the war. The place where he lay would become known as the Confederacy's "high-water mark."

John Gibbon's mounted aide, Frank Haskell, had remained with Webb and was infinitely relieved to see the enemy's breakthrough checked. But Webb's ranks had been thinned, and none of the reinforcements General Meade was assembling had arrived in his rear.

Down there under that haze of smoke, at the wall and stretching away from it to the west, were thousands of Confederates, and those in front were maintaining a strong fire. At the same time, shells supporting the assailants were shrieking over them and crashing on the ridge, this fire not impeded by Henry Hunt's guns, since these were concentrating on the Confederate infantry.

Hunt's canister, of course, was a great aid to Webb, for the terrible blasts, angling in at several points, were keeping the foe off balance.

Also helpful was the fire of the Federal infantry units curled back from the wall on either side of the abandoned section.

Webb had something else going for him—something that neither he nor Haskell was aware of. Not only Lewis Armistead, but also Pick-

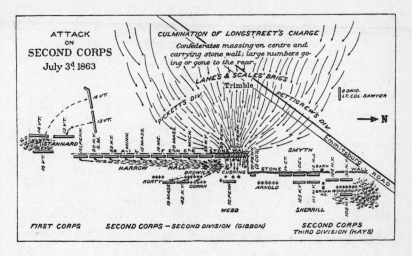

The charge in its final moments.

ett's other two brigade commanders, Richard E. Garnett and James L. Kemper, were out of the fight, Garnett dead and Kemper wounded. Moreover, Pickett's two top support commanders, Johnston Pettigrew and Isaac Trimble, were about to take hits, Trimble a severe one. The attack's leadership was being badly impaired.

But, whatever the state of their command structure, the Confederates were strong in numbers, and they might yet nerve themselves for a swarming attack up the slope. Webb and Haskell urged the men on the crest to throw themselves forward and try to repair the breach in the line, but even the bravest balked at this.

Something had to be done, very quickly! Neither Winfield Hancock nor John Gibbon was present. The two had gone southward just before the development of the crisis, feeling that the best way to stop Pickett was to increase the pressure on his still-unprotected right flank. Hancock, however, had dispatched two regiments of reserves toward Webb's position.

But more troops were needed! Frank Haskell looked to the north, where Hays was facing those men of Pettigrew's division who had not

Rushing to repel Pickett.

fled or were not interlaced with Pickett's units. Hays was obviously busy! A look to the south was more encouraging. The left wing of Gibbon's division was only lightly engaged.

Off went Haskell on Dick, galloping wildly. The only mounted officer on this section of the slope, the lieutenant attracted the enemy's special attention. Dick began taking hits but kept going without changing his gait.

Haskell's mission was successful. Most of the left-wing regiments, he found, could be spared from the front. These men were sent pounding northward, formations largely disregarded, and they came up in a press on the left of the 72nd, still on the crest, and angled themselves down the slope to the clump of trees.

The front ranks spewed musketry at the several thousand men massed at the breach, fire that was at first stoutly returned. Many were hit on both sides.

Frank Haskell was there, trying to be heard with his "Forward to the wall! Forward to the wall!"

The lieutenant was still on Dick, who continued to perform magnificently even though his bullet wounds were now accompanied by a ghastly shrapnel mutilation in his right haunch.

An unlikely figure fighting on the Union side was General Henry Hunt. This man of many cannons was at the front popping at the foe with his revolver.

It was only a matter of minutes until the Confederates who held the wall began to waver, at least partly because the supports stretching behind them, heavily hurt by the relentless artillery fire and by long-range musketry, were breaking up, with some of the men in full flight back toward Seminary Ridge.

Now the Federals on the slope moved forward en masse, and for a few moments the fighting was hand to hand. Swords were wielded, bayonets thrust home, muskets used as clubs, heads even broken by stones grabbed from the wall.

Little cheering was heard. Far more prominent were growls, oaths, shrieks of pain, and petitions to God from the mortally wounded.

Then it was over. Some of the graycoats turned and ran, but many hundreds of those in front of Webb—and equal numbers of those to the north, in front of Hays—threw down their muskets and surrendered, giving up about twenty-five sets of colors.

Observing the entire episode from Cemetery Hill was the Boston journalist Charles Carleton Coffin, who wrote later: "How inspiring the moment! How thrilling the hour! It is the high-water mark of the Rebellion—a turning point of history and of human destiny!"

This assessment, of course, was the product of an after-war focus.

Right now, even the fact that a victory had been achieved was hard to grasp. In Frank Haskell's words: "The judgment almost refused to credit the senses. Are these abject wretches about us, whom our men are now disarming and driving together in flocks, the jaunty men . . . whose steady lines and flashing arms but a few moments since came sweeping up the slope to destroy us? Are these red cloths that our men toss about in derision . . . the battle flags of the Rebellion that waved defiance at the wall? We know, but so sudden has been the transition, we yet can scarce believe."

Within minutes of the end of the mutual ferocity, some of the enemies were fraternizing.

A Confederate prisoner glanced around at the nearby slopes of Cemetery Ridge and said to a guard, "You had a lot of men killed here."

The Yankee responded, "Hell, yes! You gave us hell, and we gave you hell."

With that, a prisoner of Irish extraction put in, "An' shure, it was hell all around!"

Confederate prisoners marching under guard.

Astride Dick, Frank Haskell watched the cleanup operations from the summit of the ridge. One of the lieutenant's thighs had been struck by a spent bullet that had left a severe bruise, and he was in pain. Dick, who was still functioning with perfect faithfulness, was a tragic sight, with his sweat everywhere mingled with blood, some of it running down his legs. In addition to his surface wounds, the horse had three bullets lodged deep within him.

Haskell and Dick were on the summit when General Meade, along with the son who was serving as one of his aides, rode up from the rear. The commander had just completed his task of summoning reserves to bolster his center.

"How is it going here?" he asked Haskell.

"I believe, General, the enemy's attack is repulsed."

"What! Is the assault already repulsed?"

"It is, sir."

Meade's eyes swept the field, taking in the masses of prisoners under guard, the Confederate flags in Federal hands, and the scatterings of graycoats in full retreat.

His haggard face brightening, the general said, "Thank God!" He followed this with a controlled "Hurrah!"

The younger George Meade was more enthusiastic. Swinging his hat, he voiced three hearty cheers.

General Meade now gave Frank Haskell some orders to transmit to Second Corps officers, and Haskell rode off to find these men. At this point, Haskell and Dick leave our story, but they merit a further word.

The flagging Dick carried his master through the new round of duties, then quietly laid himself down to die, with Haskell believing that the horse had done enough for the Union cause to deserve special remembrance, perhaps even his own monument.

[Haskell himself, during the next few weeks, wrote a book-length letter about the battle for his brother, and the account rose to great fame, becoming a Harvard Classic. Unaware he had made himself into an American legend, Haskell was killed at Cold Harbor eleven months after Gettysburg.]

As Haskell and Dick were leaving the two George Meades, cheers were beginning to swell all along Cemetery Ridge. Even some of the dying added their tremulous mite. Though no one knew that the Battle of Gettysburg had been won, everyone had begun to realize that the foe had been dealt a stunning setback.

This included a secondary blow. The Confederate supports under Cadmus Wilcox, making the mistake of coming across the valley in the south while Pickett's battered attack force was retreating in the north, were thrown back by blasts from Henry Hunt's artillery abetted by the musketry of George Stannard's reinforced Vermonters. Wilcox lost about 200 men to no purpose.

Neither Winfield Hancock nor John Gibbon could enjoy the afternoon's triumph in full, for both had been severely wounded, Hancock in the thigh and Gibbon in the shoulder. Hancock had spent the last part of the fight on a stretcher set down on the ridge. He refused to go to a hospital in the rear until the issue was settled. Just before the general was carried away, an aide arrived and handed him some items tied up in a handkerchief, the personal effects of his dying Confederate friend, Lewis Armistead. The parcel came with Armistead's request that it be sent to his family, and with an apology for his work against the Union.

Across the valley, the disorganized remnants of Pickett's attack force, which included hundreds of walking wounded, were threading their way toward the woods of Seminary Ridge. The men were still under shellfire, and the dispiriting sound of the Yankee cheering carried to their ears.

Of the 15,000 who had taken part in the attack, less than half were returning. A strong part of the loss was in captured, but the fields between the ridges were heavily littered with corpses and with helpless wounded.

Although James Longstreet had predicted the failure, he was shaken by its reality. Moreover, at first he feared that Meade would hasten to launch a counterattack Lee was ill prepared for. While maintaining a calm exterior through some bad moments, Longstreet asked British observer Arthur Fremantle if he had something to drink. Fremantle gave him a silver flask of rum and told him to keep it, and the general was grateful.

Lee's conduct at this time was extraordinary. Added to his illness and weariness was now a deep discouragement, and perhaps even a foreboding that the Southern fight for independence was lost; but he

Lee after Pickett's charge had failed.

managed to project an image of placid and cheerful leadership, riding about among the returning men, offering sympathy to the wounded and encouragement to the downcast, and asking for support in handling the setback.

"All this will come right in the end," he said. "In the meantime, all good men must rally. You must help me out of this in the best way you can."

More than one lamenting officer was told: "All this has been my fault. It is I who have lost this fight."

Later, in the company of close subordinates, Lee would anguish over the defeat and try to analyze it, but he would not deviate from his acceptance of the whole of the blame.

George Pickett made his return from the battlefield with his head down and his eyes brimming. As he rode past Lee, the commander called for him to rally his division behind the ridge. With something less than a due respect, Pickett responded that he no longer had a division to rally.

He wrote Sally: "Your soldier lives and mourns, and but for you, my darling, he would rather—a million times rather—be back there with his dead, to sleep for all time in an unknown grave."

Pickett, no doubt, would have been less dejected if he could have foreseen that he'd become famous as the leader of one of the greatest do-or-die attacks in military history.

Even while Lee was reorganizing his central units, a new sound of gunfire was heard on his right, west of the Round Tops. Judson Kilpatrick's division of Union troopers had been watching the Confederate infantry there; and now, believing that Meade was planning a counterattack, Kilpatrick decided to make an attack of his own. An all-around mistake, the charges pitted the wavering carbines of mounted men against the steady muskets of foot troops; and the work closed with the sacrificial Union dead including the promising young brigadier Elon Farnsworth, whose body bore five wounds, each one mortal in itself.

Though neither side knew it, the Battle of Gettysburg was now over.

The casualty figures for this largest and most significant conflict of the Civil War would never be precisely determined, but the aggregate was probably at least 50,000 in killed, wounded, captured, and missing, with the proportions about equal.

Farnsworth's charge.

17

In Conclusion

LEE KNEW THAT his only option now was to return to Virginia, but he decided to delay his departure for a day to determine Meade's intentions regarding a counterblow. The Union commander, far from thinking in terms of such a move, was concerned that Lee might be planning another attack.

So the evening of July 3 found the armies watching one another closely over the awful debris of war that littered the valley, with the situation reminding at least one Union officer of two wild beasts that had separated after fighting one another nearly to the death, then had to stay alert for the possibility of a resumption of the struggle.

On both sides, efforts were turned to caring for the new multitudes of wounded, and the hospitals expanded again. By this time some of the surgeons were so badly overworked they were giving amputation cases to assistants who'd had no previous experience with the knife and the saw.

Weatherwise, this was a fine evening, and the survivors on both ridges enjoyed their campfires. Bands began playing. On the Union side, sad pieces like "Home, Sweet Home" were balanced by lively ones like "Yankee Doodle." Across the valley, the inspirational "Dixie" was much resorted to. But the troops were not as badly in need of cheering as might be supposed. To be sure, there was widespread dejection over Pickett's repulse, but faith in Lee was so strong that most of the men believed he'd weather this blow and achieve his invasion goals, would probably lead them to Washington itself.

The people of Gettysburg heard little exuberant talk among Dick Ewell's men that evening. Not that this would have bothered them deeply. There was a general feeling that the day had gone against the Confederates. Observers in high places had got glimpses of the return of Pickett's depleted forces to Seminary Ridge, and Yankee prisoners in the town were heard analyzing the sounds of the afternoon as those of a great Confederate attack that had failed.

There was no certainty among the civilians that the battle was over and had been a Federal success, but there was hope. And this was reinforced during the night. Lee ordered Ewell's corps to leave its eastern positions, and also to abandon Gettysburg, and to form on the Seminary Ridge line. All through the moonlit hours, troops, artillery batteries, and wagon trains crowded noisily through the town, all heading westward.

At dawn on the Fourth of July there was a general outpouring of citizens into the streets. It was learned that Confederate skirmishers still held the western edge of town but that all areas to the east were

Federals looking for holes in their colors.

Reclaiming Gettysburg on July 4.

clear. At first there was no celebrating over this, for no one was sure what it meant. Then up from the south, from Cemetery Hill, came the sound of drums and fifes heralding the approach of a column of bluecoats carrying the Stars and Stripes. By sunrise the flag was aloft in the town square, a band was under it playing "The Star-Spangled Banner," and citizens were clustered about, some of them cheering, some of them crying.

On that same Fourth of July in 1863, about 800 miles to the southwest, Ulysses Grant received a note from John Pemberton surrendering Vicksburg, which meant that the Union had gained complete control of the Mississippi River. Realization would come later that the two victories, both critical to the Northern cause, gave the nation "a new birth of freedom." It is a noteworthy coincidence that the new birth came on the same date as the original.

While Meade and Lee watched each other on the Fourth, burial details operated under flags of truce. The corpses, many already decomposing, some horribly bloated, with black tongues bulging from gaping mouths, were interred where they fell, in very shallow excavations, each wrapped in a blanket. Where the slain were found in groups, shallow trenches were utilized.

Since it was expected that most of the bodies would be removed to more appropriate resting places, identifications were made, whenever possible, on wooden slats used as head pieces. But much of the work was done with more haste than efficiency. Right now the important thing was to get the corpses out of sight, beyond scenting, and away from the flies that were gathered thick upon them.

At noon the weather turned rainy, as it often does after a great battle. Soon the burial details were working in mud, with the corpses be-

Incompleted Confederate burial.

coming more offensive in their sogginess, and with the thin layers of earth on earlier graves washing thinner.

The rain became so heavy there was flash flooding along the area's streams, and some of the wounded lying on the banks were drowned. All of the open-air hospitals, of course, were saturated, and the pace of the ministrations was impeded. Many of the wounded lay on the ground with no protection.

Despite the deluge, Lee started his trains westward that afternoon, seventeen miles of them. The ambulances carried off all the wounded Confederates able to travel. But, what with the weather and the condition of the roads, these men began a grievous ordeal, one that numbers of them would not survive.

By nightfall the entire Confederate army was under marching orders, and Lee himself took to the rainy road after indulging in a drink of liquor "for health's sake."

If the night was a wretched one for the retreating Confederates, it wasn't too much better for the encamped Federals. Even General Meade, with his headquarters cottage filled with wounded, was exposed to the elements. He divided the night between sleeping on the ground and sitting on a rock.

For the Federals, the gloom of the dawn and the lack of coffee because fires resisted starting was soon offset by big news from the picket lines: the enemy was gone!

Only now was there a full realization that Lee had been defeated.

No one found the moment more thrilling than civilian observer Tillie Pierce, back on the Jacob Weikert farm after her evacuation during the fighting of the previous day. Tillie never forgot how the army reacted.

"On the summits, in the valleys, everywhere we heard the soldiers hurrahing for the victory that had been won. The troops on our right, at Culp's Hill, caught up the joyous sound as it came rolling on from the Round Tops on our left, and soon the whole line of blue rejoiced in the results achieved."

The next logical step, most of the men believed, would be for the army to launch a vigorous offensive that would drive Lee to the wall

Union graves at Gettysburg.

and end the war. This view was also adopted by the Northern populace, now about to make the victories of Gettysburg and Vicksburg the object of religious thanksgivings and wild celebrations.

But General Meade had no plans to try to smash Lee. He retained his high respect for the Army of Northern Virginia, even in its battered condition; and he was satisfied with what he had achieved—even, it seems, a little surprised. His chief desire now was revealed in a congratulatory order he wrote to be read to the troops and released to the newspapers. It included the line: "The commanding general looks to the army for greater efforts to drive from our soil every vestige of the presence of the invader."

"My God!" cried Abraham Lincoln. "Is that all?"

It was.

Although Meade put elements of infantry and cavalry on Lee's trail at once, he kept the larger part of the army at Gettysburg for the next two days.

Aside from the great advantage to Lee, the time was well spent. Most of the rest of the 6,000 dead—Confederates included—were buried, and more was done for the wounded still on the scene, the number of which—Confederates included—came to some 22,000. Calls for civilian help were telegraphed through the Northern states, calls that were generously answered, with members of the Sanitary Commission and the Christian Commission in the fore.

The army was infinitely glad to leave Gettysburg because the battlefield stench—now mostly that of the thousands of dead horses—was becoming unbearable. Men were resorting to the use of chunks of damp turf as filters for breathing.

This sickening odor would plague the area for weeks, with a large part of the solution being provided by buzzards, crows, and millions of large green flies that grew even larger as they fed. The townspeople, who had to keep their windows closed to shut out the stench, began to regard these scavengers as friends.

Meade's pursuit of Lee was made with great deliberation, even though he was being prodded by Washington to attack before the foe crossed the Potomac.

Lee reached the river in the vicinity of Williamsport, Maryland, three days after leaving Gettysburg, but he wasn't able to cross because the flow was high as a result of the rain. His only choice was to deploy and entrench with his back to the crossings.

It took Meade until July 12 to get his whole army to the scene. Deployments were made to hem Lee in, six miles of them, with cavalry extending the flanks. But no attack orders were issued.

The next day found the river falling, and Lee decided to chance a crossing, by wading and by pontoon bridge, that night.

On the sunny morning of July 14 the Union army made a coordinated advance along its entire front.

"We move upon the enemy's works," one of the bluecoats wrote later. "Works are ours. Enemy sitting on the other side of the river performing various gyrations with his fingers—thumb on his nose."

The applause for Meade that had been sweeping the North suddenly subsided. Abraham Lincoln was so distressed in the knowledge that the war must now continue that he sat down and wrote the general a letter of censure. Though he changed his mind about sending it, the President did go as far as to tell Meade that his work during Lee's retreat reminded him ever so much of an old woman trying to shoo her geese across a creek.

Meade remained in charge of the Army of the Potomac until the end of the war, but Ulysses Grant, appointed top commander of all the Union's forces, attached himself to Meade's army and made its major decisions.

Gettysburg and Vicksburg plunged the South into gloom, but there was no thought of surrendering to the hated Yankees. Two hopes remained: the North might abandon the war through weariness with its cost; Lincoln might be defeated by a Peace Party candidate in the 1864 elections.

Robert E. Lee offered to resign his command after Gettysburg, citing his failure and his ill health. His government responded that he was irreplaceable. Lee's health improved, and he was able to carry on for five years beyond his surrender at Appomattox in 1865, dying of his heart condition, while serving as president of Virginia's Washington College, at age sixty-three. Traveller survived him.

The Battle of Gettysburg was barely over before Andrew Curtin, the governor of Pennsylvania, decided that the Union dead must be honored with a special cemetery. (The Confederate dead would have to lie in their makeshift graves until after the war, when they would be taken south.)

Use was made of a seventeen-acre plot on the north slope of Cemetery Hill, and elaborate dedication ceremonies were set for November 19, 1863, four and a half months after the battle. Since this was not a Federal affair—the cemetery would not become national until 1872—Abraham Lincoln was sent an invitation only as a courtesy, and the planners were surprised when he accepted. He was now asked to contribute a few words to the ceremonies.

After sitting through a two-hour speech by a professional orator, the President rose and gave a three-minute talk that became as famous as the three-day battle.

Address delivered at the dedication of the
Cemetery at Gettysburg.

Four score and seven years ago our fathers
brought forth on this continent, a new nation, conceived in Liberty, and dedicated
to the proposition that all men are created equal.

Now we are engaged in a great civil war,
testing whether that nation, or any nation
so conceived and so dedicated, can long
endure. We are met on a great battle field
of that war. We have come to dedicate a
portion of that field, as a final resting
place for those who here gave their lives
that that nation might live. It is altogether fitting and proper that we should
do this.

But, in a larger sense, we can not dedicate— we can not consecrate— we can not
hallow— this ground. The brave men, living and dead, who struggled here have con-
secrated it, far above our poor power to add
or detract. The world will little note, nor
long remember what we say here, but it can
never forget what they did here. It is for us
the living, rather, to be dedicated here to
the unfinished work which they who fought here have thus far so nobly advanced.
It is rather for us to be here dedicated to
the great task remaining before us— that
from these honored dead we take increased
devotion to that cause for which they gave
the last full measure of devotion— that
we here highly resolve that these dead shall
not have died in vain— that this nation,
under God, shall have a new birth of freedom— and that government of the people,
by the people, for the people, shall not perish from the earth.

                                    Abraham Lincoln.

November 19, 1863.

Facsimile of Lincoln's Gettysburg Address

Bibliography

Alleman, Tillie Pierce. *At Gettysburg; What a Girl Saw and Heard of the Battle.* New York: W. Lake Borland, 1889.

Angle, Paul M., and Miers, Earl Schenck. *Tragic Years, 1860–1865,* vol. 2. New York: Simon and Schuster, 1960.

Annals of the War. Philadelphia: The Times Publishing Company, 1879.

Battles and Leaders of the Civil War, vol. 3. Robert Underwood Johnson and Clarence Clough Buel, eds. New York: The Century Co., 1884.

Bayly, Mrs. Joseph. *Personal Stories of the Battle.* Typescript in the library of Gettysburg National Military Park. Originally published in the Gettysburg *Compiler*.

Bayly, William Hamilton. *Personal Stories of the Battle.* Typescript in the library of Gettysburg National Military Park. Originally published in the Gettysburg *Compiler*.

Bigelow, John. *The Peach Orchard, Gettysburg.* Minneapolis: Kimball-Storer Co., 1910. Butternut and Blue reprint, 1984.

Billings, John D. *Hardtack and Coffee.* Boston: George M. Smith & Co., 1889.

Blackford, W. W. *War Years With Jeb Stuart.* New York: Charles Scribner's Sons, 1945.

Blake, Henry W. *Three Years in the Army of the Potomac.* Boston: Lee and Shepard, 1865.

Boritt, Gabor S., ed. *The Gettysburg Nobody Knows.* New York: Oxford University Press, 1997.

Botts, John Minor. *The Great Rebellion.* New York: Harper & Brothers, 1866.

Bradford, Gamaliel. *Lee the American.* Boston and New York: Houghton Mifflin Company, 1927.

Broadhead, Sarah M. *Diary of a Lady of Gettysburg, Pennsylvania, from June 15 to July 15, 1863.* Self-published. Undated.

Buell, Augustus. *The Cannoneer; Recollections of Service in the Army of the Potomac.* Washington, D.C.: The National Tribune, 1890.

Caldwell, J. F. J. *The History of a Brigade of South Carolinians.* Philadelphia: King & Baird, 1866. Facsimile edition by Morningside Bookshop, Dayton, Ohio, 1974.

Carpenter, F. B. *The Inner Life of Abraham Lincoln.* New York: Hurd and Houghton, 1868.

Casler, John O. *Four Years in the Stonewall Brigade.* James I. Robertson, Jr., ed. Dayton, Ohio: Morningside Bookshop, 1971. Facsimile of 1906 edition.

Catton, Bruce. *The Army of the Potomac: Glory Road.* Garden City, N.Y.: Doubleday & Company, Inc., 1952.

———. *Never Call Retreat.* Garden City, N.Y.: Doubleday & Company, Inc., 1965.

———. *Gettysburg: The Final Fury.* Garden City, N.Y.: Doubleday & Company, Inc., 1974.

Coco, Gregory A. *On the Bloodstained Field II.* Gettysburg, Pa.: Thomas Publications, 1989.

Coffin, Charles Carleton. *The Boys of '61.* Boston: Estes and Lauriat, 1884.

———. *Marching to Victory.* New York: Harper & Brothers, 1889.

———. *Stories of Our Soldiers.* Boston: Journal Newspaper Company, 1893.

Commager, Henry Steele. *The Blue and the Gray.* Indianapolis and New York: The Bobbs-Merrill Company, Inc., 1950.

Cooke, John Esten. *The Life of Stonewall Jackson.* Freeport, New York: Books for Libraries Press, 1971. First published in 1863.

———. *Wearing of the Gray.* New York: Kraus Reprint Co., 1969. Reprint of 1867 edition.

———. *Robert E. Lee.* New York: D. Appleton & Company, 1871.

Crotty, D. G. *Four Years Campaigning in the Army of the Potomac.* Grand Rapids, Mich.: Dygert Bros. & Co., 1874.

Davis, Burke. *Jeb Stuart, the Last Cavalier.* New York and Toronto: Rinehart & Company, Inc., 1957.

Davis, Jefferson. *The Rise and Fall of the Confederate Government,* vol. 2. New York: Thomas Yoseloff, 1958.

Davis, Varina. *Jefferson Davis, a Memoir by His Wife,* vol. 2. New York: Belford Company, 1890.

DeTrobriand, P. Regis. *Four Years with the Army of the Potomac.* Boston: Ticknor and Company, 1889.

Dickert, D. Augustus. *History of Kershaw's Brigade.* Dayton, Ohio: Morningside Bookshop, 1976. Facsimile of 1899 edition.

Doubleday, Abner. *Chancellorsville and Gettysburg (Campaigns of the Civil War, vol. 6).* New York: Charles Scribner's Sons, 1882.

Douglas, Henry Kyd. *I Rode With Stonewall.* Chapel Hill: The University of North Carolina Press, 1940.

Early, Jubal Anderson. *War Memoirs.* Bloomington: Indiana University Press, 1960. Reprint of 1912 edition.

Eggleston, George Cary. *A Rebel's Recollections.* New York: Kraus Reprint Co., 1969.

Evans, Clement A., ed. *Confederate Military History: A Library of Confederate States History in Twelve Volumes, Written by Distinguished Men of the South.* New York: Thomas Yoseloff, 1962. Reprint of edition by the Confederate Publishing Company, 1889.

[Fiske, Samuel]. *Mr. Dunn Browne's Experiences in the Army.* Boston: Nichols and Noyes, 1866.

Fletcher, William A. *Rebel Private: Front and Rear.* New York: Dutton, 1995. First published in 1908.

Foote, Shelby. *Stars in Their Courses.* New York: The Modern Library, 1994.

Forney, John W. *Life and Military Career of Winfield Scott Hancock.* Philadelphia: J. C. McCurdy & Co., 1880.

Freeman, Douglas Southall. *Lee's Lieutenants,* vol. 3. New York: Charles Scribner's Sons, 1944.

Gates, Theodore B. *The War of the Rebellion.* New York: P. F. McBreen, 1884.

Gerrish, Theodore. *Army Life; A Private's Reminiscences of the Civil War.* Portland, Me.: Hoyt, Fogg & Donham, 1882.

Gilbert, J. Warren, ed. *The Blue and Gray; A History of the Conflicts During Lee's Invasion and Battle of Gettysburg.* Publisher not named. 1922.

Gilmor, Harry. *Four Years in the Saddle.* New York: Harper & Brothers, 1866.

Glazier, Willard. *Three Years in the Federal Cavalry.* New York: R. H. Ferguson & Company, 1874.

———. *Battles for the Union.* Hartford, Conn.: Dustin, Gilman & Co., 1875.

Gordon, John B. *Reminiscences of the Civil War.* New York: Charles Scribner's Sons, 1904.

Goss, Warren Lee. *Recollections of a Private.* New York: Thomas Y. Crowell & Co., 1890.

Greeley, Horace. *The American Conflict,* vol. 2. Hartford, Conn.: O. D. Case & Company, 1867.

Guernsey, Alfred H., and Alden, Henry M. *Harper's Pictorial History of the Great Rebellion,* vol. 2. Chicago: McDonnell Bros., 1866.

Hale, Edward E., ed. *Stories of War Told by Soldiers.* Boston: Roberts Brothers, 1879.

Hancock, Mrs. A. R. *Reminiscences of Winfield Scott Hancock.* New York: Charles L. Webster & Company, 1887.

Hansen, Harry. *The Civil War.* New York: Bonanza Books, 1961.

Haskell, Frank Aretas. *The Battle of Gettysburg.* Wisconsin History Commission, 1908.

[Holstein, Anna M.] *Three Years in Field Hospitals of the Army of the Potomac.* Philadelphia: J. B. Lippincott & Co., 1867.

Hopkins, Luther W. *From Bull Run to Appomattox.* Baltimore: Fleet-McGinley Co., 1908.

Jackson, Mary Anna. *Memoirs of Stonewall Jackson.* Louisville, Ky.: The Prentice Press, 1895.

Jacobs, M. *Notes on the Rebel Invasion of Maryland and Pennsylvania, and the Battle of Gettysburg.* G. E. Jacobs, 1888.

Johnson, Rossiter. *Campfires and Battlefields.* New York: The Civil War Press, 1967. First published in 1894.

Jones, John B. *A Rebel War Clerk's Diary.* Earl Schenck Miers, ed. New York: Sagamore Press, Inc., 1958. First published in 1866.

Jones, J. William. *Personal Reminiscences, Anecdotes, and Letters of Gen. Robert E. Lee.* New York: D. Appleton and Company, 1874.

Lee, Fitzhugh. *General Lee of the Confederate Army.* London: Chapman and Hall, Ltd., 1895.

Lee, Robert E. *Recollections and Letters of General Robert E. Lee, by His Son.* Garden City, N.Y.: Garden City Publishing Co., Inc., 1904.

Long, E. B., with Barbara Long. *The Civil War Day by Day.* Garden City, N.Y.: Doubleday & Company, Inc., 1971.

Longstreet, James. *From Manassas to Appomattox.* Millwood, N.Y.: Kraus Reprint Co., 1976. First published in 1896.

Lossing, Benson J. *Pictorial Field Book of the Civil War,* vol. 3. New York: T. Belknap & Company, 1868.

McClellan, H. B. *The Life and Campaigns of Major General J. E. B. Stuart.* Boston: Houghton, Mifflin & Company, 1885.

McClure, A. K. *Abraham Lincoln and Men of War Times.* Philadelphia: The Times Publishing Company, 1892.

[McGuire, Judith W.]. *Diary of a Southern Refugee During the War.* New York: E. J. Hale & Son, 1867.

Maurice, Frederick. *Robert E. Lee the Soldier.* New York: Bonanza Books (undated). Original copyright, 1925.

Miers, Earl Schenck, and Brown, Richard A. *Gettysburg.* New Brunswick, N.J.: Rutgers University Press, 1948.

Moore, Frank, ed. *The Rebellion Record,* vols. 7, 8, 10. New York: D. Van Nostrand, 1864, 1865, 1867.

——. *The Civil War in Song and Story.* New York: P. F. Collier, 1889.

Neese, George M. *Three Years in the Confederate Horse Artillery.* New York and Washington: The Neale Publishing Company, 1911.

Nesbitt, Mark. *35 Days to Gettysburg.* Harrisburg, Pa.: Stackpole Books, 1992.

Nichols, G. W. *A Soldier's Story of His Regiment.* Kennesaw, Georgia: Continental Book Company, 1961. Reprint of 1898 edition.

Nicholson, John P., ed. *Pennsylvania at Gettysburg; Ceremonies at the Dedication of the Monuments.* 2 vols. Harrisburg, Pa.: E. K. Meyers, State Printer, 1893.

Norton, Oliver Willcox. *The Attack and Defense of Little Round Top.* New York: The Neale Publishing Company, 1913.

Oates, William C. *The War Between the Union and the Confederacy.* New York: The Neale Publishing Company, 1905.

Opie, John N. *A Rebel Cavalryman with Lee, Stuart, and Jackson.* Dayton, Ohio: Morningside Bookshop, 1972. Facsimile of 1899 edition.

Our Women in the War. Charleston, S.C.: The News and Courier Book Presses, 1885.

Owen, William Miller. *In Camp and Battle with the Washington Artillery.* Boston: Ticknor and Company, 1885. Second edition by Pelican Publishing Company, New Orleans, 1964.

Page, Thomas Nelson. *Robert E. Lee, Man and Soldier.* New York: Charles Scribner's Sons, 1911.

Paris, Comte de. *History of the Civil War in America,* vol. 3. Philadelphia: Jos. H. Coates & Co., 1883.

Pennypacker, Isaac R. *General Meade.* New York: D. Appleton and Company, 1901.

Pfanz, Harry W. *Gettysburg: The Second Day.* Chapel Hill and London: The University of North Carolina Press, 1987.

Pickett, George E. *The Heart of a Soldier.* New York: Seth Moyle, Inc., 1913.

Pollard, Edward A. *The Second Year of the War.* New York: Charles B. Richardson, 1864.

———. *The Lost Cause.* New York: E. B. Treat & Co., 1866.

———. *The Early Life, Campaigns, and Public Services of Robert E. Lee; with a Record of the Campaigns and Heroic Deeds of His Companions in Arms.* New York: E. B. Treat & Co., 1871.

[Putnam, Sarah A.]. *Richmond During the War.* New York: G. W. Carleton & Co., 1867.

Ratchford, J. W. *Some Reminiscences of Persons and Incidents of the Civil War.* Austin, Texas: Shoal Creek Publishers, 1971. Facsimile of 1909 edition.

Reardon, Carol. *Pickett's Charge in History and Memory.* Chapel Hill and London: The University of North Carolina Press, 1997.

Riggs, David F. *East of Gettysburg; Custer vs. Stuart.* Ft. Collins, Colo.: The Old Army Press, 1985.

Robert L. Brake Collection. A treasury of early Gettysburg items in transcript: letters, diaries, book excerpts, magazine articles, and newspaper clippings, many of the last from the Gettysburg *Compiler*. United States Army Military History Institute, Carlisle, Pennsylvania.

Shay, Ralph S., ed. *Reflections on the Battle of Gettysburg.* Lebanon, Pa.: Lebanon County Historical Society, 1963.

Smart, James G., ed. *A Radical View: The "Agate" Dispatches of Whitelaw Reid, 1861–1865,* vol. 2. Memphis, Tenn.: Memphis State University Press, 1976.

Stackpole, Edward J. *They Met at Gettysburg.* New York: Bonanza Books, 1956.

Stephenson, Nathaniel W. *The Day of the Confederacy.* New Haven: Yale University Press, 1920.

Stern, Philip Van Doren. *Robert E. Lee, the Man and the Soldier.* New York: McGraw-Hill Book Company, Inc., 1963.

Stevens, George T. *Three Years in the Sixth Corps.* New York: D. Van Nostrand, 1870.

Stewart, George R. *Pickett's Charge.* Dayton, Ohio: Morningside Bookshop, 1983.

Stiles, Robert. *Four Years Under Marse Robert.* New York and Washington: The Neale Publishing Company, 1903.

Stine, J. H. *History of the Army of the Potomac.* Philadelphia: J. B. Rogers Printing Co., 1892.

Stowe, Harriet Beecher. *Men of Our Times.* Hartford, Conn.: Hartford Publishing Company, 1868.

Swinton, William. *The Twelve Decisive Battles of the War.* New York: Dick & Fitzgerald, 1867.

———. *Campaigns of the Army of the Potomac.* New York: Charles Scribner's Sons, 1882.

Tarbell, Ida M. *The Life of Abraham Lincoln,* vol. 2. New York: McClure, Phillips & Co., 1902.

Taylor, Walter H. *Four Years with General Lee.* New York: D. Appleton and Company, 1878.

Tenney, W. J. *The Military and Naval History of the Rebellion.* New York: D. Appleton & Company, 1865.

The War of the Rebellion: A Compilation of the Official Records of the Union and Confederate Armies, Series I, Volume 27. 3 vols. Washington, D.C.: Government Printing Office, 1889.

Thomas, Emory M. *Bold Dragoon; the Life of J. E. B. Stuart.* New York: Harper & Row, 1986.

Thomason, John W., Jr. *Jeb Stuart.* New York and London: Charles Scribner's Sons, 1930.

Under Both Flags: A Panorama of the Great Civil War. Chicago: W. S. Reeve Publishing Co., 1896.

Urban, John W. *Battle Field and Prison Pen.* Edgewood Publishing Company, 1882.

Von Borcke, Heros. *Memoirs of the Confederate War for Independence,* vol. 2. New York: Peter Smith, 1938. Reprint of 1866 edition.

Walker, Francis A. *History of the Second Army Corps in the Army of the Potomac.* New York: Charles Scribner's Sons, 1886.

Wallace, Francis B. *Memorial of the Patriotism of Schuylkill County in the American Slaveholder's Rebellion.* Pottsville, Pa.: Benjamin Bannan, 1865.

Wheeler, Richard. *Voices of the Civil War.* New York: Thomas Y. Crowell Company, 1976.

———. *We Knew Stonewall Jackson.* New York: Thomas Y. Crowell Company, 1977.

———. *Witness to Gettysburg.* New York: Harper & Row, 1987.

———. *Lee's Terrible Swift Sword.* New York: HarperCollins Publishers, 1992.

Williams, T. Harry. *Lincoln and His Generals.* New York: Alfred A. Knopf, Inc., 1952.

Wood, William. *Captains of the Civil War.* New Haven: Yale University Press, 1921.

Young, Jesse Bowman. *What a Boy Saw in the Army.* New York: Hunt & Eaton, 1894.

———. *The Battle of Gettysburg.* Dayton, Ohio: Morningside Bookshop, 1976. Facsimile of 1913 edition.

Index

Note: Page numbers in italics refer to illustrations.